I0792895

IMAGES
of America

OCEAN VIEW

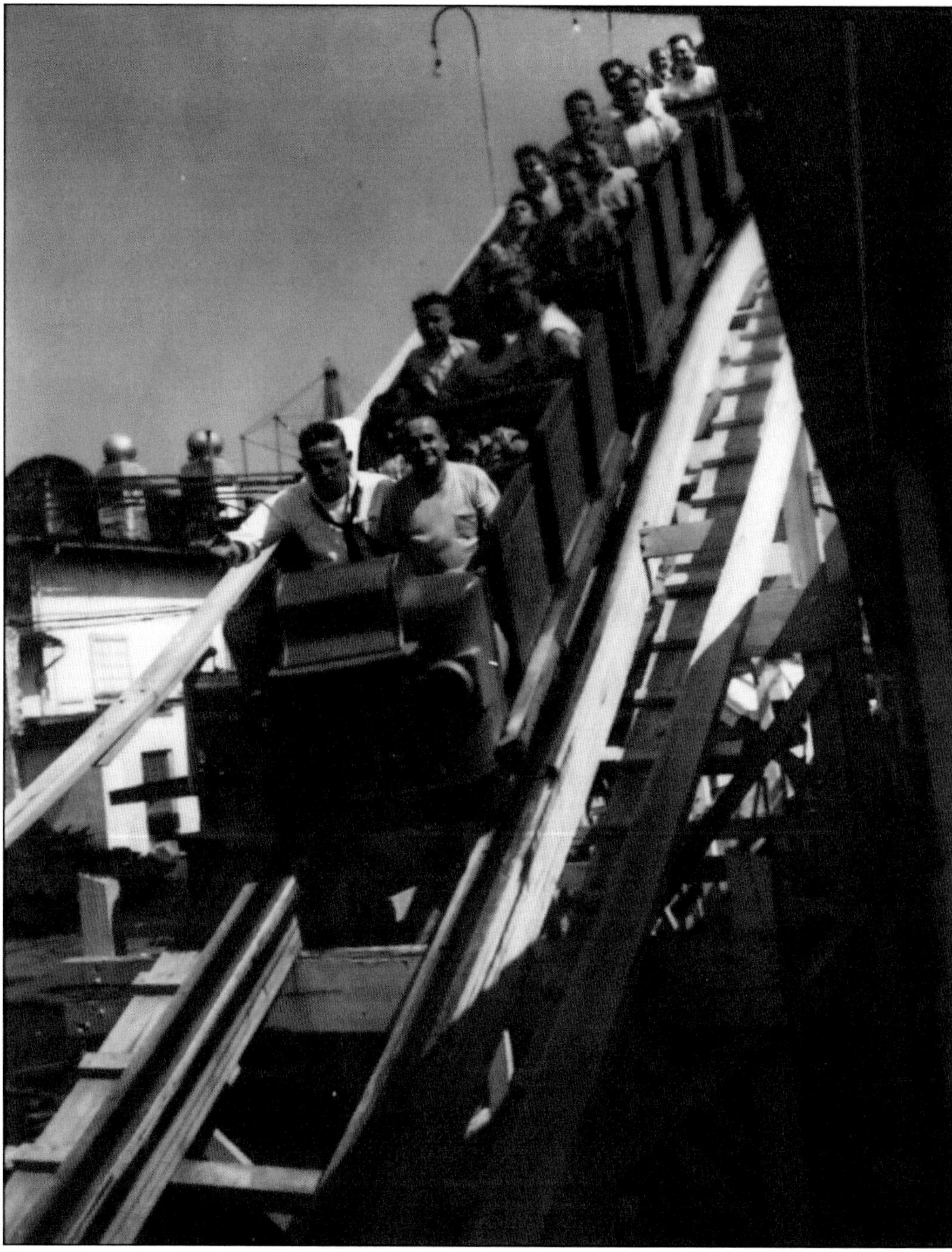

Eleven boys from the Portsmouth Orphanage were taken to Ocean View Amusement Park as guests of the Portsmouth Lions Club on August 27, 1955. The boys had an opportunity to ride the park's famous roller coaster, Leap-the-Dips, and enjoy the many rides throughout the facility. They had obviously hit one of the steeper dips on the ride when the picture was taken. The park provided all the rides for free. (Jim Mays, photographer.)

IMAGES
of America

OCEAN VIEW

Amy Waters Yarsinske

ARCADIA
PUBLISHING

Copyright © 1998, 2000 by Amy Waters Yarsinske
ISBN 978-0-7385-6826-3

Published by Arcadia Publishing
Charleston, South Carolina

Printed in the United States of America

For all general information contact Arcadia Publishing at:
Telephone 843-853-2070
Fax 843-853-0044
E-Mail sales@arcadiapublishing.com
For customer service and orders:
Toll-Free 1-888-313-2665

Visit us on the Internet at www.arcadiapublishing.com

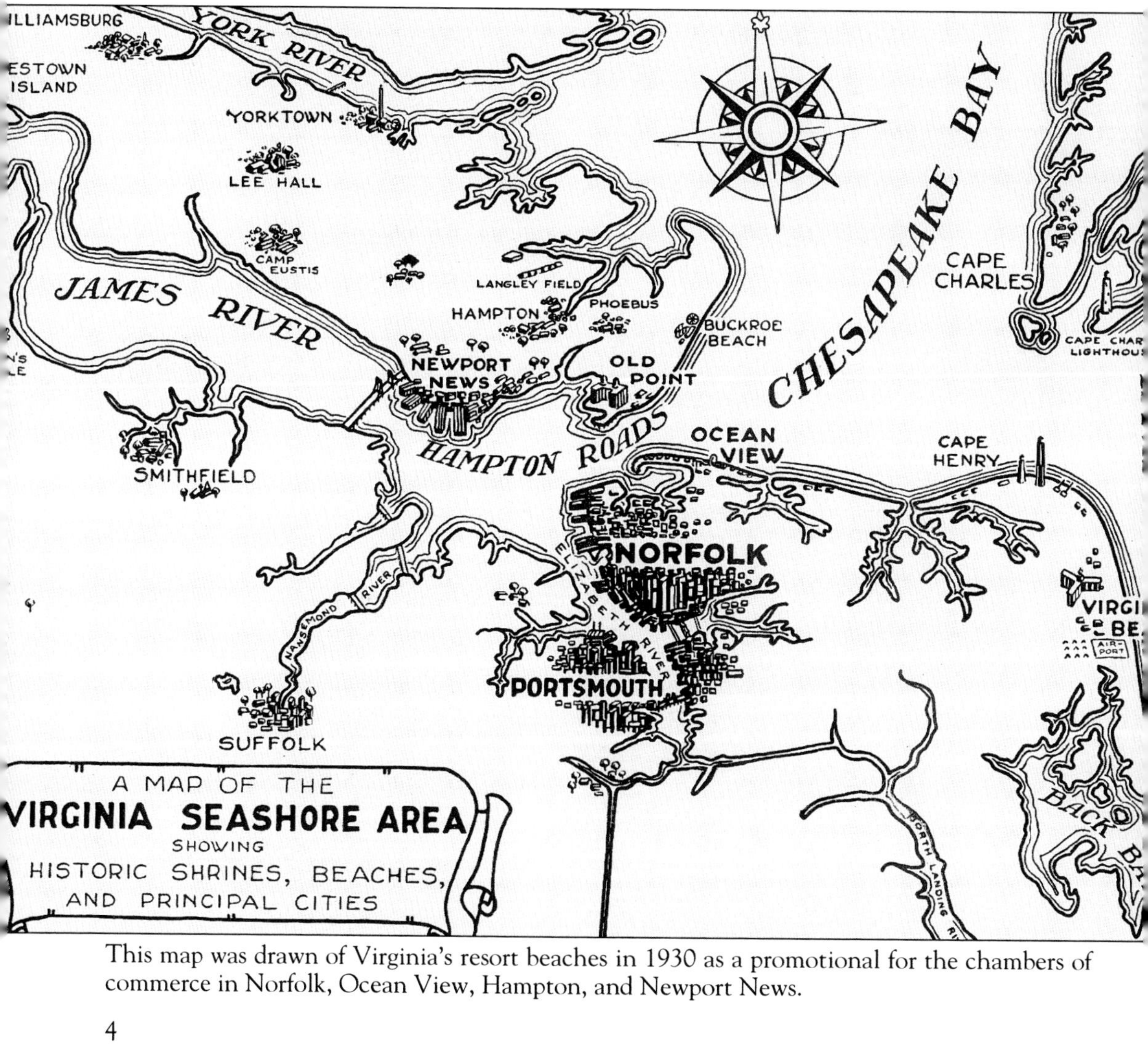

This map was drawn of Virginia's resort beaches in 1930 as a promotional for the chambers of commerce in Norfolk, Ocean View, Hampton, and Newport News.

Contents

Acknowledgments 6

Introduction 7

1. Mr. Lincoln Walks the Beach 9
2. The Ocean View Company 15
3. By the Bay 27
4. Hurricane! 63
5. Fisherman's Paradise and the Coney Island of the South 73
6. World War II and the Big Band Era 101
7. Ocean Viewites 109

ACKNOWLEDGMENTS

So often I have thought of what it means to be a caretaker of people's memories and photographs, and the responsibility of telling the stories that constitute our collective history and successfully reaching the public with the information. None of us achieves success without the efforts of other people. I recently heard from a friend that we all stand on the shoulders of giants to reach the plateau of success that makes us happy. My giants are many, but the first person I will always feel supported my work and success the best is my husband, Raymond, and he shares that place with the children of our hearts, Ashley, Allyson, and Raymond III. They bear the greatest burden of my caretaker work. I thank them now and always more than words can adequately express.

Professionally, and personally, I am fortunate to have a supportive cast of knowledgeable and committed people to make my vision for a book become reality. I would like to express my deepest thanks to Joseph M. Judge, curator, Hampton Roads Naval Museum; Peggy A. Haile, Sargeant Memorial Room, Kirn Library; Sarah Maineri, senior editor, Arcadia Publishing; and my friends in the Rotary Club of Norfolk, who provide me with a weekly dose of encouragement and fellowship that means more than anyone can know. Finally, there are people who remember Ocean View as it was and believe in what it can still become with the right amount of care and planning; I thank each of them for their interest in Ocean View's past and commitment to its future.

While the Sargeant Room at the Kirn Library was able to supply a number of images for the book, many photographs on file, labeled over the years as Ocean View, were actually of Virginia Beach. "Sand is not sand," from one resort to another. Ocean View and Virginia Beach may have shared their births by railroad, but the maturation of each area occurred under completely different sets of economic and social parameters. The Virginia Beach resort and its surrounding environs were photographed more heavily and the jewel of East Coast excursion destinations has enjoyed continuous growth and prosperity since its nineteenth-century birth. Ocean View's heyday came and went on the wave of amusement park popularity. The area also fell victim to rapid urbanization and limited real estate to accommodate automobile patrons. Photographs of old Ocean View are not found in large numbers in any single public collection.

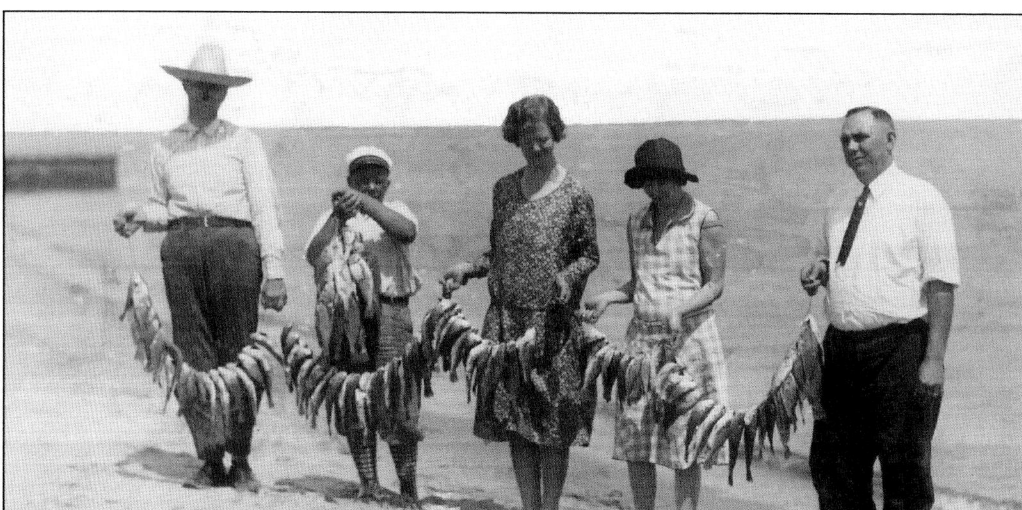

Fishing was good at Ocean View the day this picture was taken in the summer of 1930. It is a pretty impressive string of fish, too. (Photographer unknown.)

INTRODUCTION

Norfolk at one time had two seaside resorts on its Chesapeake Bay shore: Ocean View and Willoughby Beach. The first, Ocean View, was developed as early as 1854, and by January 1855, the city's first seaside resort was being advertised for tourists. The Ocean View Company promoted the area on the basis of its beautiful, cool water, its actual views of the Atlantic Ocean beyond Cape Henry, Old Point Comfort, Fort Wool, and, of course, the visual education found only by gazing upon the diverse and powerful ships of the United States Navy and merchant service that daily passed the shore of "the View." Forty-two businessmen bought lots at Ocean View, and three of them were from out of town—Edward S. Pegram, Baltimore, Maryland; Dr. George W. Peete, Portsmouth, Virginia; and Dr. Thomas D. Warren, Edenton, North Carolina. The Civil War temporarily suspended development of Ocean View. There were only five summerhouses standing in Ocean View at that time and these were clustered near the present-day northern terminus of Granby Street. After the war, people began to return to Ocean View for relaxation and recreation. There was an influx of vacationers from the North by 1880, and as the resort's reputation spread, so did the geographic diversity of its patrons. As soon as the railroad connection to Ocean View was established, the Norfolk and Ocean View Railroad Company began constructing a hotel and pavilions, and a few cottages, the start of what would eventually become the Ocean View Amusement Park. Ocean View's star began to rise. People were attracted to its mild climate and opportunities for bathing, boating, fishing, hunting, camping, and recreational pursuits of diverse description. While Lynnhaven was famous for its oysters and Hampton for the blue crab, Ocean View was renowned for spot, a fish that was so plentiful off its shore that fishermen could catch several hundred in an hour's time. While Ocean View was a resort for visitors, it was also a popular playground for Norfolk citizens.

Willoughby Beach was not developed as a resort until the turn of the century, and today, its name is inextricably linked to the area of Norfolk popularly called Ocean View. Willoughby has a much longer history than Ocean View. The first Thomas Willoughby owned land there prior to 1626, and constructed his manor house in 1635. The location of the house was Willoughby's Point, north of Ocean View Elementary School on Mason Creek Road. Willoughby's estate extended to Mason Creek on the west and nearly all the way to Little Creek to the east. Willoughby's Point was not the area known today as Willoughby Spit, leading one to believe that the formation of Willoughby Spit occurred as a result of a hurricane in 1749. Subsequent generations of Willoughbys lost their family estate. The Willoughby plantation and fishery on Willoughby Point, an estate of 360 acres, was sold in 1826. This tract was bordered by the Chesapeake Bay, Third View Street, United States Naval Air Station Norfolk, and residential developments Pamlico, Lenox, and Pinewell. Though Willoughby was largely undeveloped until 1900, the Jamestown Exposition of 1907 led to construction of additional cottages, the Hampton Roads Yacht Club on the western tip of the beach, and a small marina. Willoughby, like Ocean View, was annexed by Norfolk in 1923. This book is about Ocean View, fisherman's paradise and Coney Island of the South, and its adjacent resort beaches and vistas.

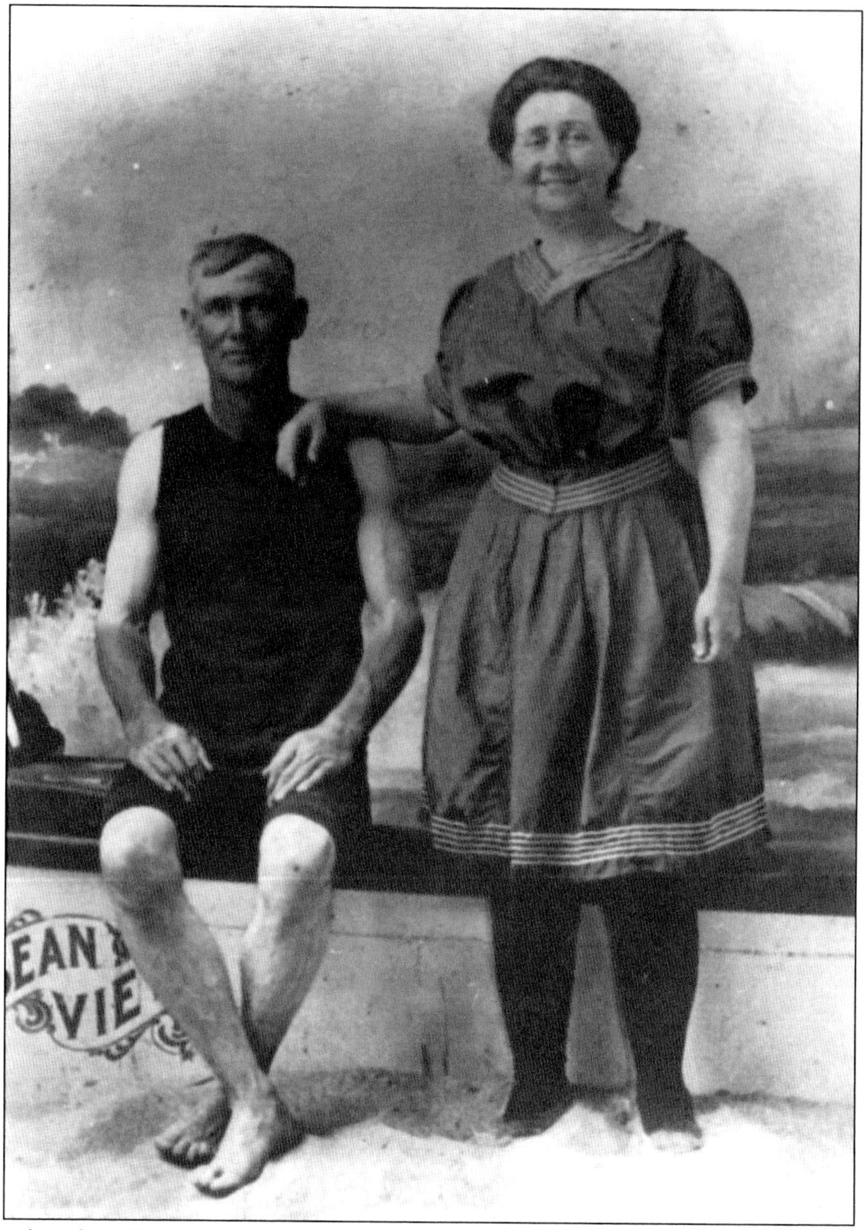

The growth of public transportation and improved waterborne connections to resort communities were the main factors in the development of amusement parks in the United States in the nineteenth century. Railroads deserve much of the credit for building an entire industry out of games and rides. Traction companies, responsible for the construction of the first streetcar lines, built amusement parks at the end of the line to build ridership and make money. In the early twentieth century, amusement parks drew the attention of big business because they raked in profits that were nothing less than impressive. The greatest inspiration for the parks built in Norfolk and Virginia Beach was the Philadelphia Centennial Exposition in 1876, which is, even today, considered a model for amusement parks across the country. The exposition featured a miniature railway 4 miles long that emptied into an amusement park. The couple in this photograph had traveled to Ocean View for vacation, c. 1900.

One

Mr. Lincoln Walks the Beach

"I remember the bulwarks by the shore,
    And the fort upon the hill,
The sunrise gun, with its hollow roar,
The drum-beat repeated o'er and o'er,
    And the bugle wild and shrill."
        —From My *Lost Youth*, 1855
        Henry Wadsworth Longfellow, American poet
        (1807–1882)

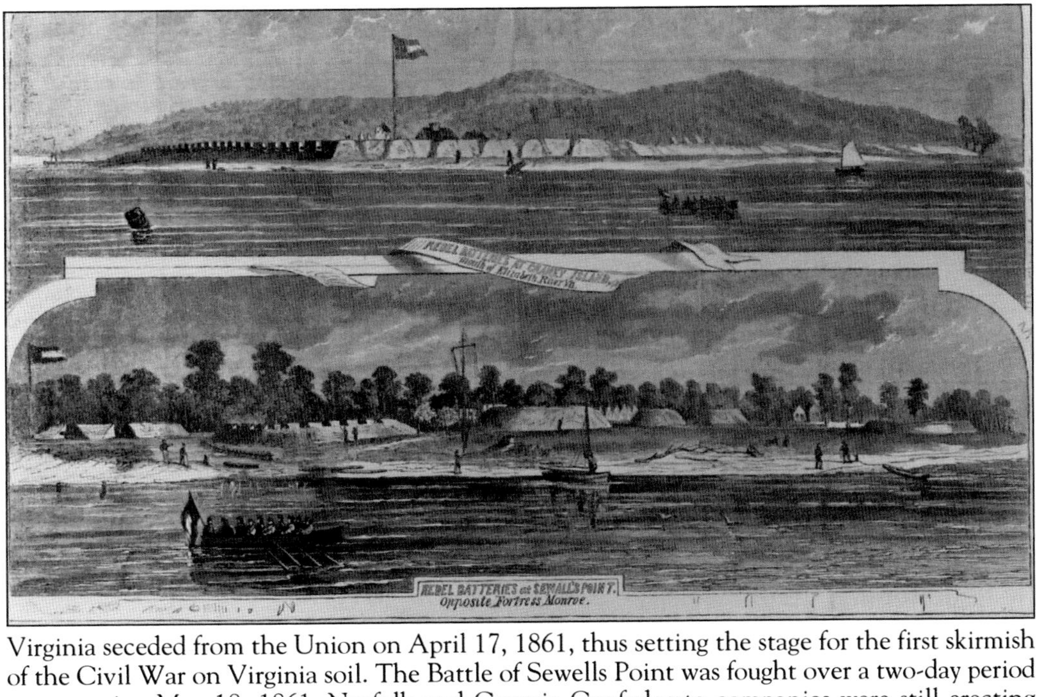

Virginia seceded from the Union on April 17, 1861, thus setting the stage for the first skirmish of the Civil War on Virginia soil. The Battle of Sewells Point was fought over a two-day period commencing May 18, 1861. Norfolk and Georgia Confederate companies were still erecting their fortifications at Sewells Point when the USS *Monticello*, berthed at Fort Monroe and commanded by Captain Henry Eagle, opened fire and a shell exploded within the breastwork. The *Monticello* would continue to bombard the breastworks as efforts were underway to complete construction. The *Monticello* could not claim victory. Confederate gunners had cut several holes in her hull with well-aimed gunfire, and the Union warship hobbled back to Fort Monroe. The Confederate batteries at Sewells Point, depicted in a *Frank Leslie's Illustrated*, 1862, provided only a modicum of protection for the northern approach to Norfolk. (Courtesy of the Hampton Roads Naval Museum.)

The President Takes Charge of the Norfolk Campaign

On the morning of May 8, 1862, President Abraham Lincoln left the confines of Fortress Monroe to view Confederate positions at Sewells Point aboard his tug. Among U.S. naval vessels making way in the waters off Sewells Point and vicinity was the ironclad USS *Monitor*, which, in full-view of the president, fired incendiary shells at Confederate batteries. Exploding shells destroyed a number of wood-frame structures, including a barracks, supply stores, and command buildings. During the firing, witnesses to this extraordinary piece of Civil War history noted that the *Monitor*'s guns were diverted from Confederate positions by the appearance of the CSS *Virginia*. Though her presence on May 8 forebode her destruction, the *Virginia* did keep Lincoln from landing at Norfolk until the following day, and stumped Union plans to take Norfolk on schedule. The Confederate ironclad's fate was sealed as an angry Lincoln, frustrated and more determined than ever to destroy her, regrouped and conferred with his advisors. The decision was made to assault Norfolk at the Willoughby end of Ocean View, clear of Confederate fortifications at Sewells Point, thus sparing Norfolk from complete destruction in a major land battle.

A President of the United States Comes under Hostile Fire

Union intelligence reported that the Confederates were evacuating the city. Lincoln met with his advisors on the wharf at Fortress Monroe and boarded the tugboat *Lionness*. He was anxious to reach Ocean View. As his tug and launch boats came close to shore, Confederate cavalry galloped onto the beach and opened fire. This did not deter Lincoln, who, upon being in the line of fire for the second time in as many days, became the first chief executive of the nation to come under direct enemy gunfire. After chasing away the enemy, the 99th New York escorted President Lincoln in a six-oared boat to shore, and it was at that time he made his recommendations for an amphibious assault of Norfolk. The date was May 9, 1862. Upon his return to Fortress Monroe, Lincoln mounted a horse and headed for Camp Hamilton to supervise General John E. Wool's amphibious assault preparations. Troops left Fortress Monroe at midnight on May 9; the final regiment landed on Ocean View beach at eight o'clock the following morning, and were accompanied by President Lincoln, Secretaries Salmon P. Chase and Edwin M. Stanton, General Wool, and Brigadier General Egbert Vièle, later the military governor of Norfolk. Lincoln would watch most of the Norfolk campaign unfold from the safety of Fortress Monroe, pacing angrily as great plumes of smoke and flame arose over the city, a sign of either fierce street fighting or the Confederate's razing the city in retreat. The President was also deeply troubled over thoughts of losing several top Union officers, at least four senior generals and Secretary Chase. This weighed heavily on his mind. Lincoln would later learn that his troops never fired a shot and most of the destruction was caused by the Confederates.

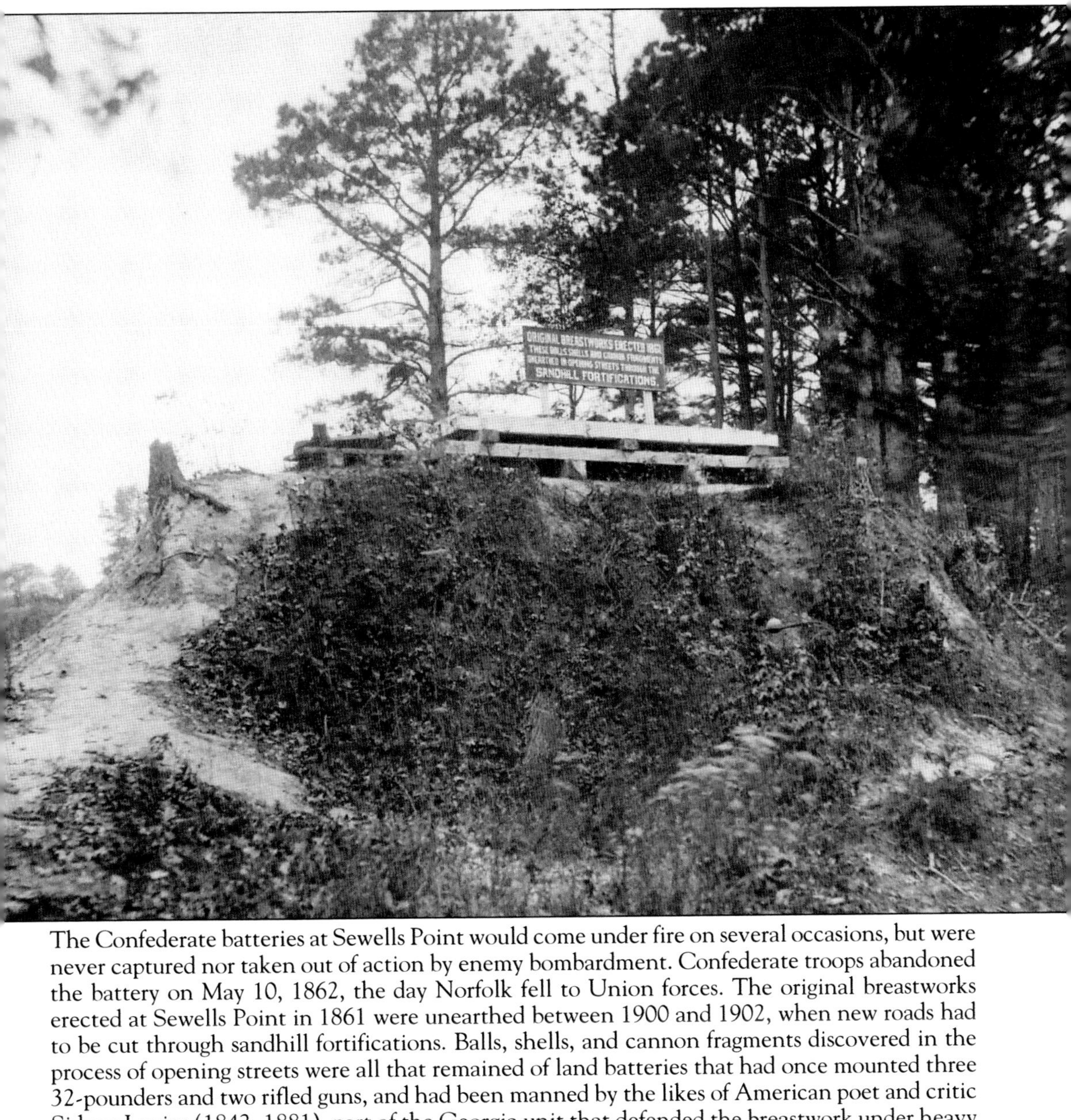

The Confederate batteries at Sewells Point would come under fire on several occasions, but were never captured nor taken out of action by enemy bombardment. Confederate troops abandoned the battery on May 10, 1862, the day Norfolk fell to Union forces. The original breastworks erected at Sewells Point in 1861 were unearthed between 1900 and 1902, when new roads had to be cut through sandhill fortifications. Balls, shells, and cannon fragments discovered in the process of opening streets were all that remained of land batteries that had once mounted three 32-pounders and two rifled guns, and had been manned by the likes of American poet and critic Sidney Lanier (1842–1881), part of the Georgia unit that defended the breastwork under heavy fire from the *Monticello*. Lanier has been called the most cultivated of all the nineteenth-century authors of the South, and this line from *The Marshes of Glynn* (1878), with its lyric richness, reveals the soul of a man who could fight for his cause yet transcend moments in history with his gift for fervent words:

> "I will fly in the greatness of God as the marsh-hen flies,
> In the freedom that fills all the space 'twixt the marsh and the skies."

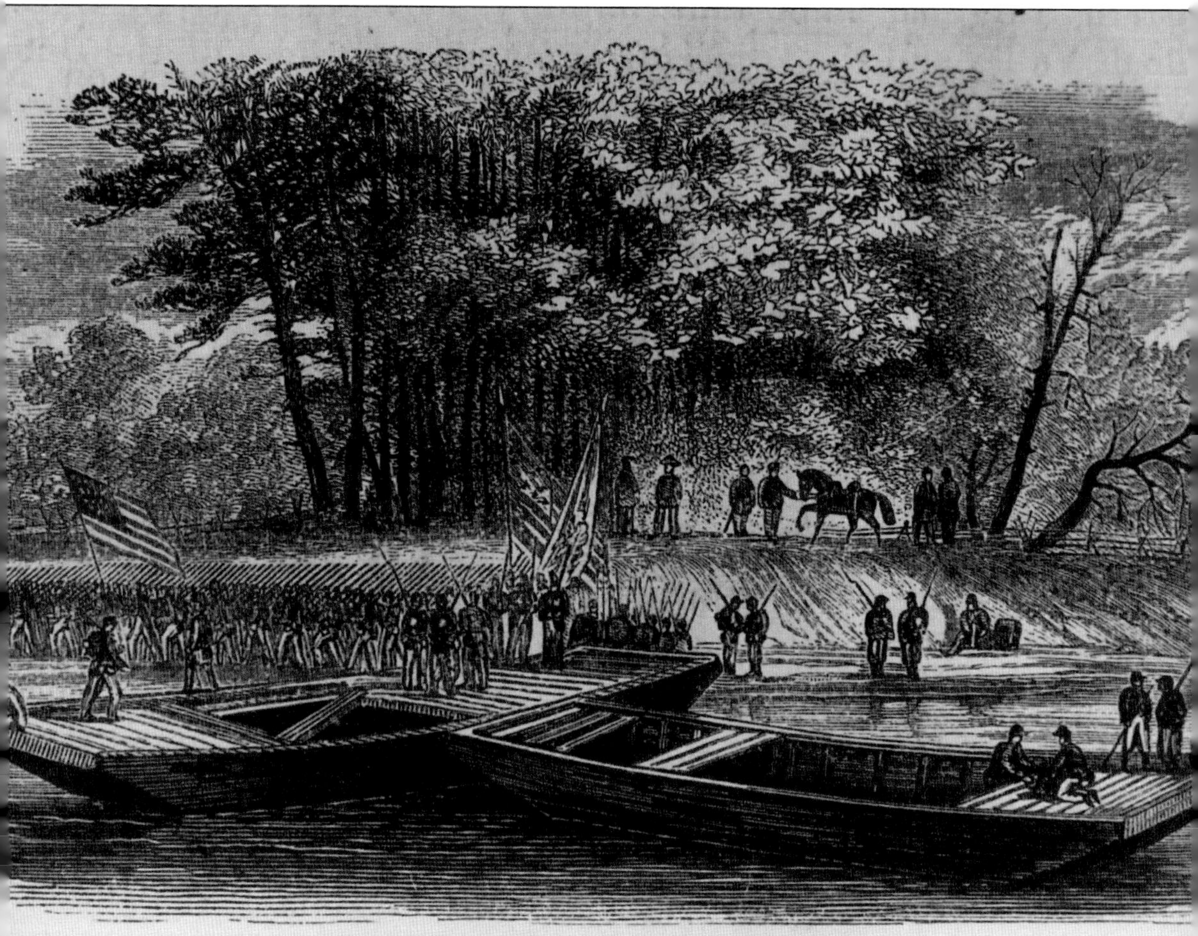

WOOL'S LANDING-PLACE AT OCEAN VIEW.

General John E. Wool and his troops landed at Ocean View near Willoughby, flanking Confederate positions at Sewells Point on May 10, 1862. *Harper's Weekly* covered the events at Ocean View for its readers, and this illustration clearly depicts the landing barges and Wool himself standing near his horse. (Courtesy of Hampton Roads Naval Museum.)

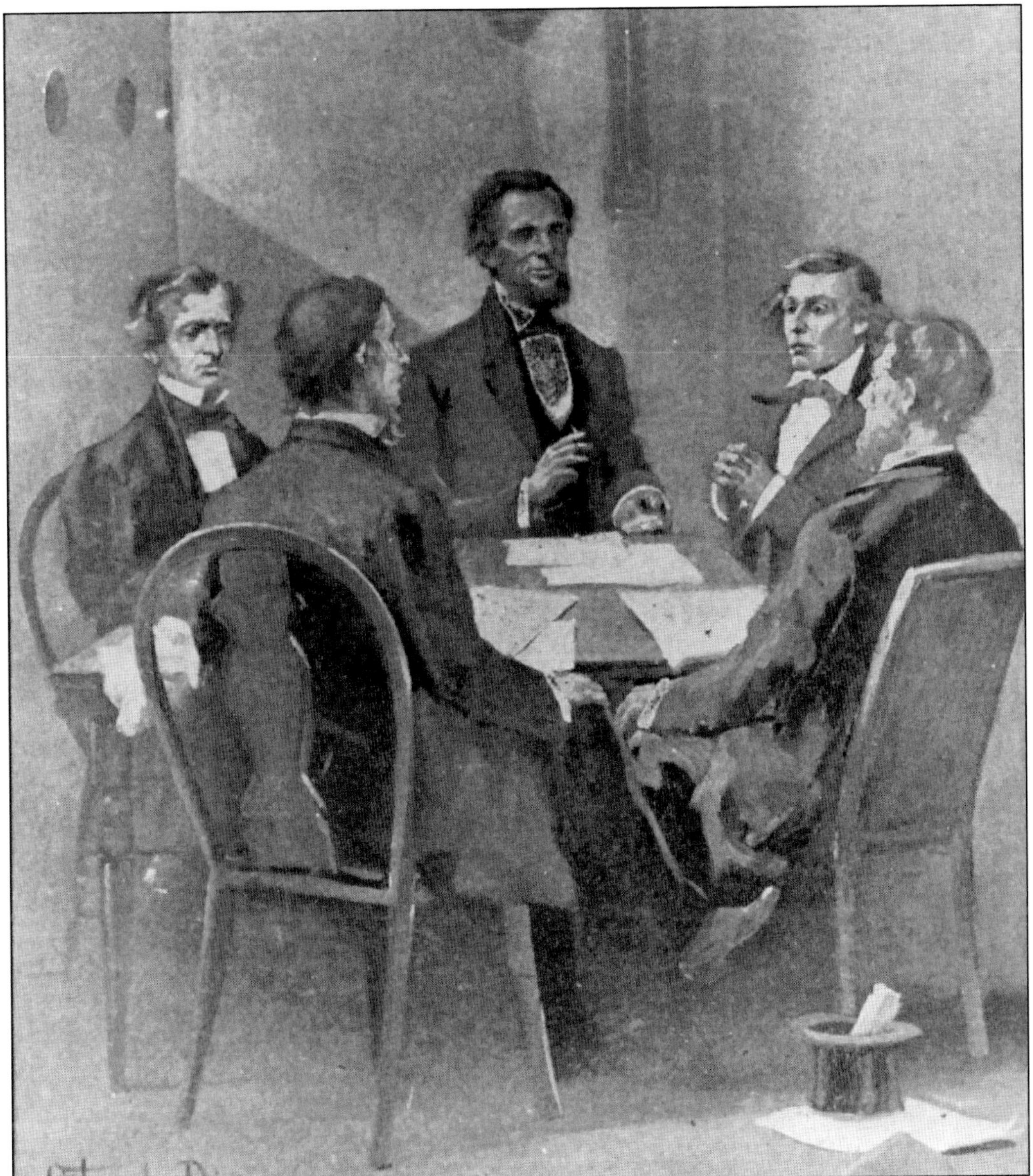

This painting depicts President Abraham Lincoln at the peace conference in Hampton Roads aboard the USS *Baltimore*. He boarded the *Baltimore* at 8:30 a.m. on the morning of May 11, 1862, and proceeded to Town Point in full view of the Norfolk waterfront, but he declined an opportunity to set foot in the captured city; whether this was due to advice given him by Chase, Stanton, or his generals is uncertain. Lincoln's life may have been in danger had he chosen to come ashore. He skirted the captured city by ship, and later in the day returned to Washington, D.C. The Norfolk campaign was Lincoln's first veridical experience as commander in chief in battle, and some military historians would say his last in terms of field exposure. Lincoln considered the taking of Norfolk and the destruction of the CSS *Virginia* that occurred in the early hours of May 11, 1862, at the hand of her crew near Craney Island, the most important accomplishments of the war to that date, and he would, as the fighting progressed, consider it one of the most important campaigns of the war. (Courtesy of Hampton Roads Naval Museum.)

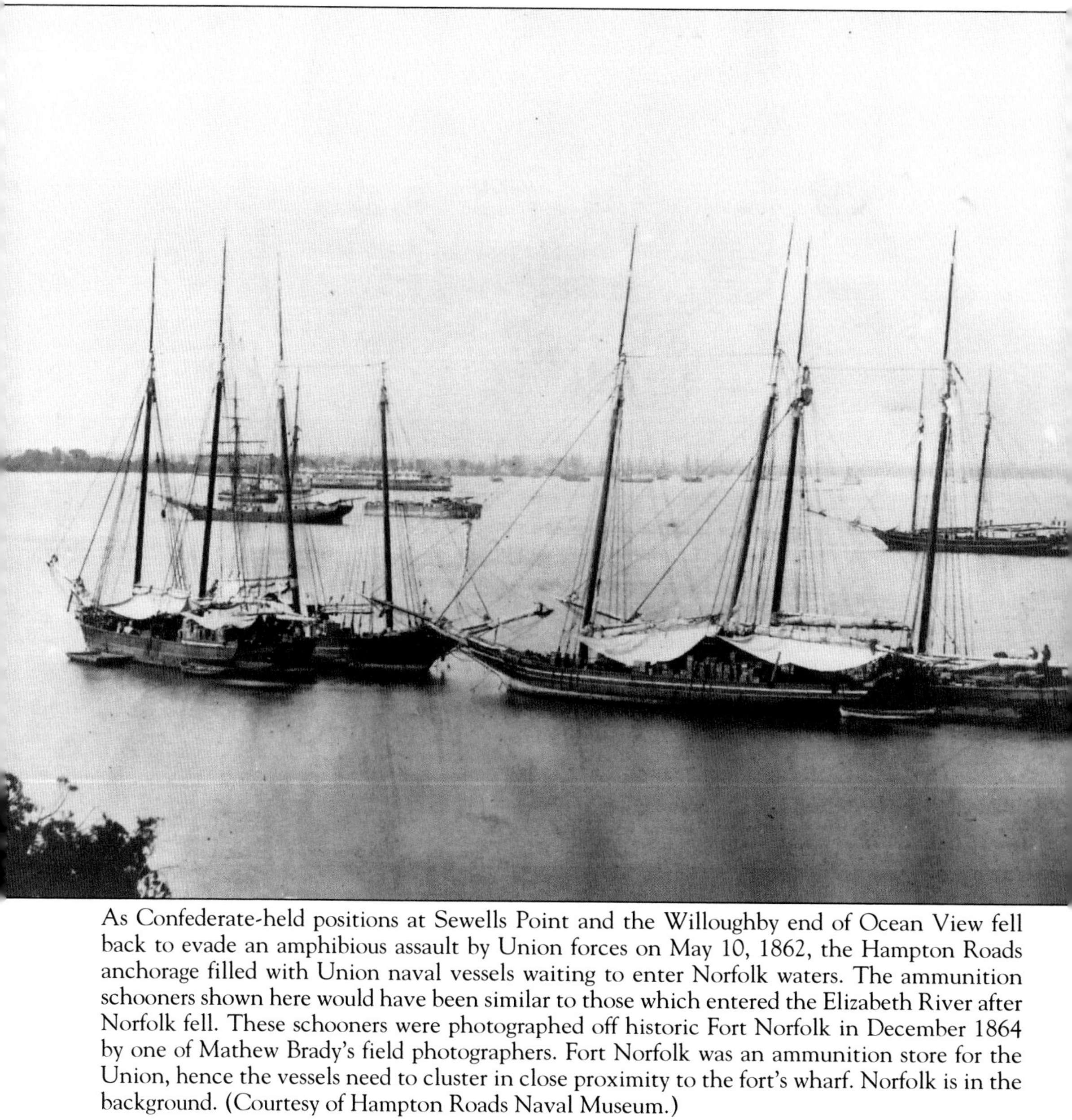

As Confederate-held positions at Sewells Point and the Willoughby end of Ocean View fell back to evade an amphibious assault by Union forces on May 10, 1862, the Hampton Roads anchorage filled with Union naval vessels waiting to enter Norfolk waters. The ammunition schooners shown here would have been similar to those which entered the Elizabeth River after Norfolk fell. These schooners were photographed off historic Fort Norfolk in December 1864 by one of Mathew Brady's field photographers. Fort Norfolk was an ammunition store for the Union, hence the vessels need to cluster in close proximity to the fort's wharf. Norfolk is in the background. (Courtesy of Hampton Roads Naval Museum.)

Two

The Ocean View Company

"A Sandy Beach with waves so blue,
A thousand bathers—not a few—
A gala crowd—diversions new—
And there you have—Old Ocean View."
—Author Unknown, c. 1910

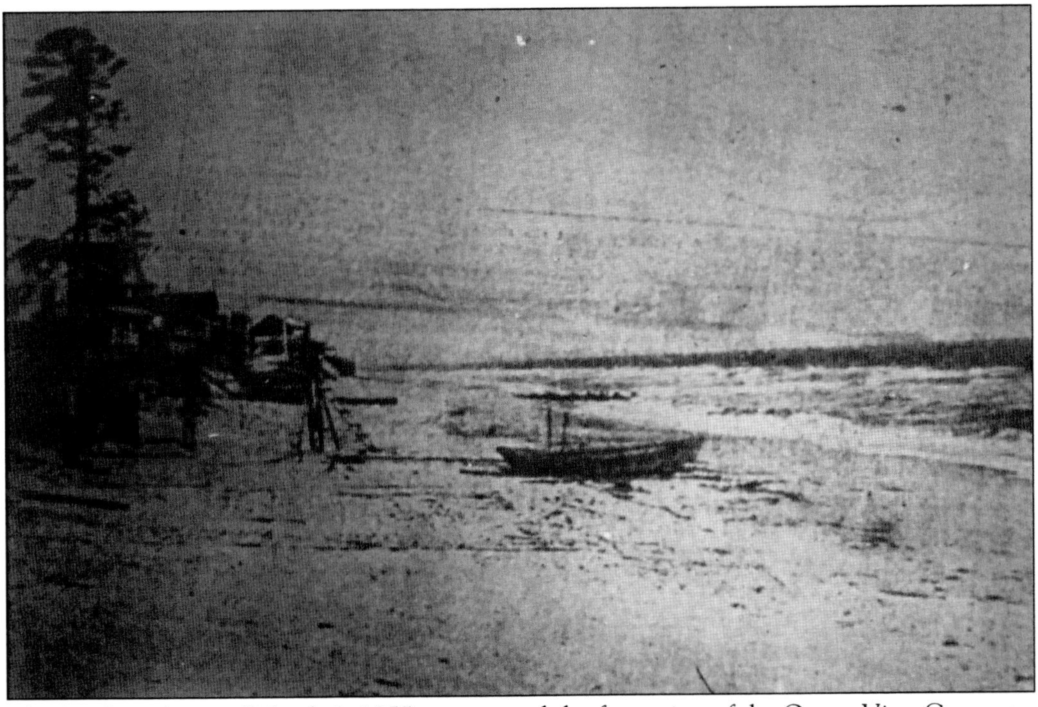

The *Southern Argus* of March 1, 1855, announced the formation of the Ocean View Company, which had purchased 10 acres of waterfront property at Ocean View in order to build a private summer resort. Though the company started building their resort, the Civil War stopped the project well-beyond the war's end in 1865. By the early 1870s, the notion of a resort at Ocean View became popular once again and people started to come back, enticed by the possibilities to start anew. Tourists from as far away as Florida stopped at Ocean View and stayed. The picture, taken in 1878, shows the beach and a few summer cottages.

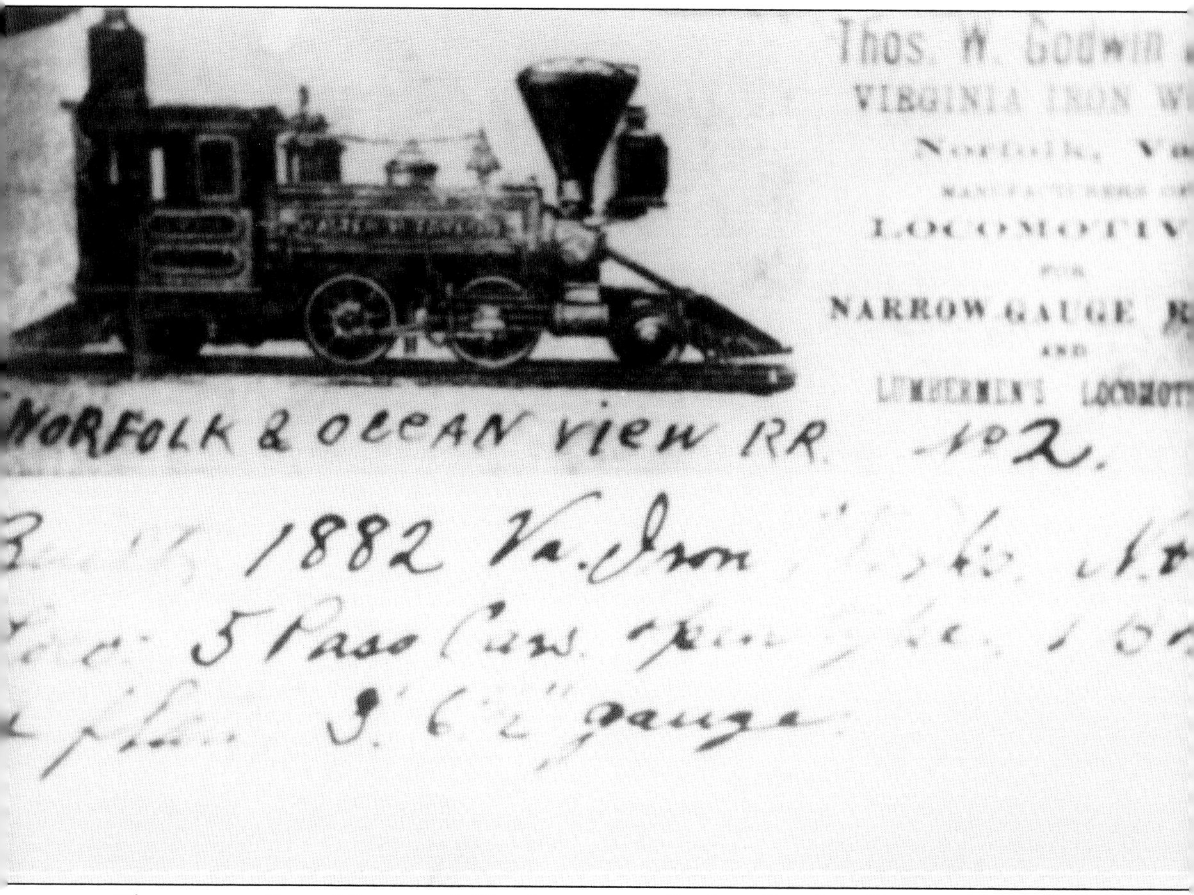

The resort at Ocean View, much like the resorts at Buckroe Beach in Hampton and at Virginia Beach, grew because of the railroad development. In 1879, the first railroad to Ocean View was constructed under the auspices of the Norfolk and Ocean View Railroad Company, a narrow-gauge, single-track line. A narrow-gauge was only 3 feet, 6 1/2 inches across, rail to rail. The first company locomotive was named for Colonel Walter H. Taylor, president of the line and former adjutant general to General Robert E. Lee. The engine (shown here the year of construction) was built in 1882 by the Thomas W. Godwin and Company, Virginia Iron Works, of Norfolk. Thomas W. Godwin and Company was located on Water Street from 1868 to 1924. The *Walter H. Taylor*, No. 2, though a small engine, could haul ten to twelve passenger cars on one trip. Another engine was added shortly thereafter and was named the *John B. Whitehead* in honor of Norfolk's mayor between 1874 and 1876.

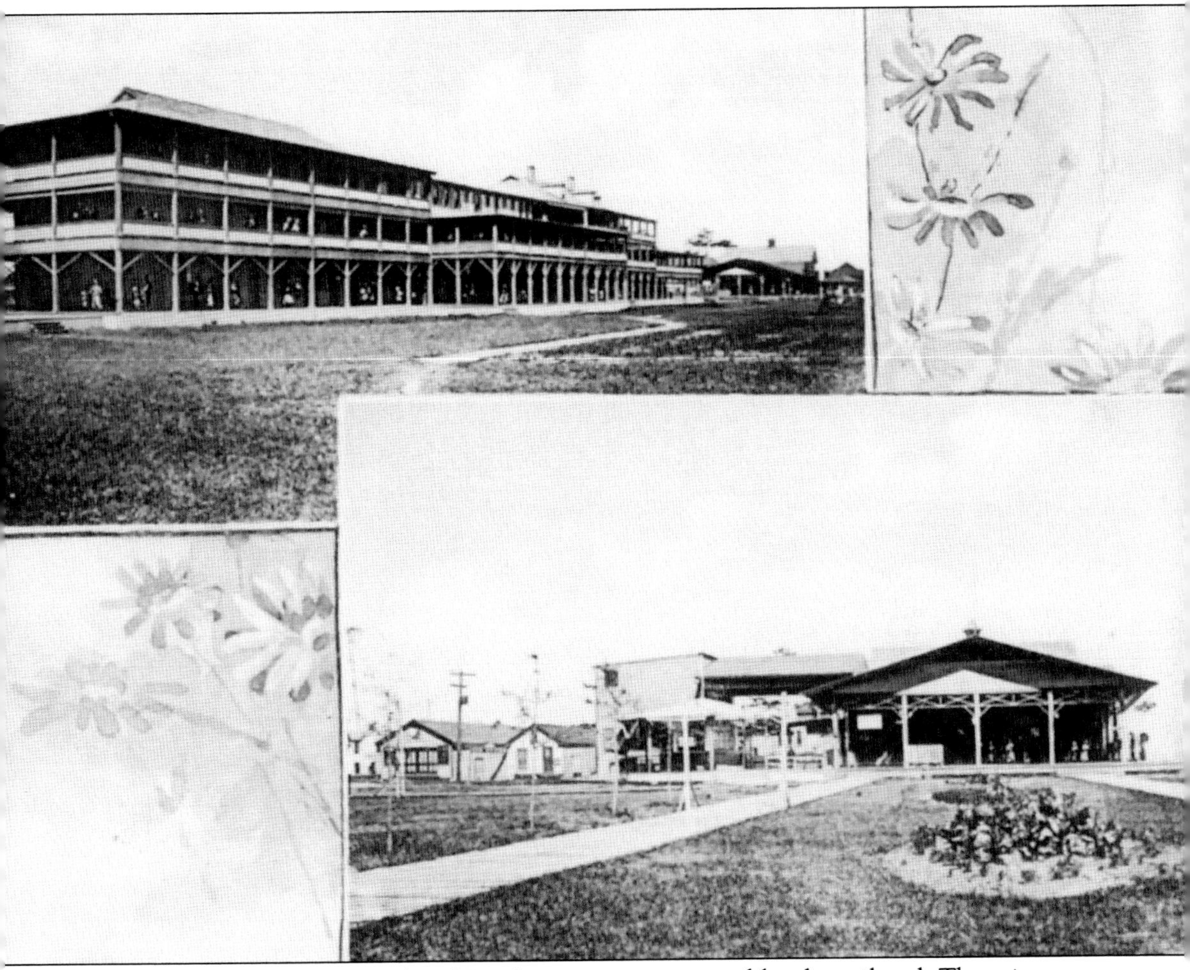

The original Ocean View Hotel and Pavilion were constructed by the railroad. These images depict the hotel and pavilion as they appeared in 1896. By 1904, an amusement entrepreneur from Richmond, Virginia, Otto Wells, visited Ocean View and saw its moneymaking potential. He purchased the resort facilities from the railroad and by 1905 had pushed the amusement business at Ocean View to new heights. There was a roller coaster at the resort as early as 1905, though it was much smaller than the famous Leap-the-Dips to come. The oldest and first Leap-the-Dips was destroyed by fire in 1914.

The Last Stop

A decade and a half after the end of the Civil War, urbanization gave rise to electric traction or trolley companies. Railroad cars gave way to trolleys. Utility companies made electric lines available to trolley companies by charging a flat fee for the electricity. It did not matter whether passenger usage was greater on weekdays or weekends, the cost was the same. In order to stimulate use of the lines on weekends, traction companies constructed a point of destination at the last stop. The point of destination was an amusement park. The first amusement parks were simple affairs. Ocean View Amusement Park was no different, consisting of picnic areas, a dance hall, eateries, souvenir shops, and a few games and rides. The parks were so successful that they began opening across the United States. Ocean View, Seaside Park in Virginia Beach, and Buckroe Beach in Hampton were three of the most successful post–Civil War attractions on the Atlantic coast.

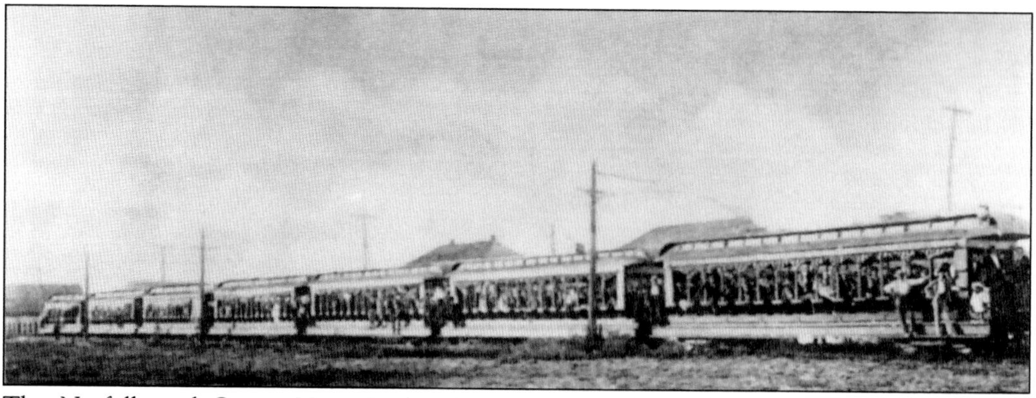

The Norfolk and Ocean View Railroad Company established the resort at Ocean View and operated all the amusements for patrons. The *Ocean View Special*, pictured here in two images from 1897, carried carloads of visitors to and from the resort. The rail line was initially constructed in 1878 as a narrow-gauge track by the Norfolk & Ocean View Narrow Gauge Railroad Company, but had to be converted to standard-gauge when the tracks were electrified in 1894.

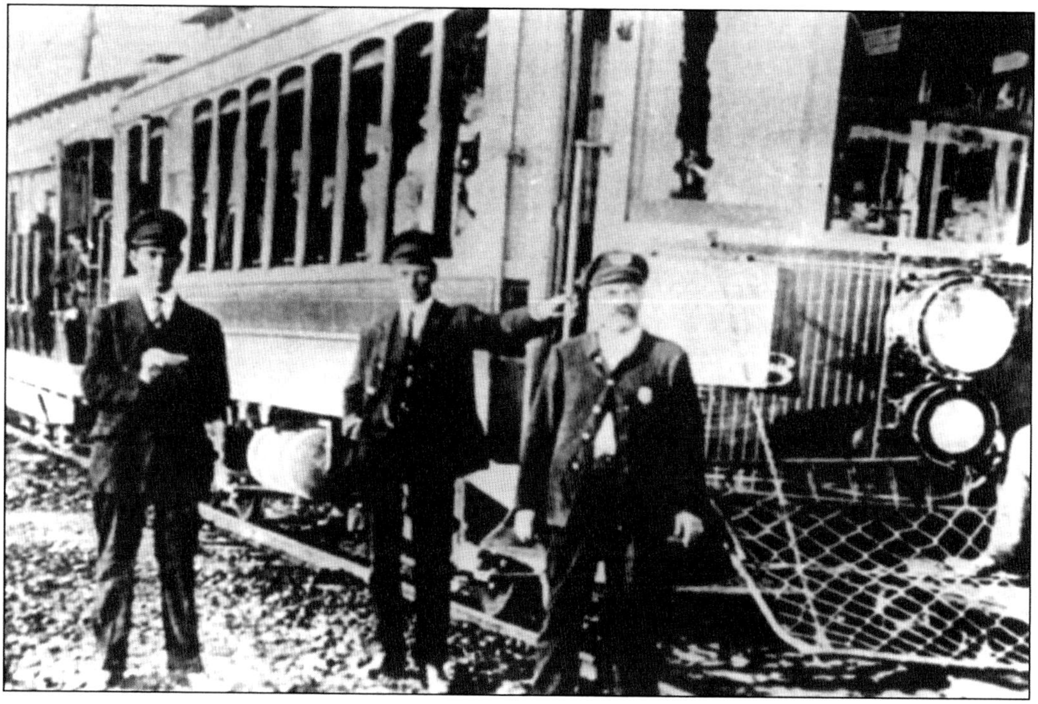

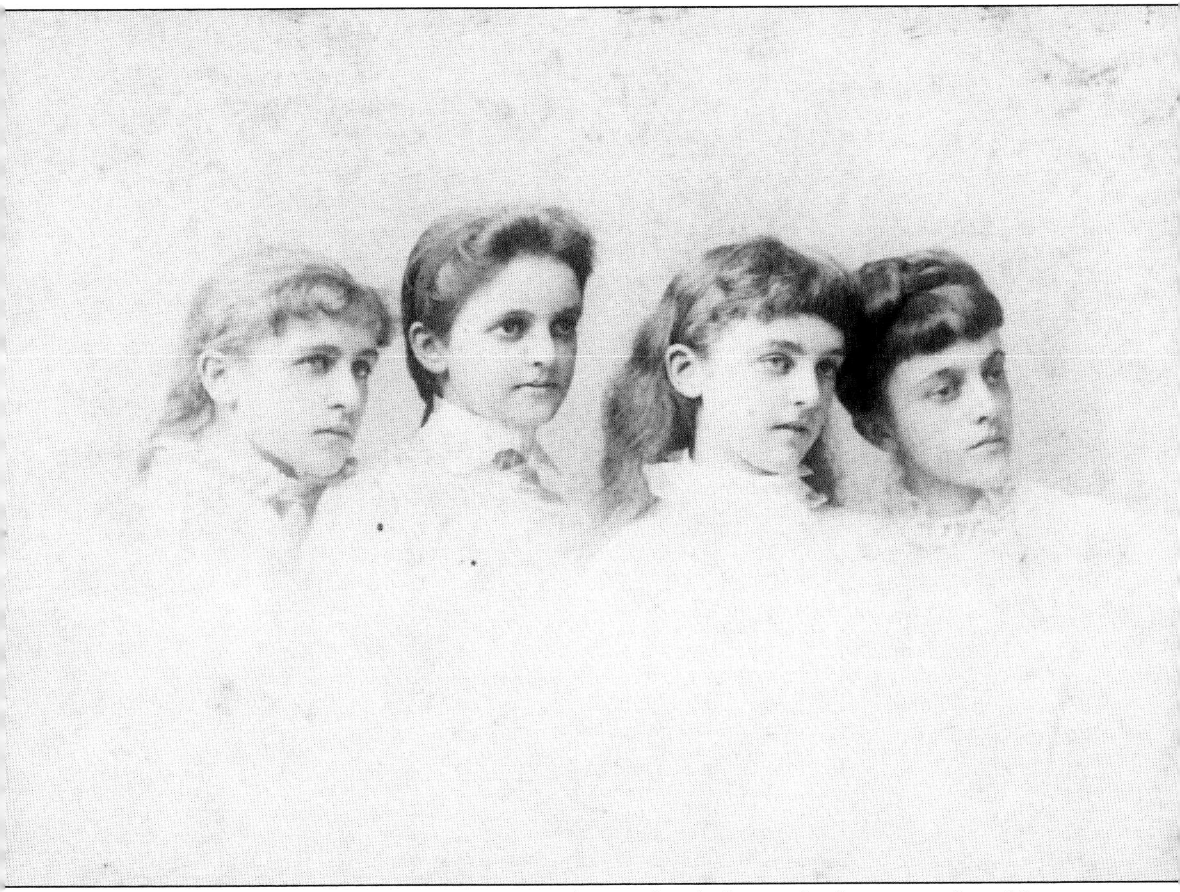

These lovely young ladies had their picture made together before embarking on a day of fun at Ocean View, *c.* 1898. (J.J. Faber, photographer.)

WHAT'S IN A NAME?

The naming of roller coasters had as much to do with the local nomenclature as it did the designer of the coaster. Whether it was the Big Dipper at Woodlawn Beach, Buffalo, New York, or the Deep Dipper, Rockaway Beach, Long Island, New York, or the Sky Rocket at Coney Island Park in Cincinnati, Ohio, the name of the roller coaster was determined by the construction of the ride, the thrill it provided its riders, and the impression the ride made upon its community. In Norfolk, the roller coaster at Ocean View was dubbed Leap-the-Dips for its sharp up-and-down ride in which the rider experienced the sensation of nearly leaping one dip to the next. The roller coaster at Seaside Park in Virginia Beach was called the Camel Back Coaster for its distinct double humps. Most of the great roller coasters of the early twentieth century were designed by John A. Miller, considered by historians to be the father of the roller coaster. Miller held over one hundred patents, many of which pertained to safety devices used on today's high-speed, looping roller coasters. Miller was issued the patent for the most crucial set of wheels on a roller coaster car, its friction wheels, in 1912. There are three sets of wheels on a roller coaster and the third set locks the car to the track. Without friction wheels, there would not be looping and inverting roller coasters, the bread and butter of the amusement business, in American theme parks.

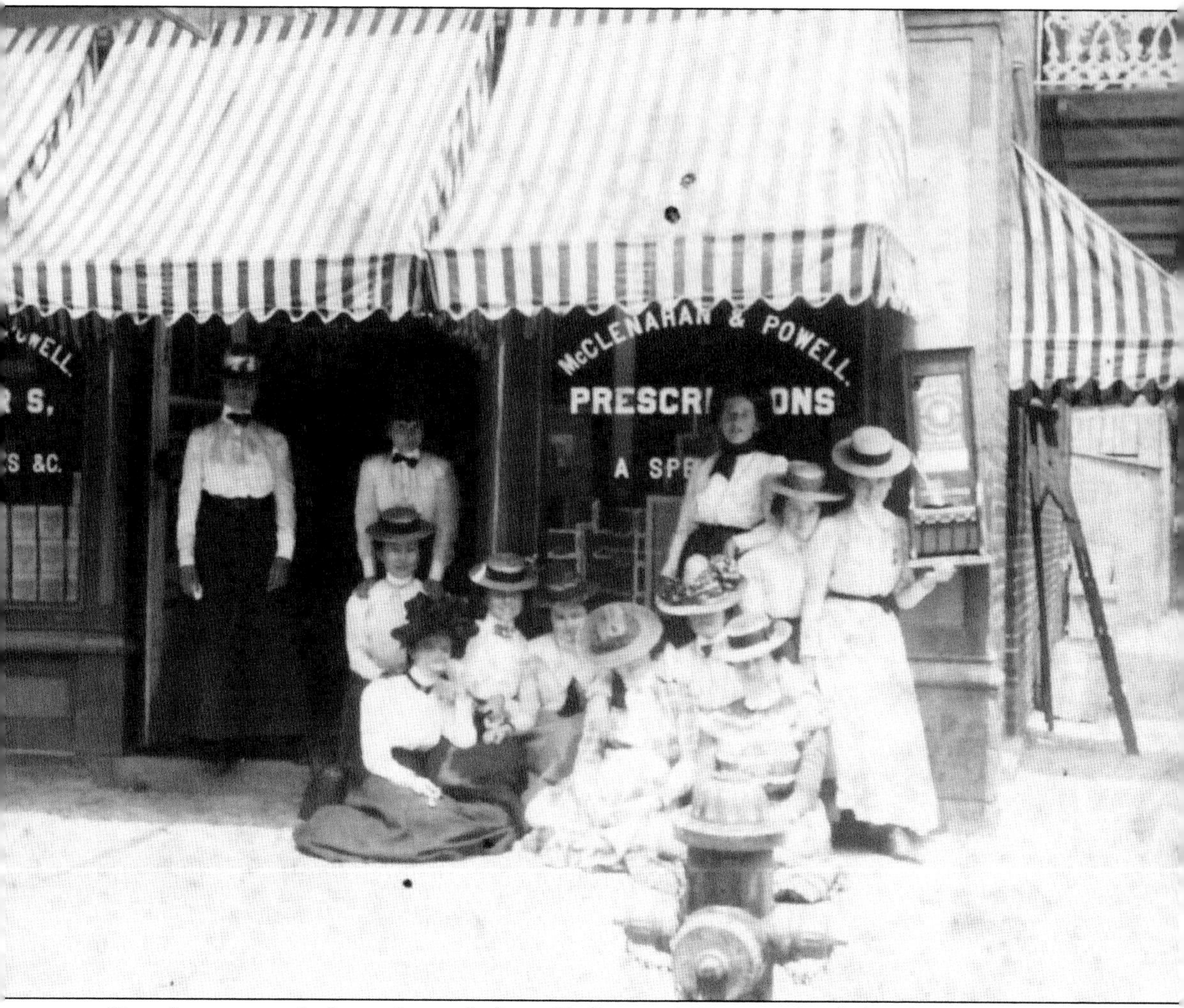

On a hot summer's day, a few girls from Phillips and West's School decided to go for a bottle of soda water at McClenahan & Powell's drugstore during recess in June 1900. The drugstore was located at the corner of Freemason and Bank Streets. These girls, all friends, were known to frequent Ocean View together on the excursion trains with their families. Pictured here, from left to right, are as follows: Baynie Taylor, Cornelia Calvert Truxton, Bessie Guy, Lizzie Foster, Eva Land, Lola Stroud, Mary Louise Jones, Eloise Taylor Waldrop, Bertha Scott, Mary Franklin Duncan, Hildegarde Lucas Chamberlaine, and Mona Lee Whittle. (Photographer unknown.)

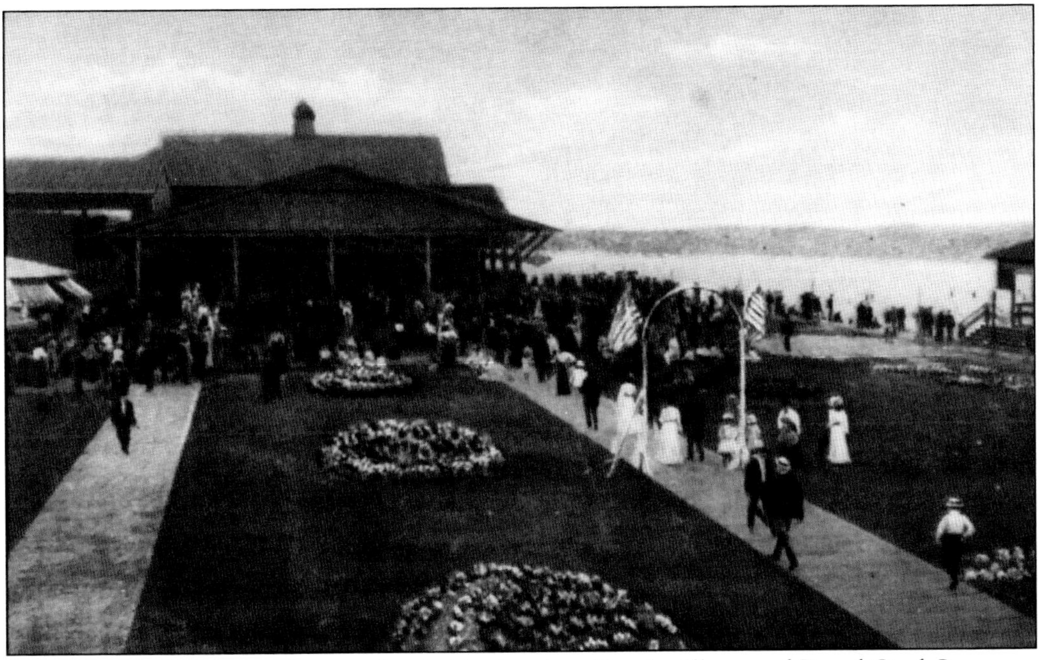

The scene on this postcard, an undivided back printed by the Illustrated Postal Card Company of New York and Leipzig, portrayed the old lawn and pavilion of Ocean View as it looked in 1901. Undivided backs were published between 1901 and 1907 and did not permit messages written on the backs, a practice then forbidden by the postal service.

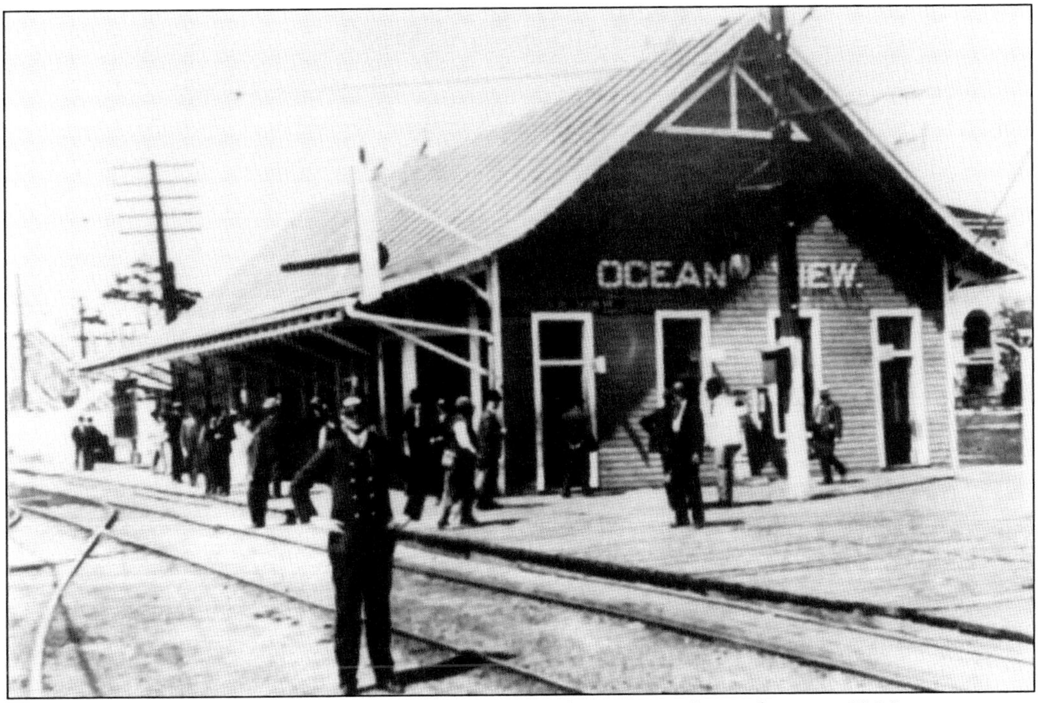

Visitors to Ocean View disembarked their train at the station shown here, c. 1908.

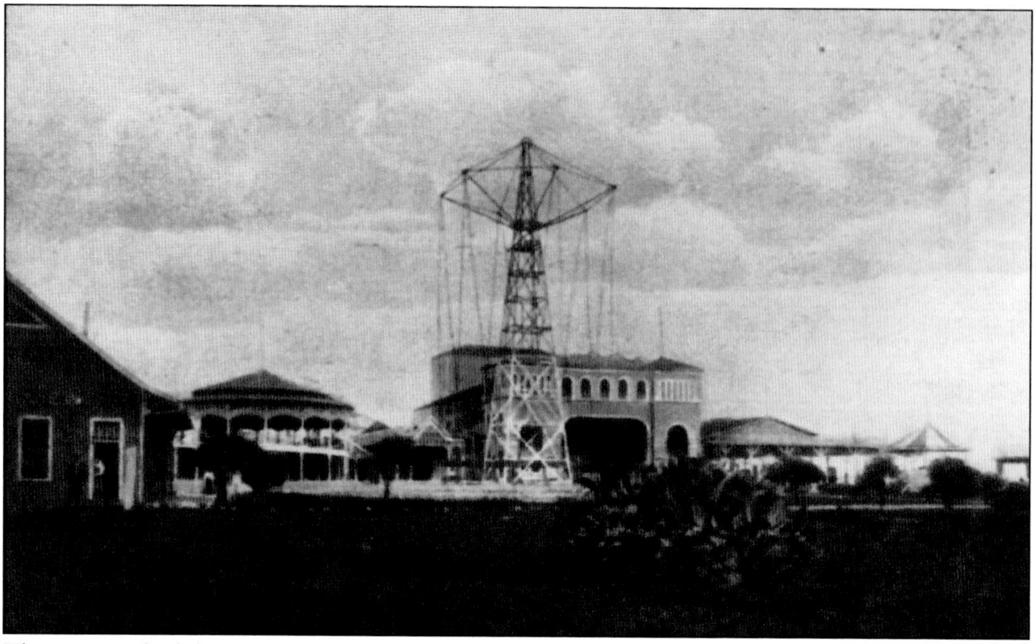

This postcard of the Ocean View Amusement Park was published about 1908 and depicts the Circle Swing ride, an amusement that remained popular until the park's business began to decline in the early 1960s.

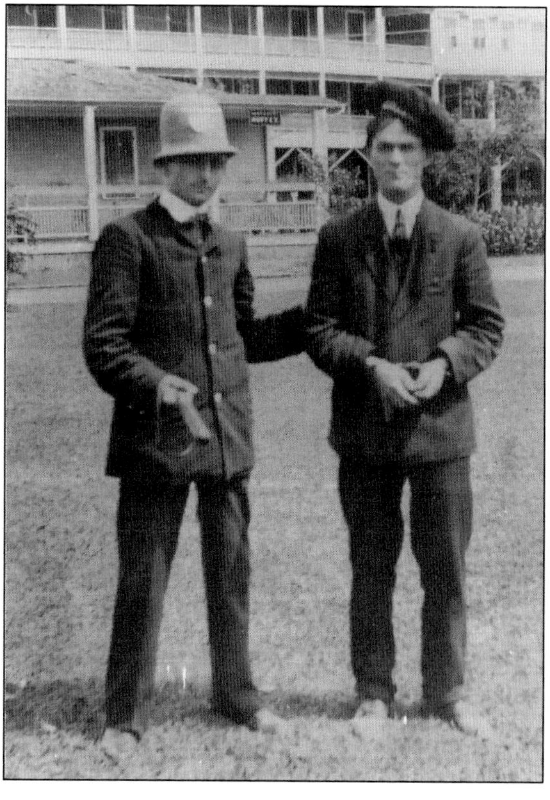

Streetcar conductors Johnson (left) and Reams (right) were photographed at Ocean View in 1908. They were standing in front of the Ocean View Hotel. The sign on the porch overhang indicated a "Gentlemen's Buffet" was available inside. (Photographer unknown.)

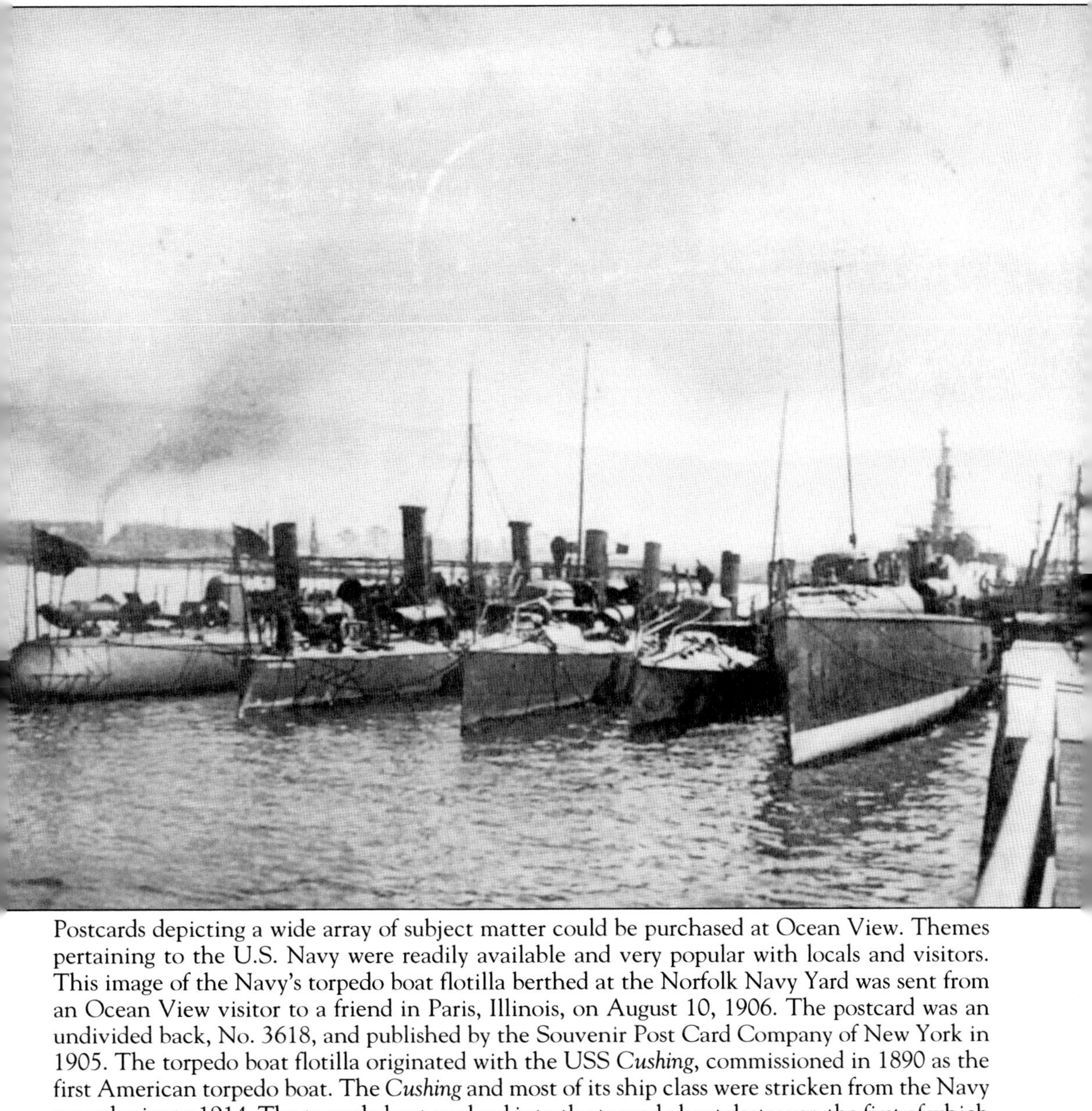

Postcards depicting a wide array of subject matter could be purchased at Ocean View. Themes pertaining to the U.S. Navy were readily available and very popular with locals and visitors. This image of the Navy's torpedo boat flotilla berthed at the Norfolk Navy Yard was sent from an Ocean View visitor to a friend in Paris, Illinois, on August 10, 1906. The postcard was an undivided back, No. 3618, and published by the Souvenir Post Card Company of New York in 1905. The torpedo boat flotilla originated with the USS *Cushing*, commissioned in 1890 as the first American torpedo boat. The *Cushing* and most of its ship class were stricken from the Navy record prior to 1914. The torpedo boat evolved into the torpedo boat destroyer, the first of which was the USS *Bainbridge*, commissioned in 1902. From the family of *Bainbridge*-class torpedo boat destroyers came the first Navy destroyers of the first-line authorized during the First World War. The *Bainbridge*, however, is known in naval history as the first U.S. destroyer.

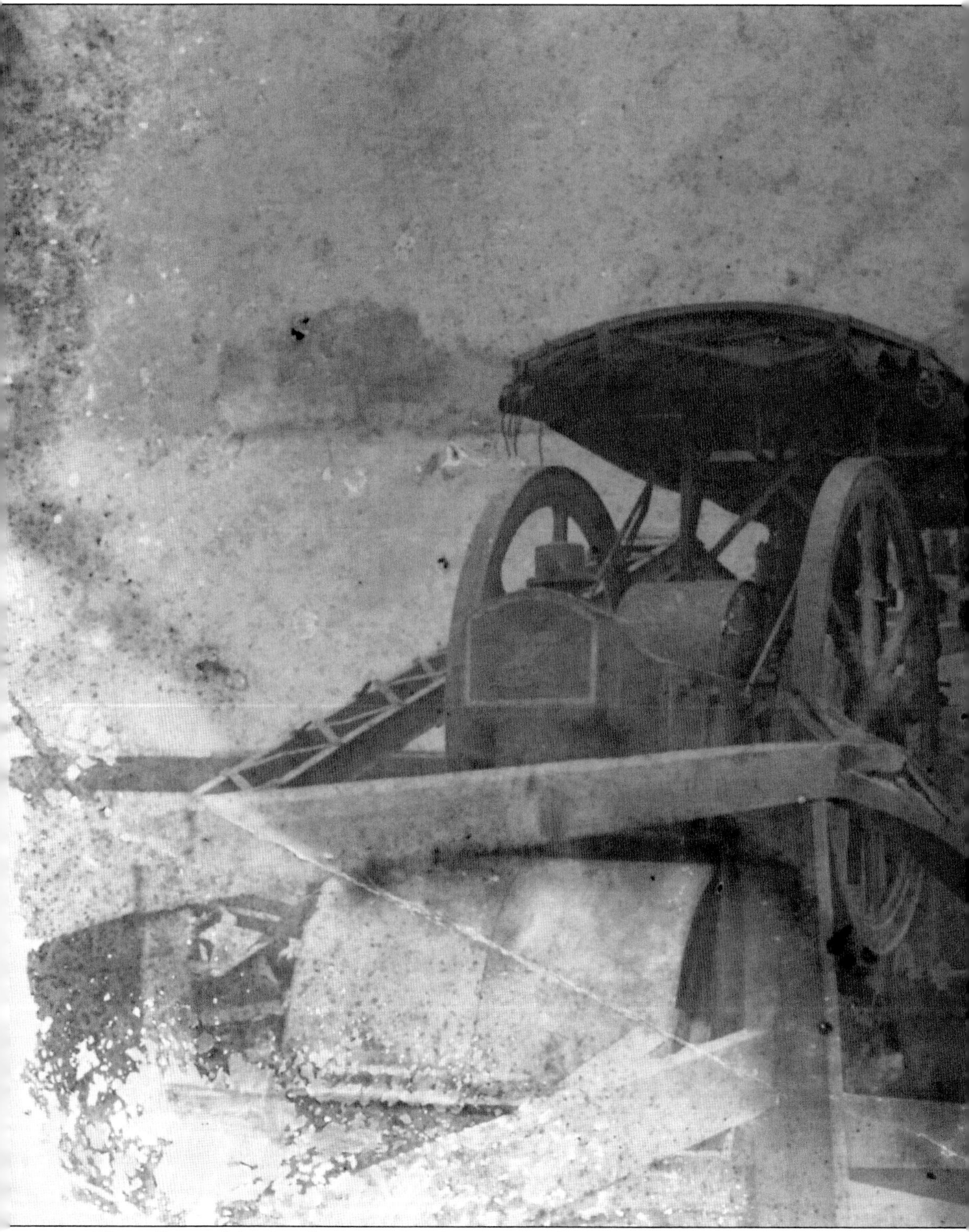

The collapse of the Granby Street or Indian Pole Bridge in 1916 left cars of the Bay Shore Line

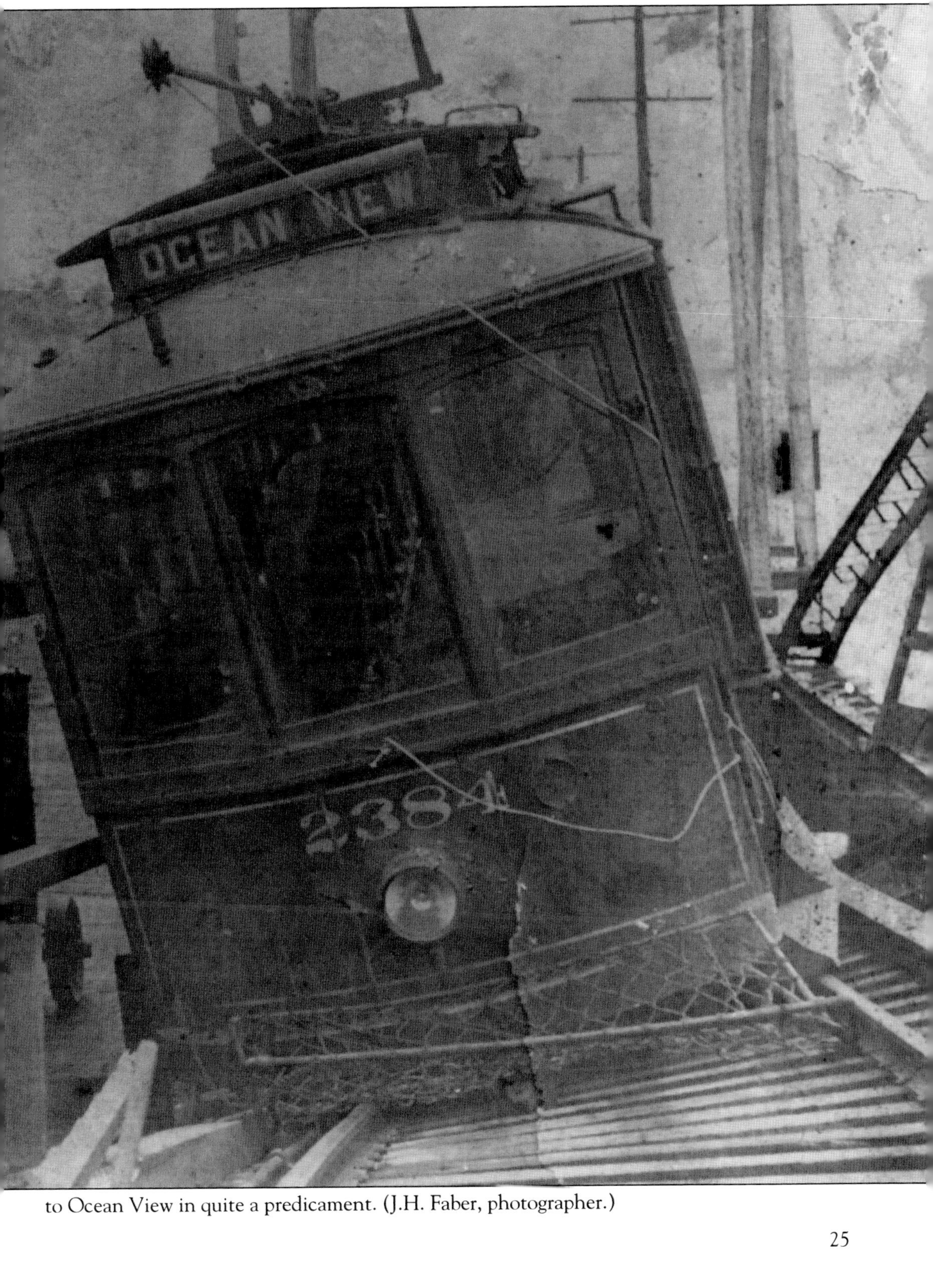

to Ocean View in quite a predicament. (J.H. Faber, photographer.)

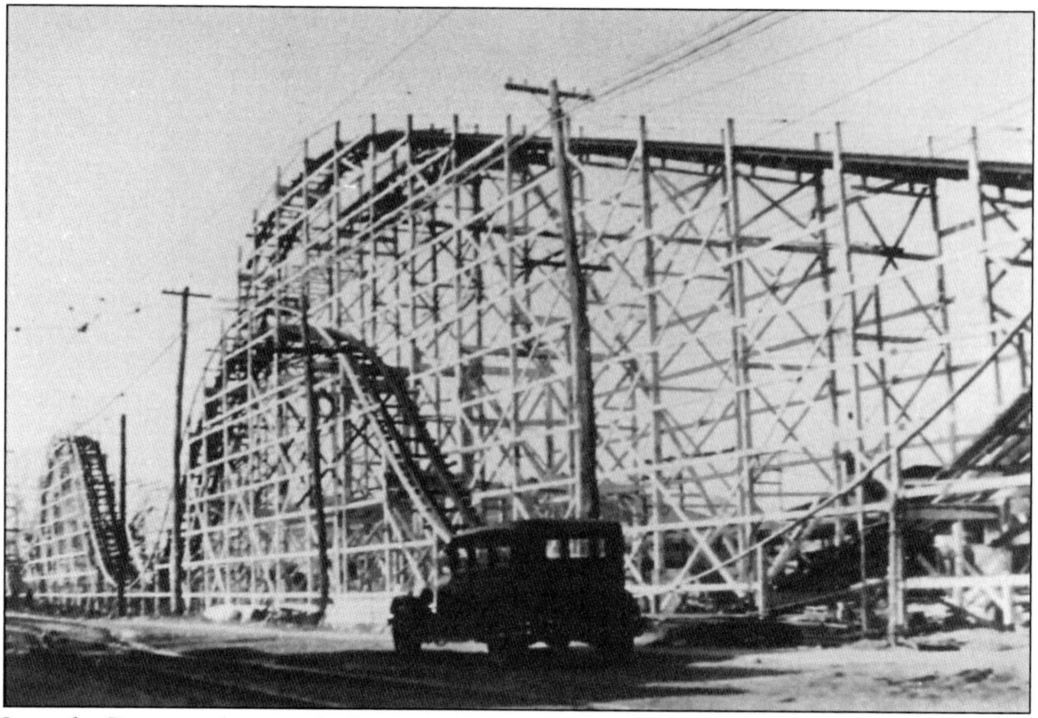

Leap-the-Dips was photographed in 1914 by an unknown cameraman standing on Ocean View Avenue. The famed roller coaster burned that year and was replaced by a new and improved version that incorporated the latest in roller coaster technology and safety devices.

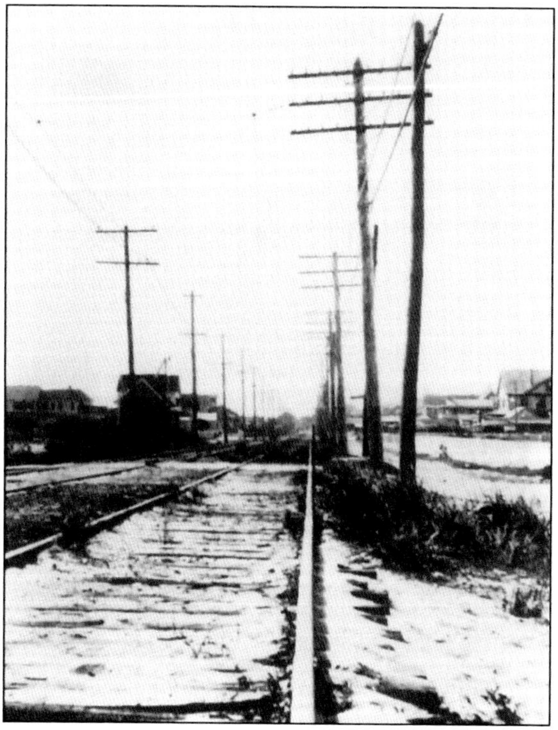

This photograph was taken in June 1915 looking west between the Fourth and Fifth Street stops at Willoughby. Stops were where the trolleys picked up and off-loaded their passengers. The road on the right was unpaved until Willoughby was annexed by the city of Norfolk in 1923. (Photographer unknown.)

Three

By the Bay

"The tide rises, the tide falls,
The twilight darkens, the curlew calls;
Along the sea-sands damp and brown
The traveller hastens toward the town,
And the tide rises, the tide falls."
—From *The Tide Rises, the Tide Falls*, 1879, 1880
Henry Wadsworth Longfellow, American poet
(1807–1882)

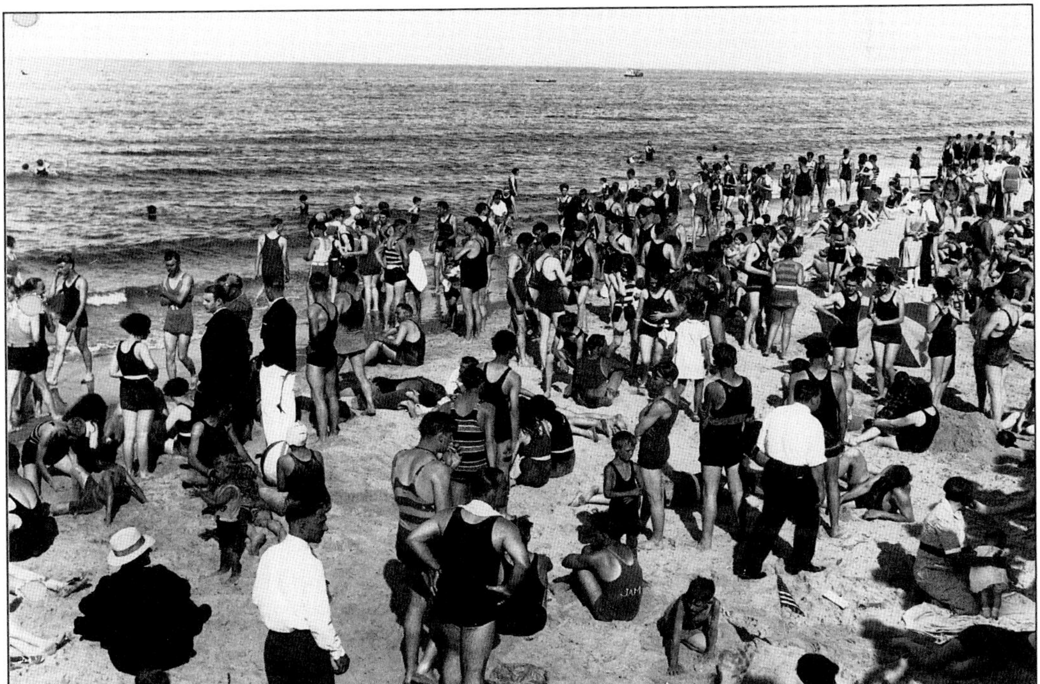

Electric cars delivered people to Ocean View in droves on July 4, 1929. Nearly all the railroads serving Norfolk had connectors to the electric trains headed for Ocean View. The Baltimore Steam Packet Company, the Chesapeake Steamship Company, the Eastern Steamship Line, and other transportation providers offered attractive water routes with excellent connections to the electric trains, while the Norfolk Southern Bus Lines and the North Carolina Bus Lines entered the city of Norfolk with direct connections, as in the case with trains and steamship lines, direct to the electric lines. (Charles S. Borjes, photographer.)

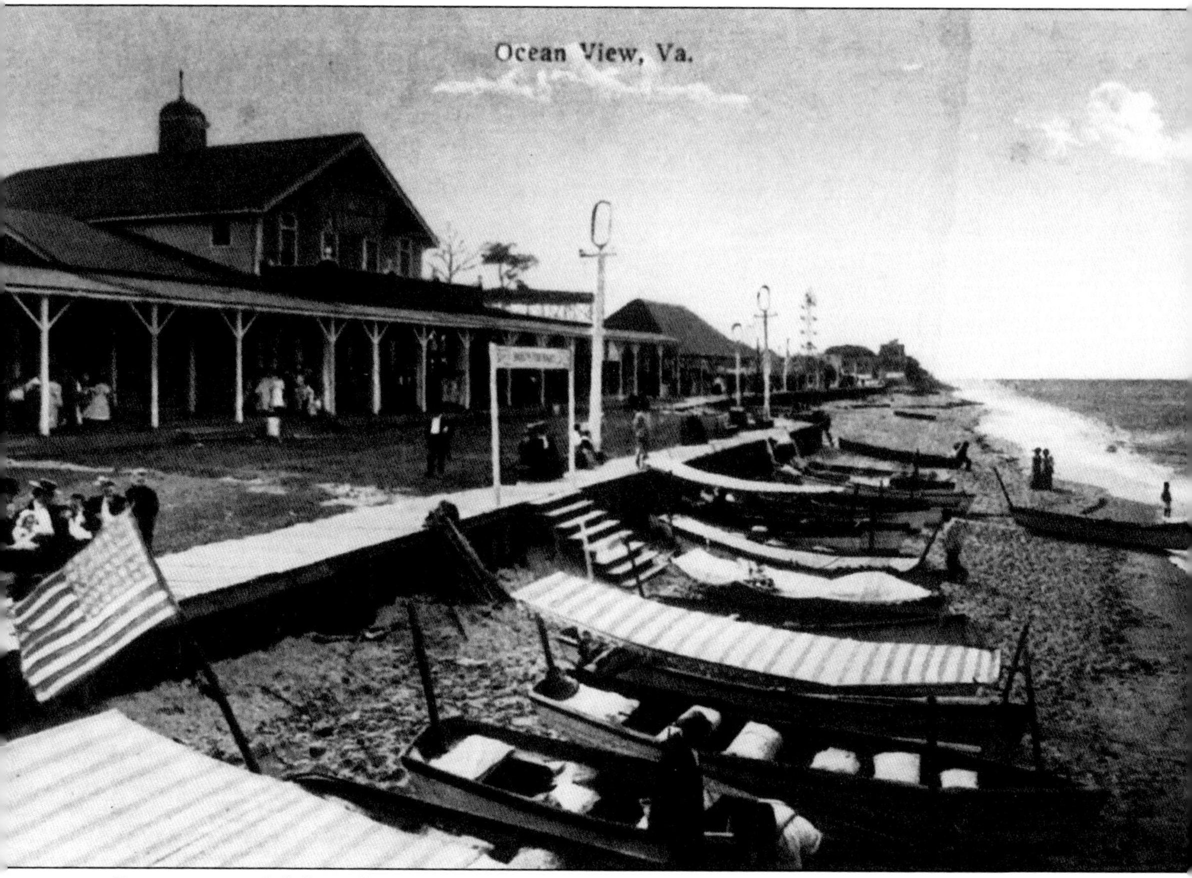

Excursion and fishing boats were very popular throughout Ocean View's resort history. The boats depicted here appeared on a postcard postmarked November 14, 1909.

SANDHILLS

The easternmost portion of Ocean View is today bordered by the Little Creek Naval Amphibious Base. Part of the base was once called Camp Bradford and on this property stood a Georgian-style home on the inlet, near a lake. Long before the U.S. Navy occupied the site, this house had been the country residence of Governor Littleton Waller Tazewell (1774–1860) of Virginia and Major Edmund Bradford (1820–1869), married to Governor Tazewell's daughter, Anne. When Tazewell and Bradford owned the property, it was called Sandhills and, later, the Bradford Farm. Though the land had been, more or less, absorbed by Princess Anne County before the Civil War, it was considered a continuation of Ocean View's view of the Atlantic Ocean. Some of the best beaches and fishing grounds associated with this historically significant part of old Ocean View's past were along the 2 1/4 miles of waterfront now occupied by the naval amphibious base. Sandhills and its farmland had fallen into disrepair and neglect by the time the Navy acquired the acreage under a takings filed July 29, 1942, in U.S. District Court, Norfolk, but the history of Sandhills remains an important chapter of Ocean View's past. By July 1945, the four separate bases established during World War II at Little Creek—Camp Bradford, Camp Shelton, Frontier Base, and Little Creek Base—were consolidated into the Little Creek Amphibious Training Command.

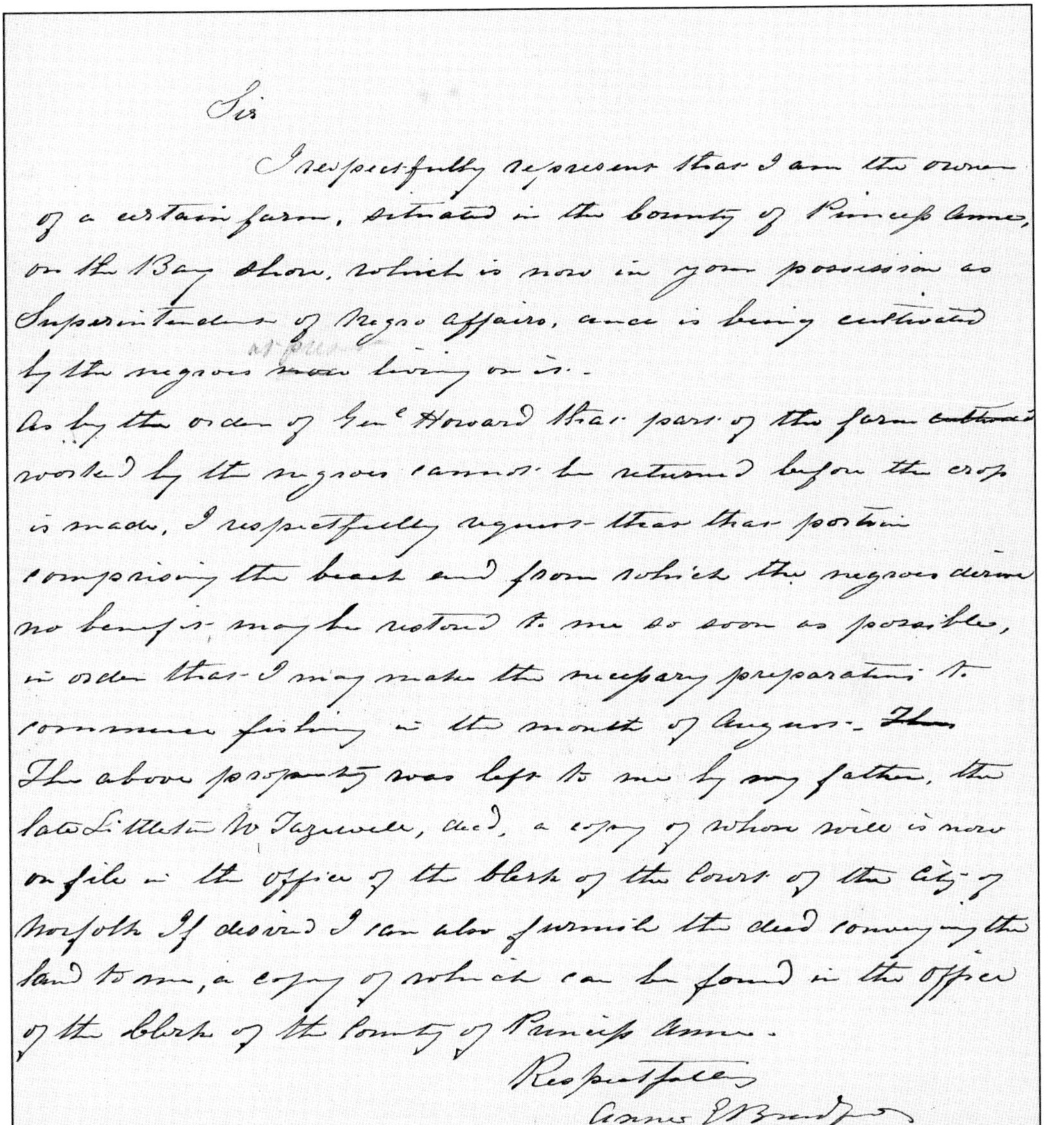

Sir

I respectfully represent that I am the owner of a certain farm, situated in the County of Princess Anne, on the Bay Shore, which is now in your possession as Superintendent of Negro affairs, and is being cultivated by the negroes ~~now~~ at present living on it.

As by the order of Genl Howard that part of the farm ~~cultivated~~ worked by the negroes cannot be returned before the crop is made, I respectfully request that that portion comprising the beach and from which the negroes derive no benefit may be restored to me as soon as possible, in order that I may make the necessary preparations to commence fishing in the month of August. ~~The~~

The above property was left to me by my father, the late Littleton W Tazewell, decd, a copy of whose will is now on file in the Office of the Clerk of the Court of the City of Norfolk. If desired I can also furnish the deed conveying the land to me, a copy of which can be found in the Office of the Clerk of the County of Princess Anne.

Respectfully

Anne E Bradford

Edmund Bradford was a graduate of the U.S. Military Academy at West Point and a distinguished U.S. Army officer who had served with distinction in the Mexican War. The citizens of Philadelphia, his city of birth, had presented Bradford with a ceremonial sword for his service. With the outbreak of the Civil War in April 1861, Bradford felt compelled to place his loyalties with Virginia. He resigned his Army commission and joined the Confederate States Army. Major Bradford's property, Sandhills, was occupied by Union forces from 1862 until the end of the war, and these troops turned the land over to emancipated slaves to farm for their subsistence. Major Edmund Bradford requested a pardon from President Andrew Johnson after hostilities ended, a pardon he was eventually granted, but his health had declined in the interim and administration of Sandhills affairs fell on Anne E.T. Bradford. She wrote to the superintendent of Negro Affairs on June 17, 1865, requesting that "the portion of her land comprising the beach and from which the negroes derive no benefit may be restored to me as soon as possible, in order that I may make the necessary preparations to commence fishing in the month of August." A copy of the letter is shown here. Edmund Bradford died in 1869.

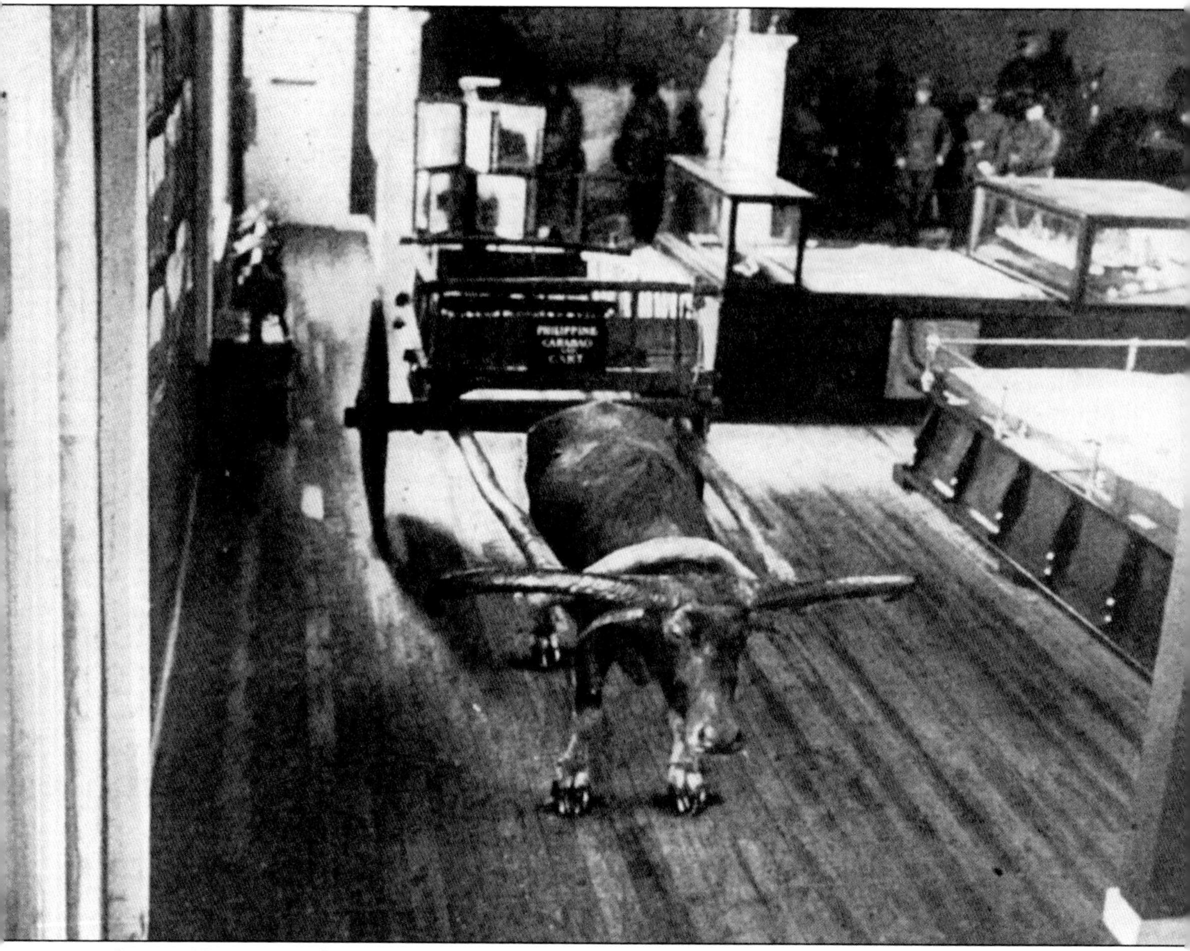

Ocean View earned its name in the nineteenth century. Though today residents and visitors to Ocean View can see only the lower end of the Chesapeake Bay from their windows and beaches, there was a time when houses at the eastern end of the resort area could look upon the Atlantic Ocean beyond Cape Henry. The outermost, eastern portion of Ocean View is now occupied by the Little Creek Naval Amphibious Base. The location of the naval base forced most of Ocean View's residential development into areas off Granby Street and down Willoughby Spit. On a good day, the Atlantic Ocean is still visible from Moore's Point at Harbor View Drive. The first person to establish a home, not a summer cottage, at Ocean View and the first promoter of the shore community was William F. Johnson (1840–1925). When he died on December 3, 1925, Johnson was eighty-five years old and had resided at 1121 Granby Street for forty-two years. He had come to the United States from London, England, and was an expert taxidermist and prominent Ocean View florist. During the Jamestown Exposition, Johnson was in charge of the exhibition of birds and animals. Johnson curated the water buffalo exhibit from the Philippines, shown here, in the Governments Building at the exposition in 1907.

Robert Mayo Hancock (left) and two of his friends had their picture made at Ocean View on June 23, 1901. The backdrop for the picture had a painting of the amusement park Ferris wheel and some of the low-level buildings by the shore. The first Ferris wheel was introduced at the 1893 Colombian Exposition.

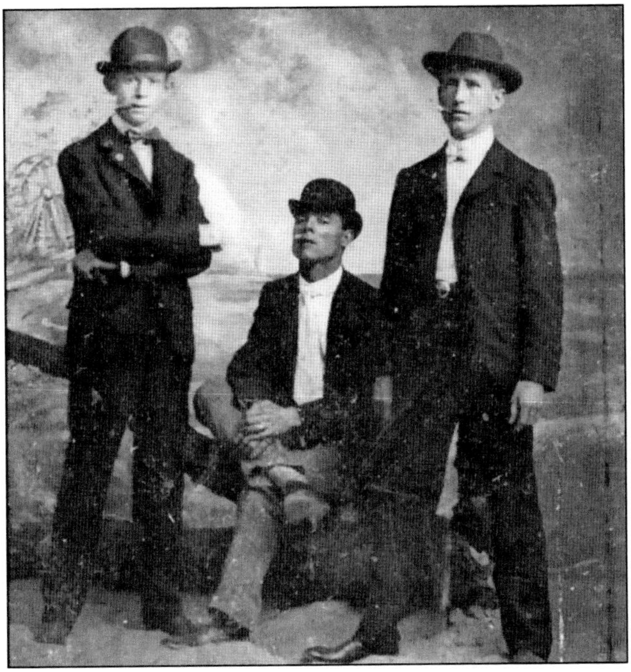

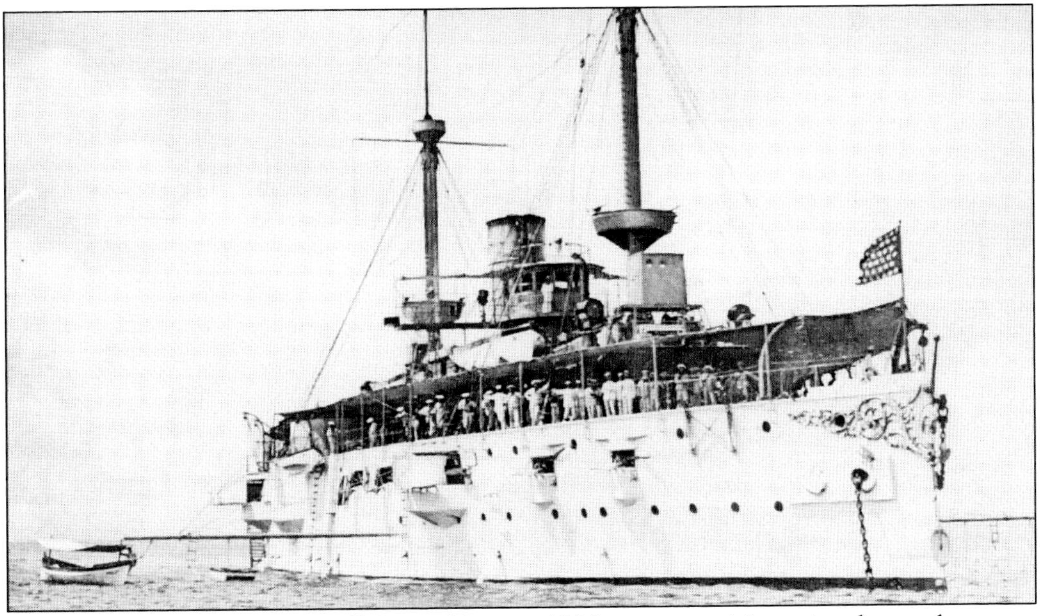

The USS *Texas*, shown here off Ocean View in 1896, was a participant in what ranks as one of the greatest sea fights in American history in the sheer power of the flying squadrons that engaged Spanish Admiral Cervera in the fight off Santiago, Cuba, on July 3, 1898. During the heat of battle, it was Captain Philip of the USS *Texas* who is quoted as saying: "Don't cheer, the poor devils are dying." The North Atlantic Squadron, under the command of Rear Admiral William T. Sampson, summarily defeated the Spanish fleet, thereby ending Spain's resistance at sea and bringing the Spanish-American War to a hasty end. The keel of this twin-screw battleship was laid on June 1, 1889, at the Norfolk Navy Yard. On June 28, 1892, the *Texas* was launched with great fanfare, as she became the U.S. Navy's first battleship.

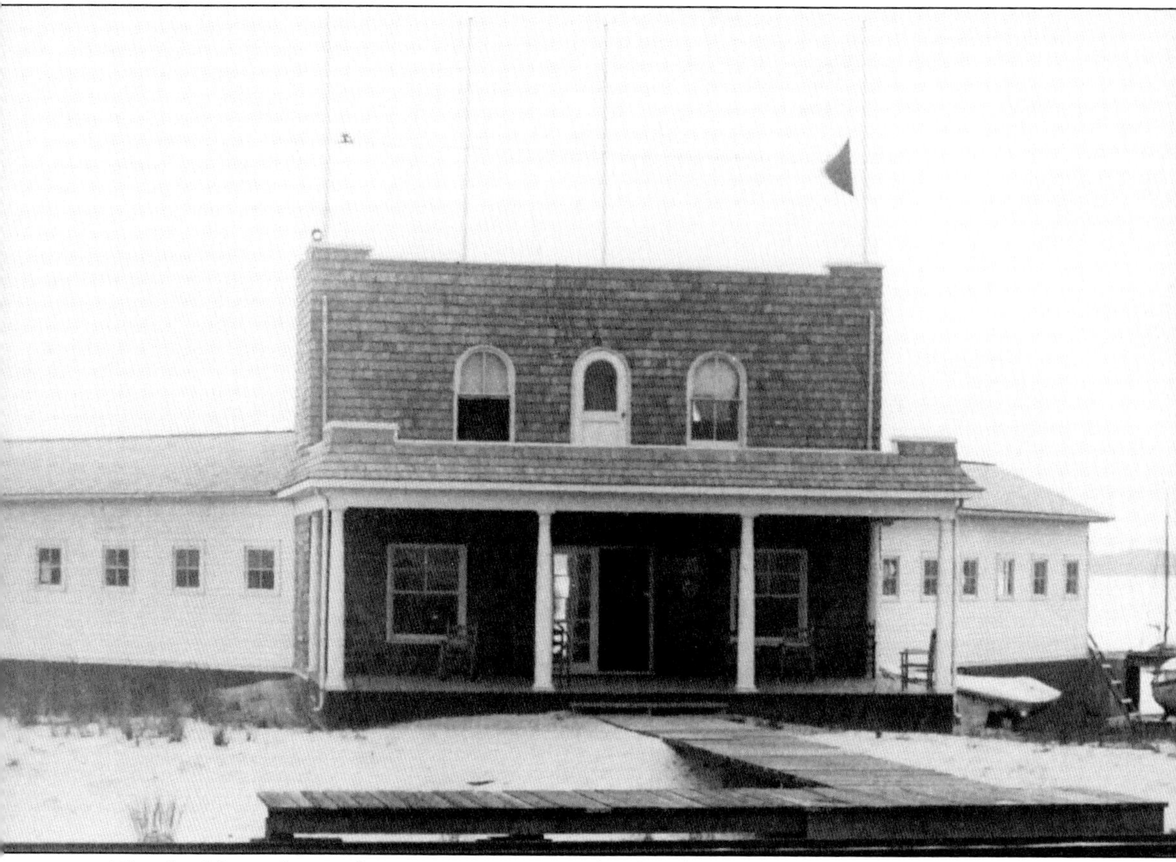

The building shown here, c. 1902, was the headquarters of the Hampton Roads Yacht Club until a larger clubhouse was completed in 1904. After the new building was finished, the old clubhouse became a boathouse. Streetcars had a stop at the club's front door. (Photographer unknown.)

Robert Mayo Hancock posed with these lovely young ladies at Ocean View, c. 1910. Hancock was a resident of Lafayette-Winona at the time. Young men could take the ladies for a Sunday afternoon to the park at Ocean View, partaking of the amusements, dancing, and seaside walks.

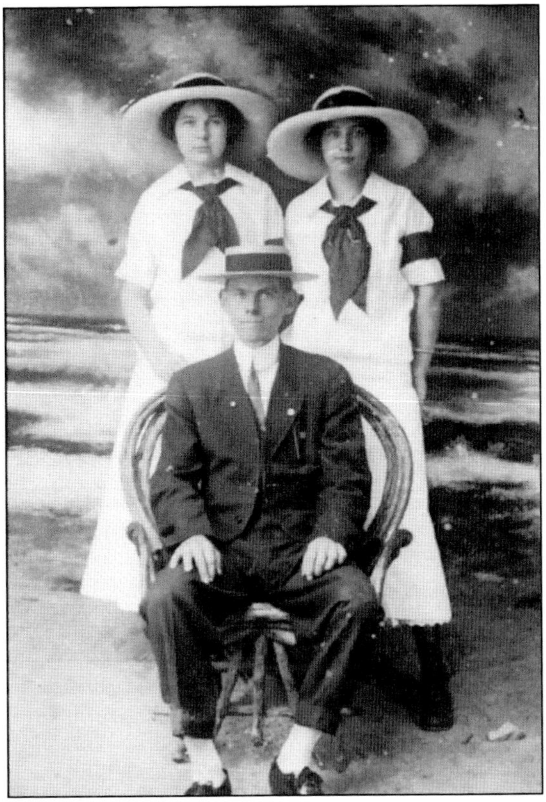

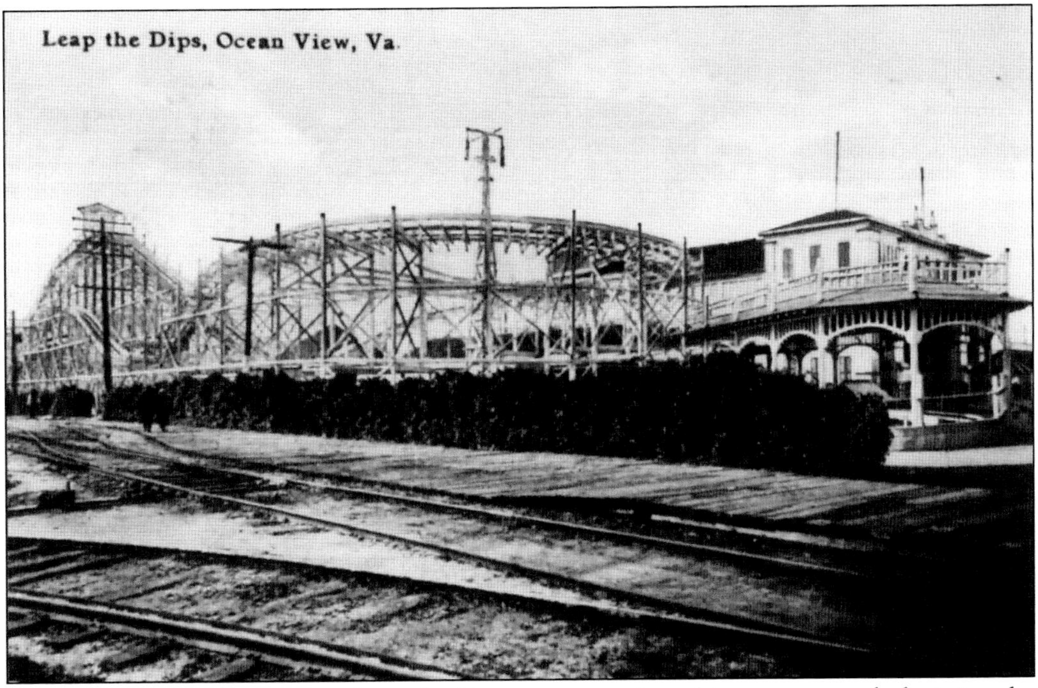

The Ocean View roller coaster, Leap-the-Dips, was a popular subject on postcards depicting the park in its early days. The postcard shown here was sent September 28, 1912, from Ocean View.

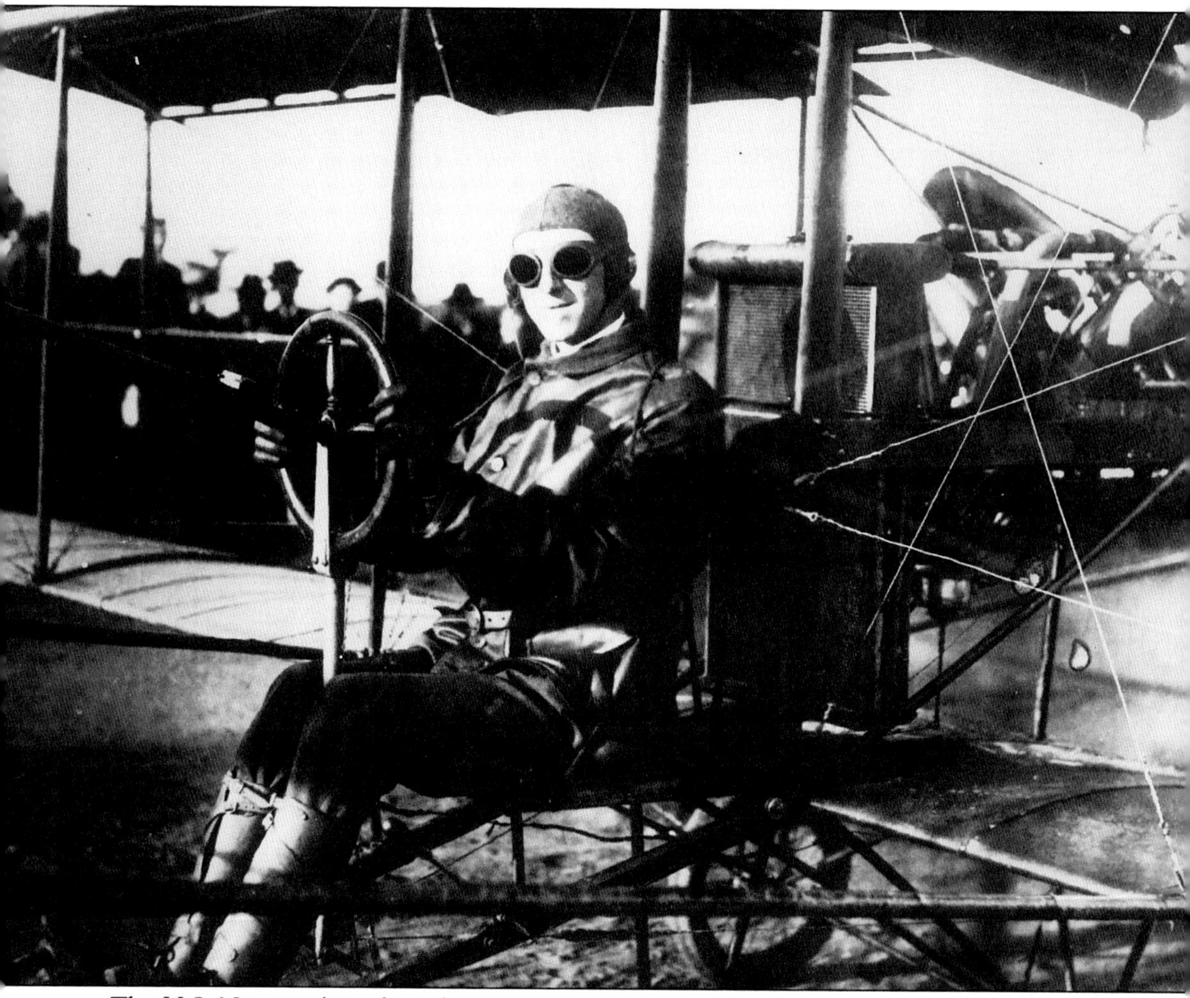

The U.S. Navy took its first plunge into aeronautics with a fixed-wing aircraft on November 14, 1910, when aviator Eugene Barton Ely, in the Curtiss biplane *Hudson Flyer*, made his way into the Chesapeake Bay aboard the scout cruiser USS *Birmingham* (CL-2) and took flight, effectively giving birth to naval aviation at Hampton Roads, Virginia. Though the flight lasted only a few minutes, it became not only the first successful aircraft launched from a ship, but the first flight from ship to shore. Ely made landfall next to the Hampton Roads Yacht Club at Willoughby Spit in Ocean View. Ely is pictured here with the *Hudson Flyer*, c. 1910. (Courtesy of the Hampton Roads Naval Museum.)

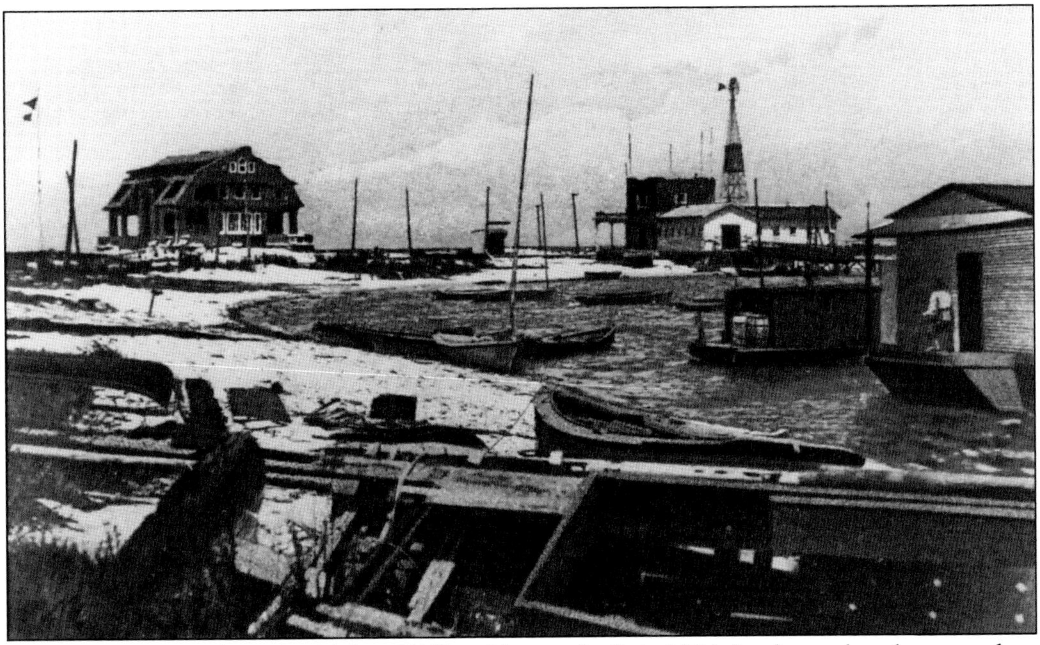

The Hampton Roads Yacht Club at Willoughby was built in 1904, but burned to the ground on September 3, 1913. The building complex to the right was the boathouse for the club. Private residences were down the beach to the left of the club. This hand-colored photograph was manufactured as a postcard and published in 1910.

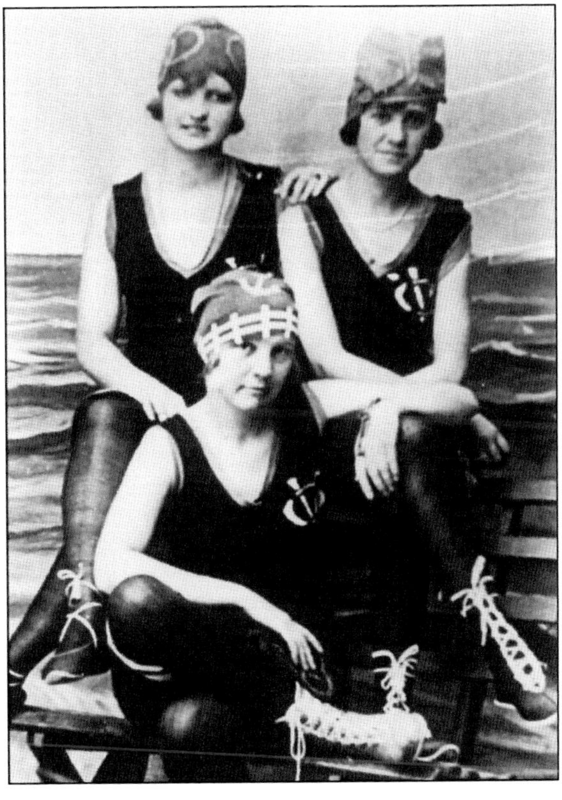

These three bathing beauties posed for a picture at Ocean View about 1915. (Photographer unknown.)

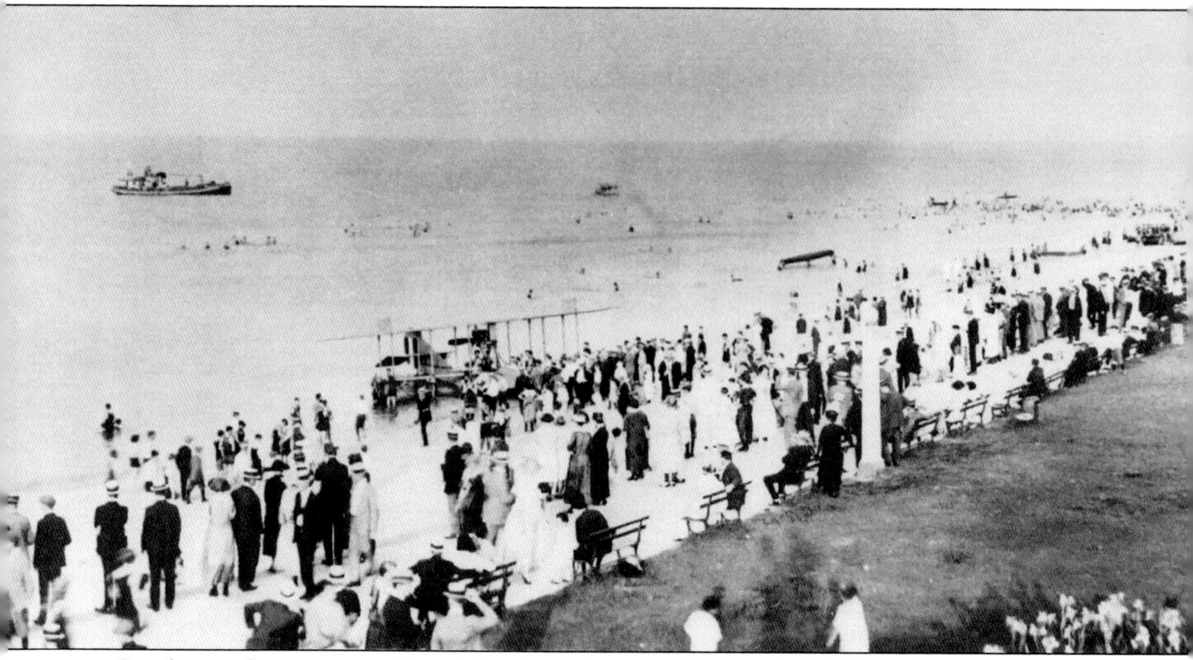

Seaplane rides were popular at Ocean View from 1915 through the 1920s. Here, a Curtiss F-boat was surrounded by potential customers, *c.* 1916. The Curtiss F-boat could accommodate one passenger and the pilot, both seated forward of the power plant. The aircraft shown in the picture might very well have come from the Atlantic Coast Aeronautical Station in Newport News, Virginia, aircraft designer and pioneer Glenn H. Curtiss' experimental station and flight school. His Newport News facility was in operation from 1915 to 1922. It would not have been unusual for a Curtiss instructor pilot to earn extra money taking weekend passengers on joy rides up and down the shore. (Photographer unknown.)

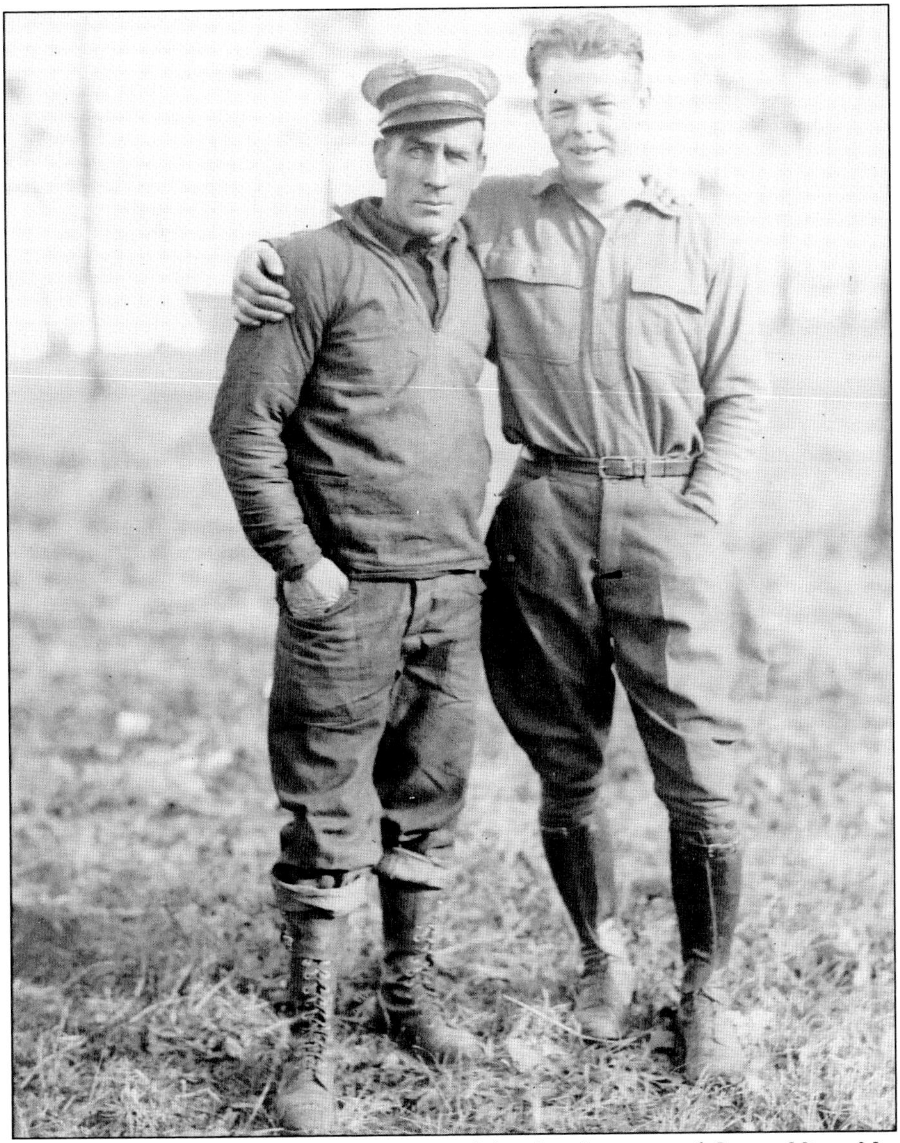

The U.S. Navy was, and is, an important part of the development of Ocean View. Naval Air Detachment Hampton Roads was established on land adjoining the naval base in May 1917. Student naval aviators and their instructors trained informally at the base until September 2, when their work was officially acknowledged. On August 27, 1918, Naval Air Station Hampton Roads was commissioned and simultaneously became a separate command from the naval base. From May 1917 through November 1918, the air station trained 622 pilots and 1,000 mechanics. With the exception of Naval Air Station Pensacola, Florida, as of June 1918, the air station at Norfolk had become the most important in the nation. The "birdmen," as they were dubbed, participated in the lifeblood of the city of Norfolk and remained faithful patrons of the resort at Ocean View. Within twenty years of its commissioning, the naval air station had acquired considerable lands around Willoughby Bay through a combination of property purchase and landfill. Navy seaplanes used the protection of Willoughby Bay for training and practice exercises. A chief and student naval aviator were photographed by Frank J. Conway c. 1918 at the air station.

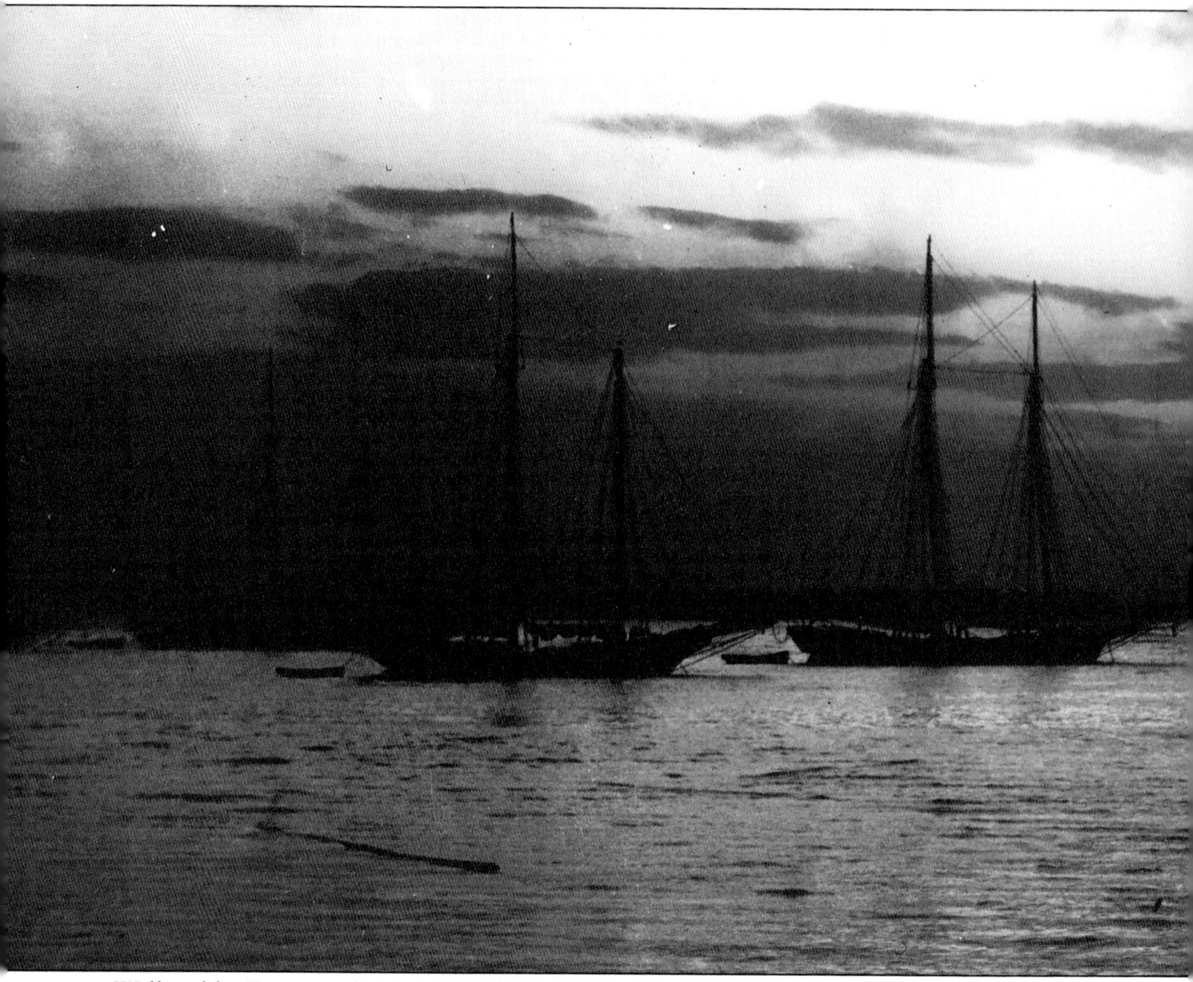

Willoughby Bay was photographed by Harry C. Mann about 1918. The bay was filled with sail boats at sunset.

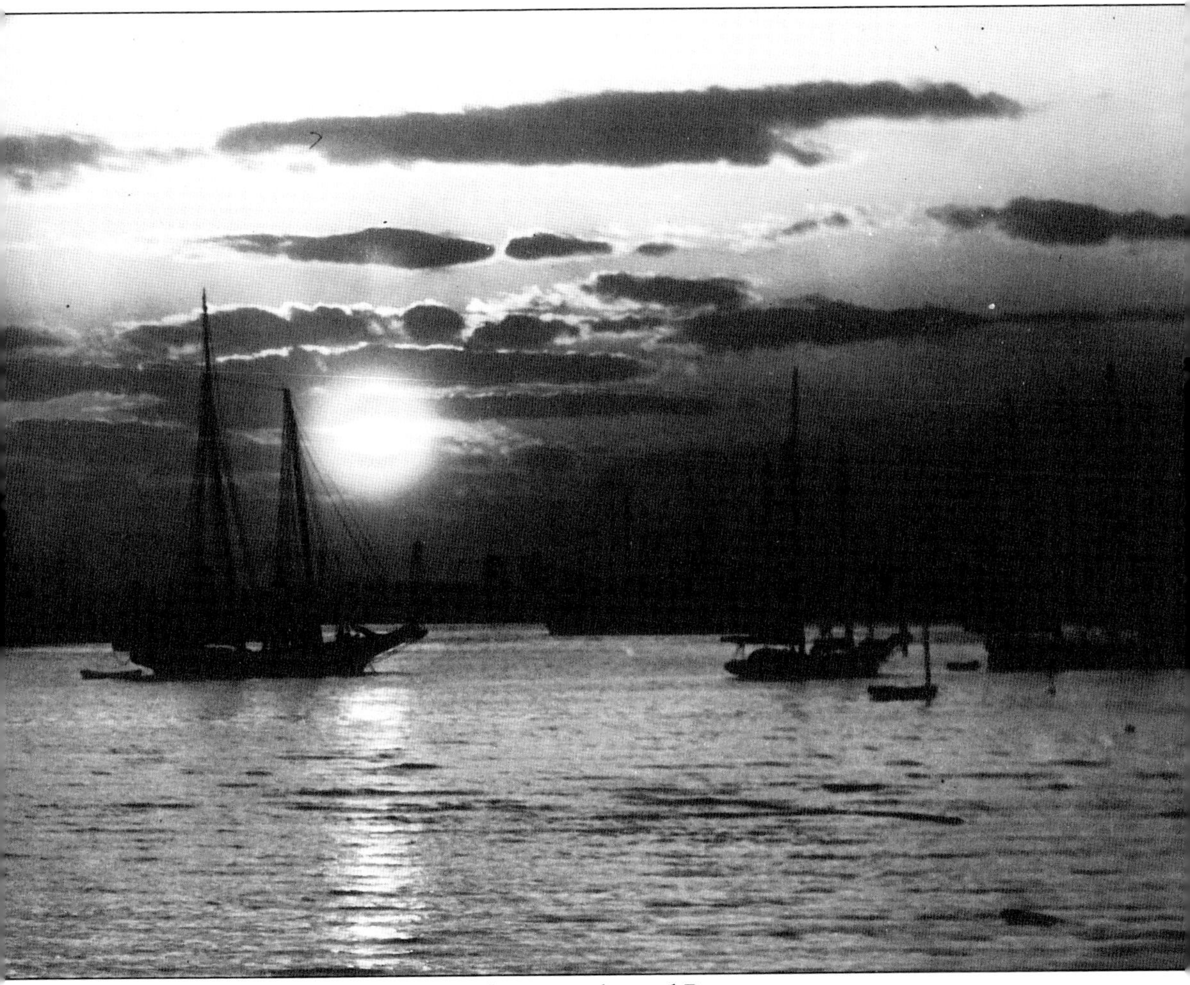

"My soul is an enchanted Boat,
Which, like a sleeping swan, doth float."
—From "My Soul Is an Enchanted Boat,"
Prometheus Unbound, 1818–1819
Percy Bysshe Shelley, English poet
(1792–1822)

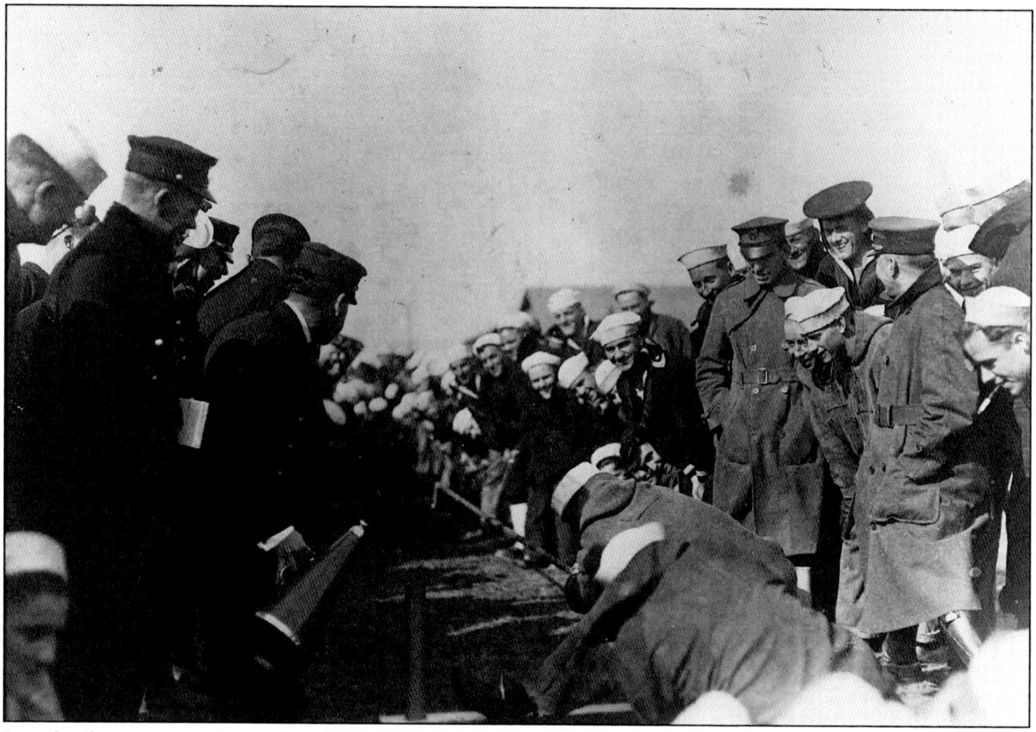

Just for fun, airmen from Naval Air Station Hampton Roads and corpsmen from the Naval Base Hospital Unit A competed at tug-of-war on Field Day, March 1, 1918, Old Chambers Field. (Official United States Navy Photograph.)

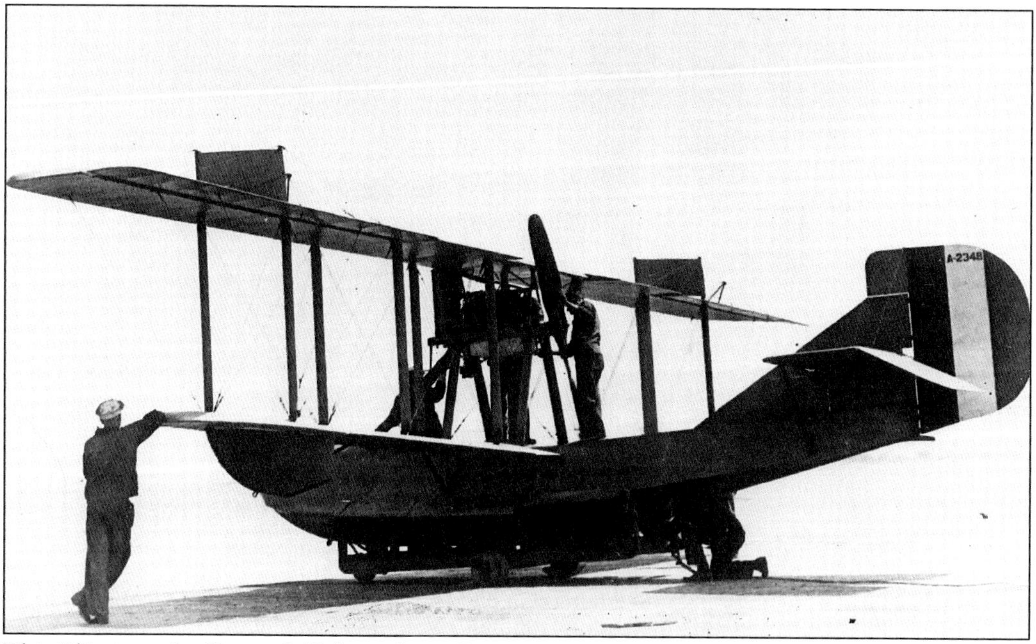

This 3/4 view of a Curtiss MF flying boat, Bureau No. A2348, was taken on the ramp at Naval Air Station Hampton Roads on April 28, 1919. Seaplanes dotted the waters of Willoughby Bay. (Photographer unknown.)

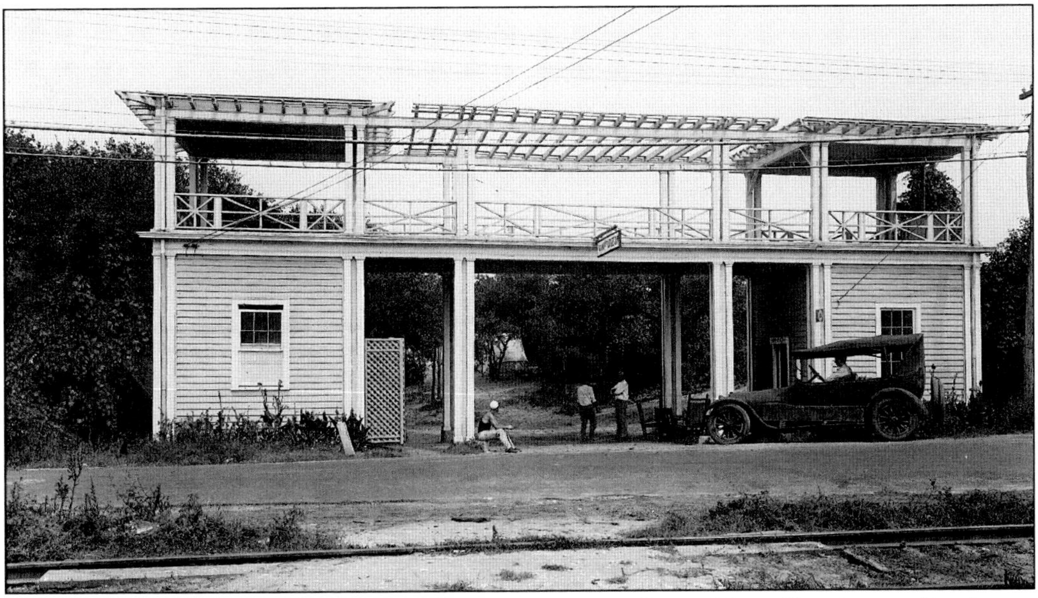

This was the entrance to the automobile tourist camp at Ocean View. People traveling by car could frequent such camps up and down the East Coast. Ocean View's tourist camp proved a particularly popular destination for travelers. Located across the street from the beach, the camp was within easy walking distance of the amusement park and resort strip. The photograph was taken in 1925. (Photographer unknown.)

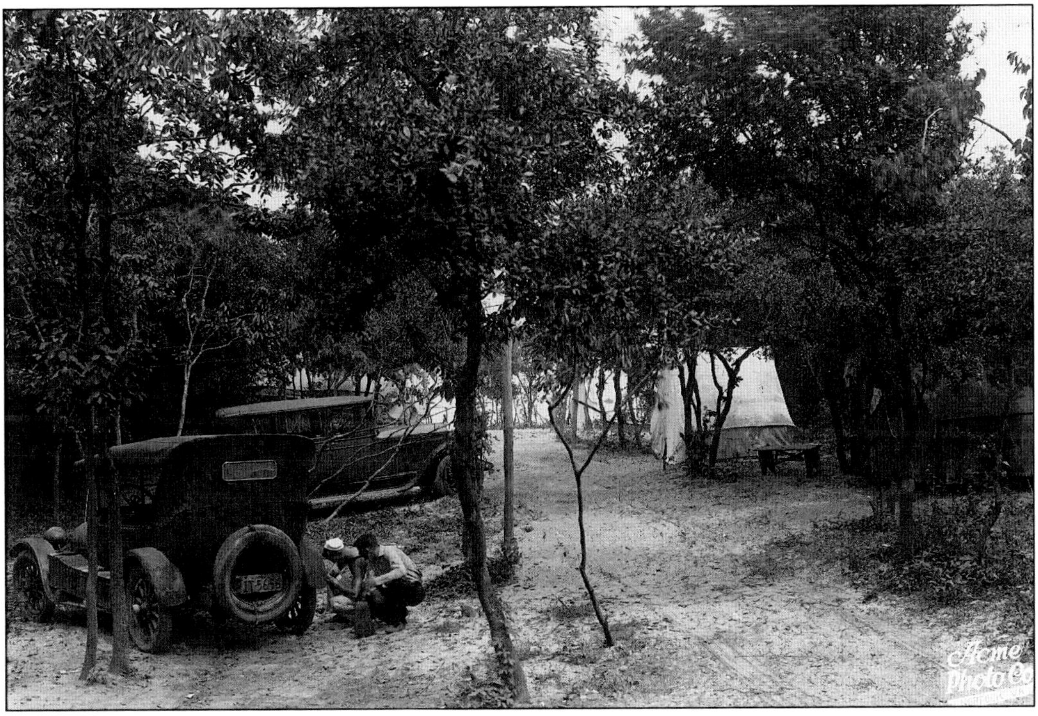

Once inside the automobile tourist camp, visitors assembled their tents, left their belongings, and could take a sojourn down to the water. The photograph, also taken in 1925, depicts the simplicity of the camp's layout and its tranquility.

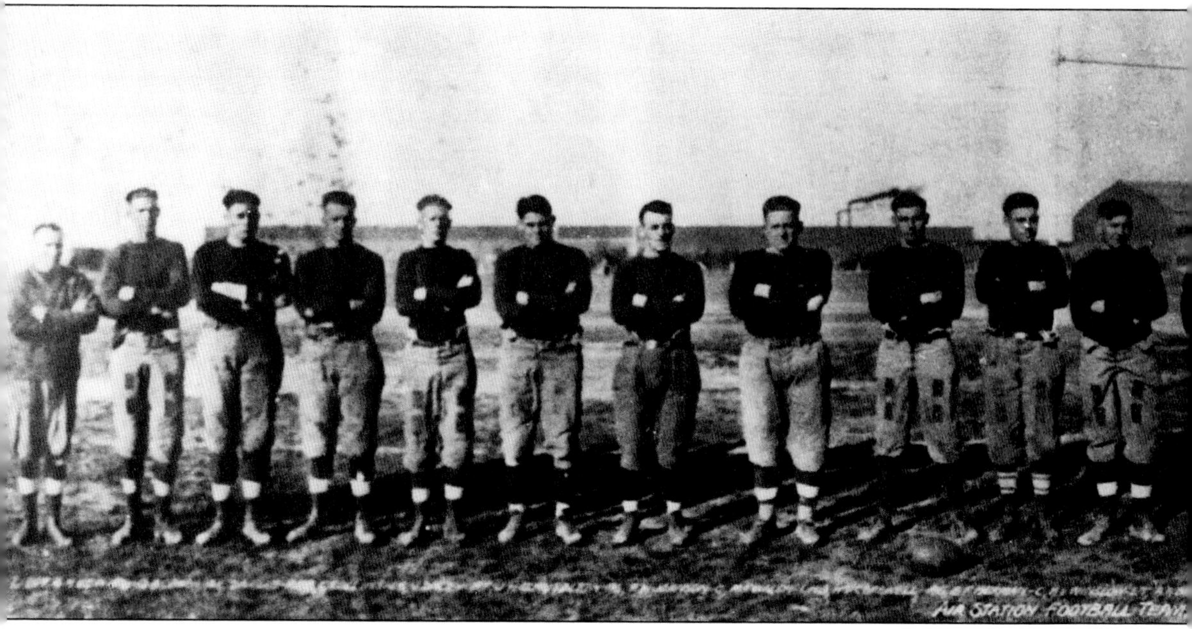

The Naval Air Station Hampton Roads football team, champions of the Fifth Naval District,

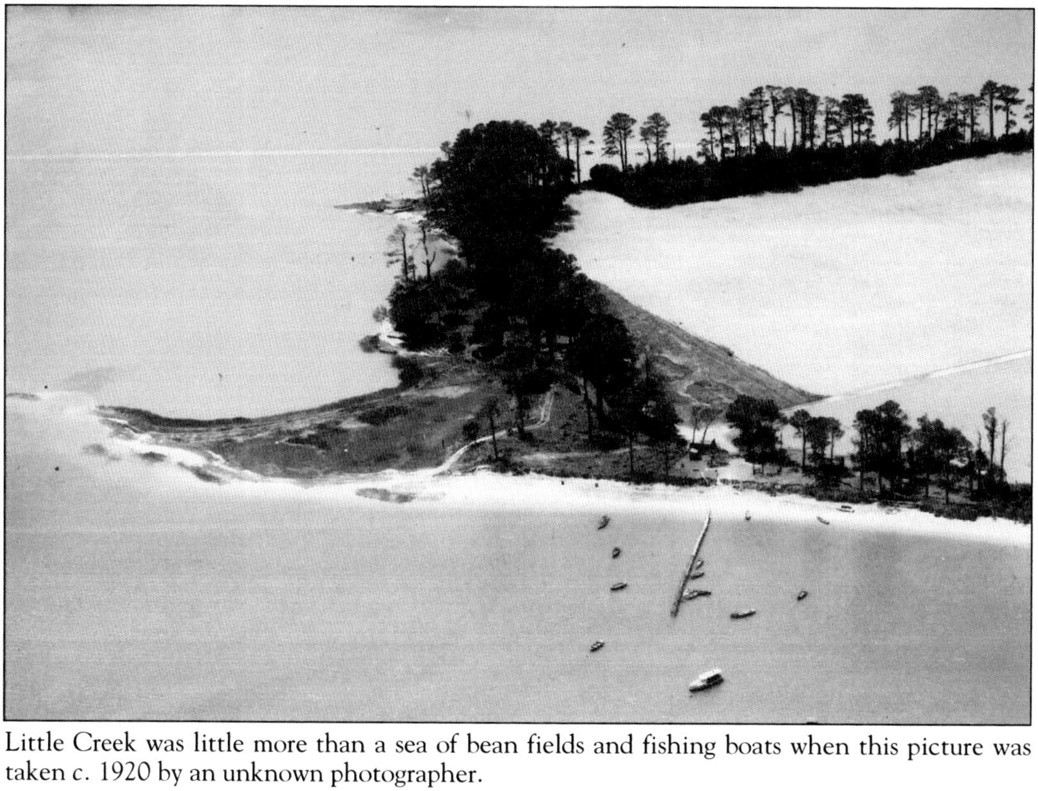

Little Creek was little more than a sea of bean fields and fishing boats when this picture was taken *c.* 1920 by an unknown photographer.

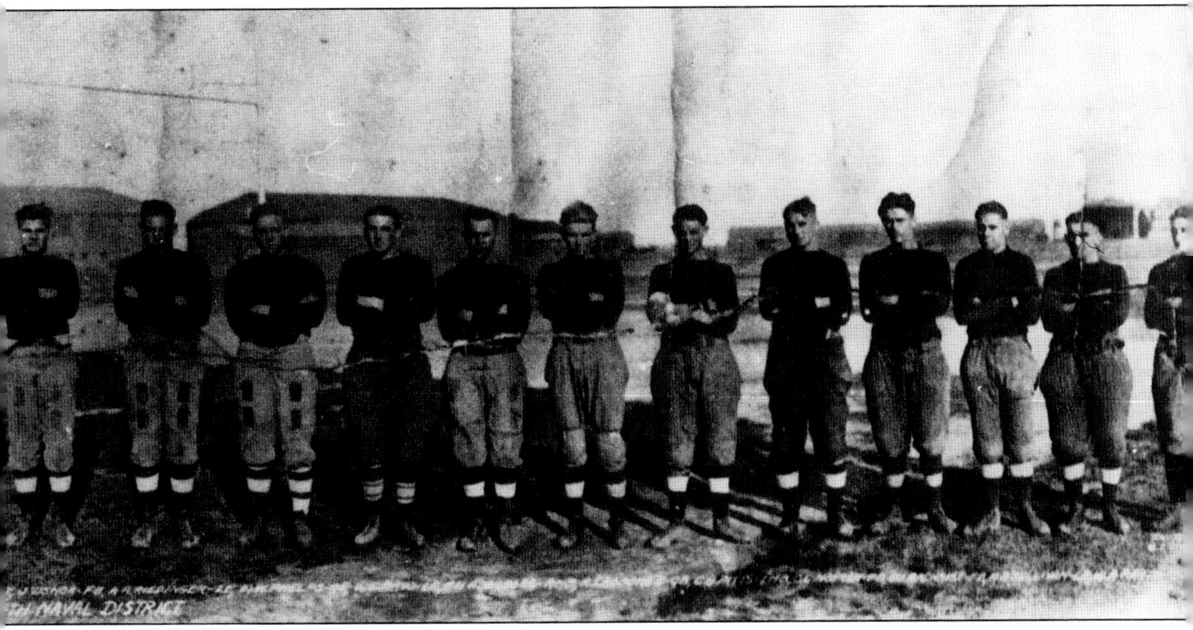

posed for this picture in 1927.

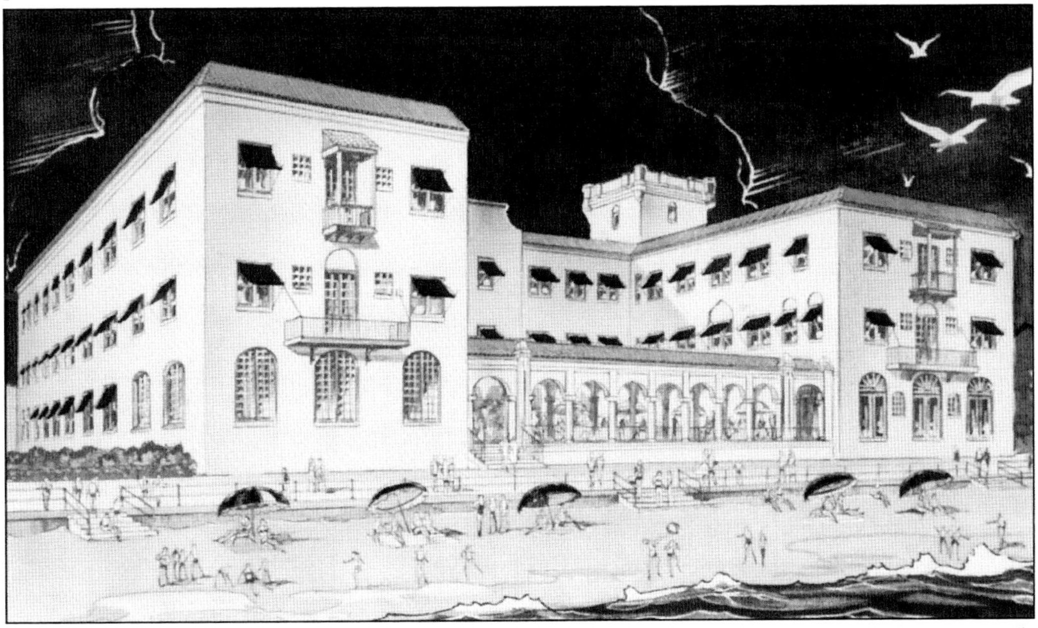

The 114-room Nansemond Hotel opened on June 23, 1928, on Ocean View Avenue with a perfect view of the Chesapeake Bay. The hotel was designed by local architect Bernard Spigel, and its first owners, Mr. and Mrs. C.A. Baker, were longtime residents of Ocean View. The three-story hotel had a Spanish influence in its design, and was constructed at a cost of $250,000. A fire destroyed the Ocean View hostelry in October 1978. This postcard image of the hotel originated in the post–World War II period. It is made of cardstock with a high rag content, cross-hatched like a linen. Cheaper inks could be used on these postcards, making them inexpensive moneymakers for manufacturers. The "linens" were popular between 1939 and 1955.

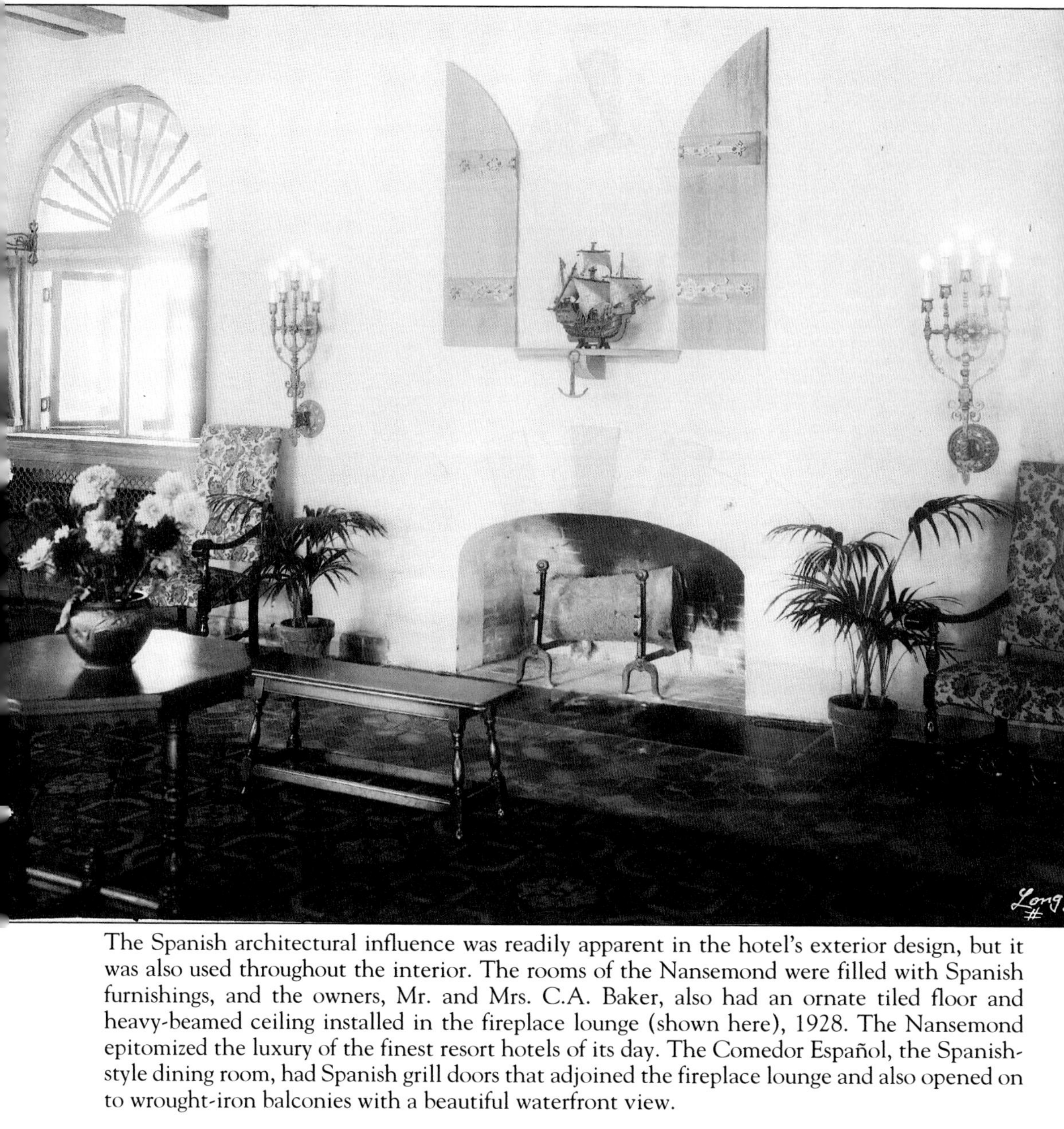

The Spanish architectural influence was readily apparent in the hotel's exterior design, but it was also used throughout the interior. The rooms of the Nansemond were filled with Spanish furnishings, and the owners, Mr. and Mrs. C.A. Baker, also had an ornate tiled floor and heavy-beamed ceiling installed in the fireplace lounge (shown here), 1928. The Nansemond epitomized the luxury of the finest resort hotels of its day. The Comedor Español, the Spanish-style dining room, had Spanish grill doors that adjoined the fireplace lounge and also opened on to wrought-iron balconies with a beautiful waterfront view.

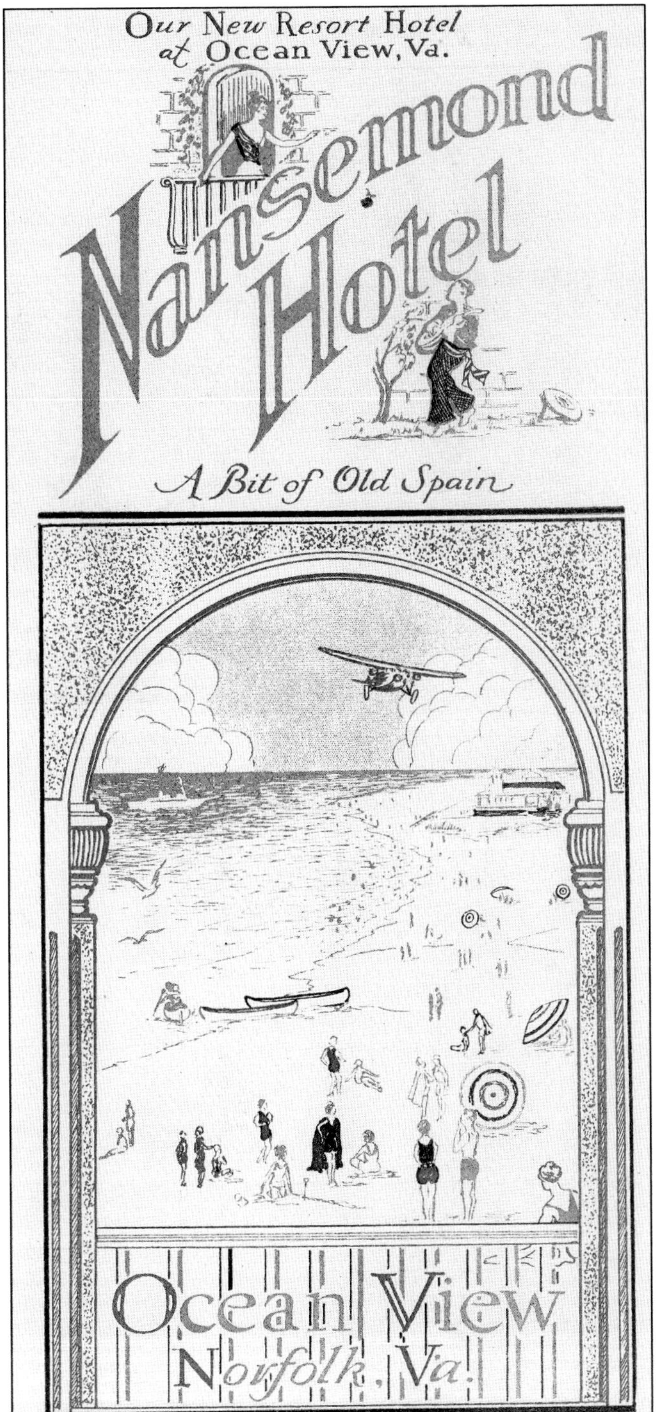

The Nansemond Hotel was situated on a site that fronted 200 feet of prime beach property. This brochure from 1928 promoted the Nansemond as the newest resort hotel at Ocean View, one with "A Bit of Old Spain" to offer patrons. Seaplane rides were popular, as were canoeing, fishing excursions, golf at the Ocean View Golf Course, and water sports.

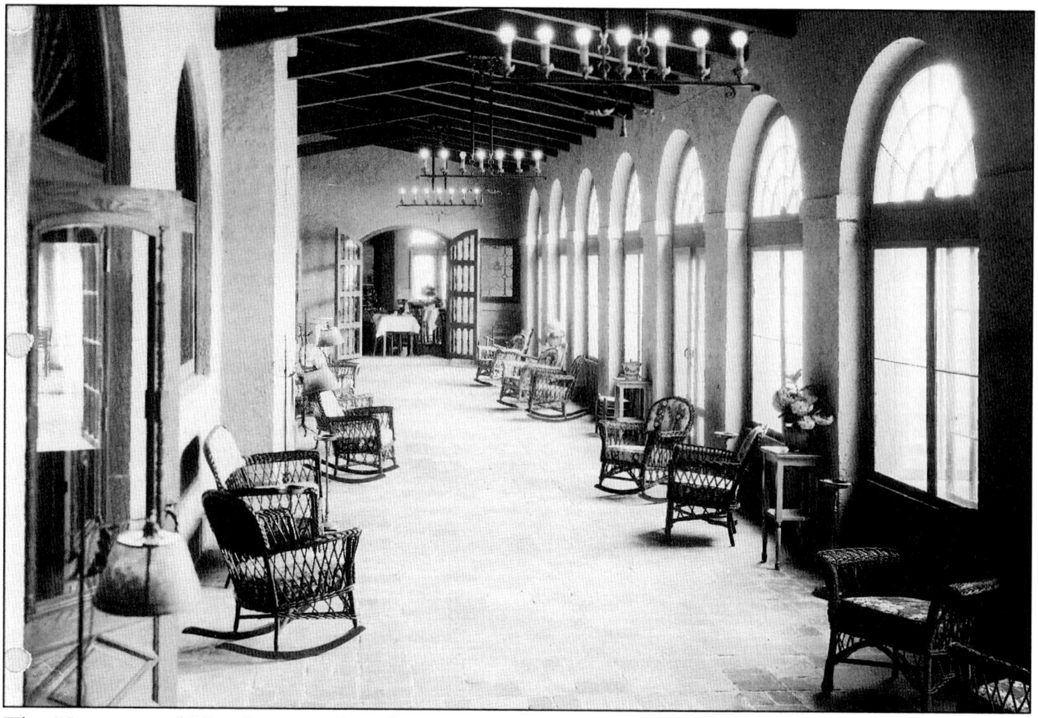

The Nansemond Hotel sun parlor, shown as it appeared in 1928, adjoined the fireplace lounge and dining room. It, too, was of Spanish design with its beamed ceiling and antique tile floor. (Photographer unknown.)

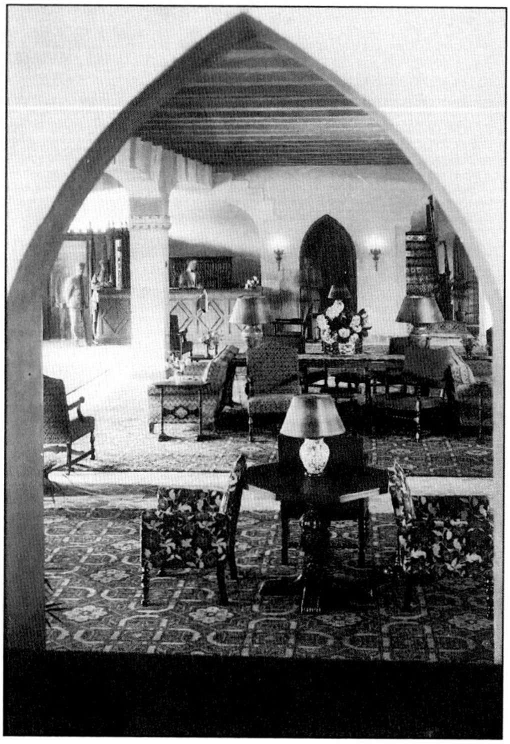

The hotel's Spanish influence was readily apparent as guests entered the lobby of the Nansemond Hotel, shown here in 1928. Archways and architectural details throughout the hotel had a Moorish appearance, and the furnishings, carpets, and fabric coverings had the warm appearance of a hostelry in Spain. The Spanish, though specifically Moorish, appearance of the Nansemond set it apart in style and prestige amongst resort hotels in the South. The Moors were one of the mixed Arab and Berber conquerors of Spain in the eighth century. The impact of the Arab patterns found in Spanish architecture of Moorish influence is unmistakable; this image of the Nansemond lobby best illustrates this point. (Photographer unknown.)

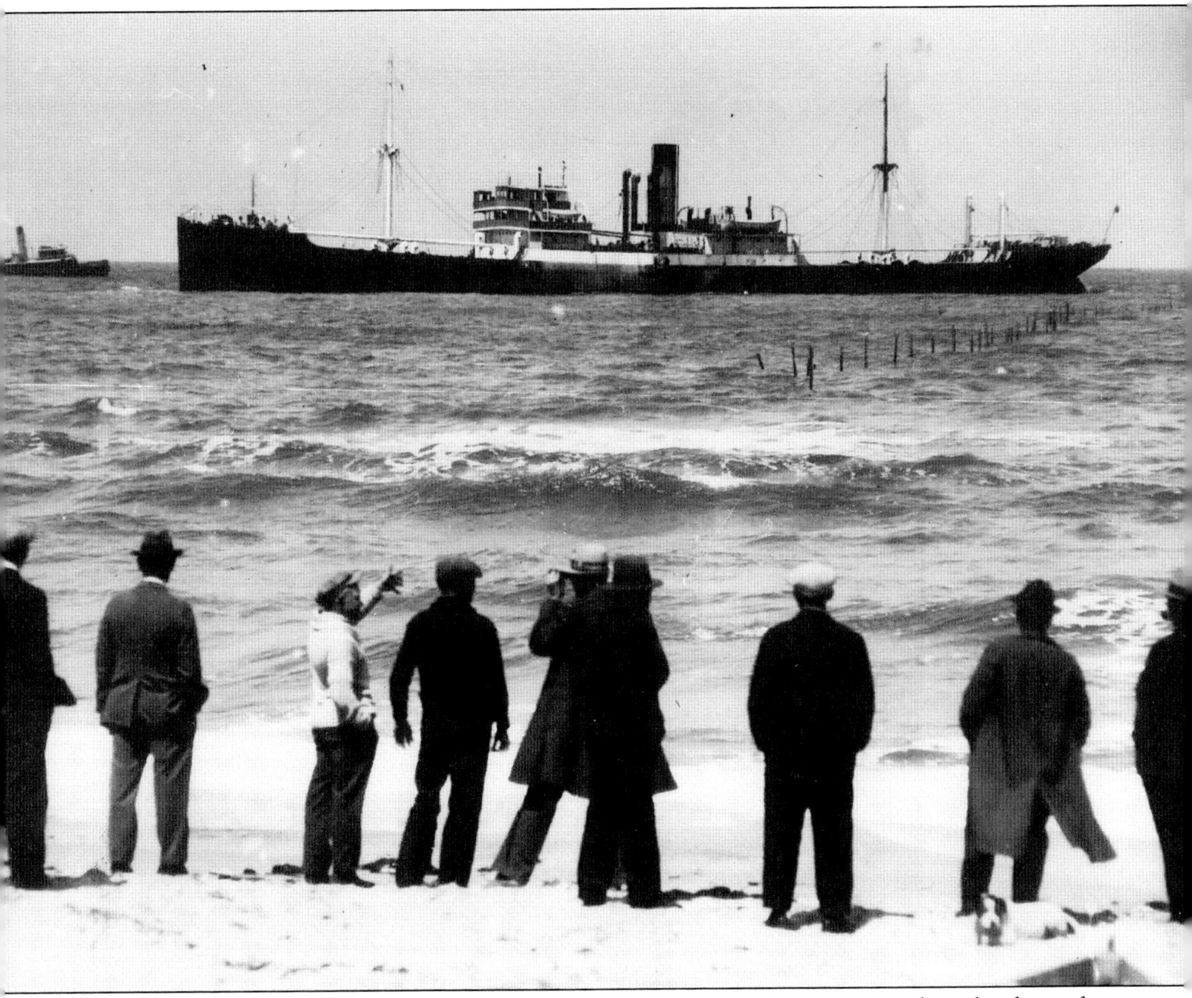

The British steamer *Errington Court*, laden with a cargo of grain, ran aground at the foot of First Street in Ocean View the morning of May 5, 1926, the day this picture was taken. The 2,988-ton *Errington Court* was 380 feet long and a little over 52 feet wide. Built in Newcastle, England, in 1907, she was owned by the Court Line, Limited, of London. The *Errington Court* was the only vessel of her size that had ever come so close to the shores of the Ocean View resort. Just a few hundred yards offshore and her bow securely wedged in the sand, the steamer was stranded in 20 feet of water with a load line draft requirement of 22 feet. The steamer was headed for Sewells Point to load bunker coal. She had departed Vancouver, Canada, on April 10, with a full load of grain for delivery to British ports. Neither pilots of the Virginia Pilots Association nor representatives of Hasler and Company, agents for the ship, could determine with any certainty why the steamer's captain was 3 miles off course when the steamer stranded. Four Wood Towing Company tugs, the *Helen*, *Dauntless*, *John G. Chandler*, and *Joseph* M. *Clark*, worked to float the ship to deeper water. They were eventually successful. (Charles S. Borjes, photographer.)

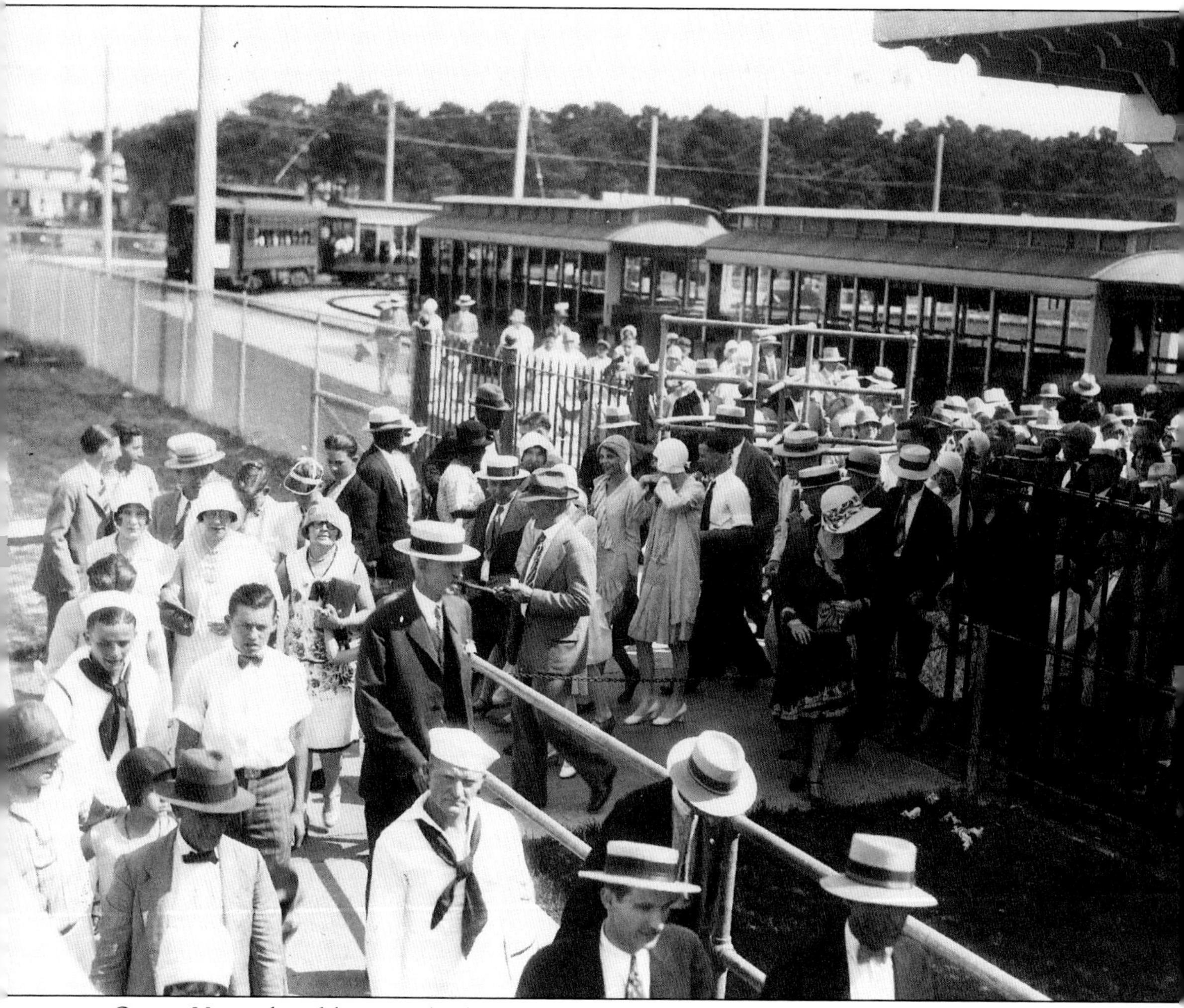

Ocean View played host to the largest crowd in its history on July 4, 1928, when thirty-five thousand people came to take in sun and relaxation. There were no serious accidents to mar the pleasant passing of Independence Day. At Ocean View, a young man and a young woman were rescued after being overcome in the water. Hotels and cottages were booked to capacity with holiday crowds from out of town. The guest register at the Nansemond Hotel listed patrons from thirty-two states. The Virginia Electric and Power Company had to draw on reserve equipment to carry crowds to Ocean View. Extra service was also provided by the Norfolk Southern electric division. The two lines to Ocean View began in the morning on a ten-minute headway, but before noon, this had to be doubled to provide one car over each line every five minutes. Private automobiles rivaled the streetcar lines in bringing crowds into the Ocean View Amusement Park. (Charles S. Borjes, photographer.)

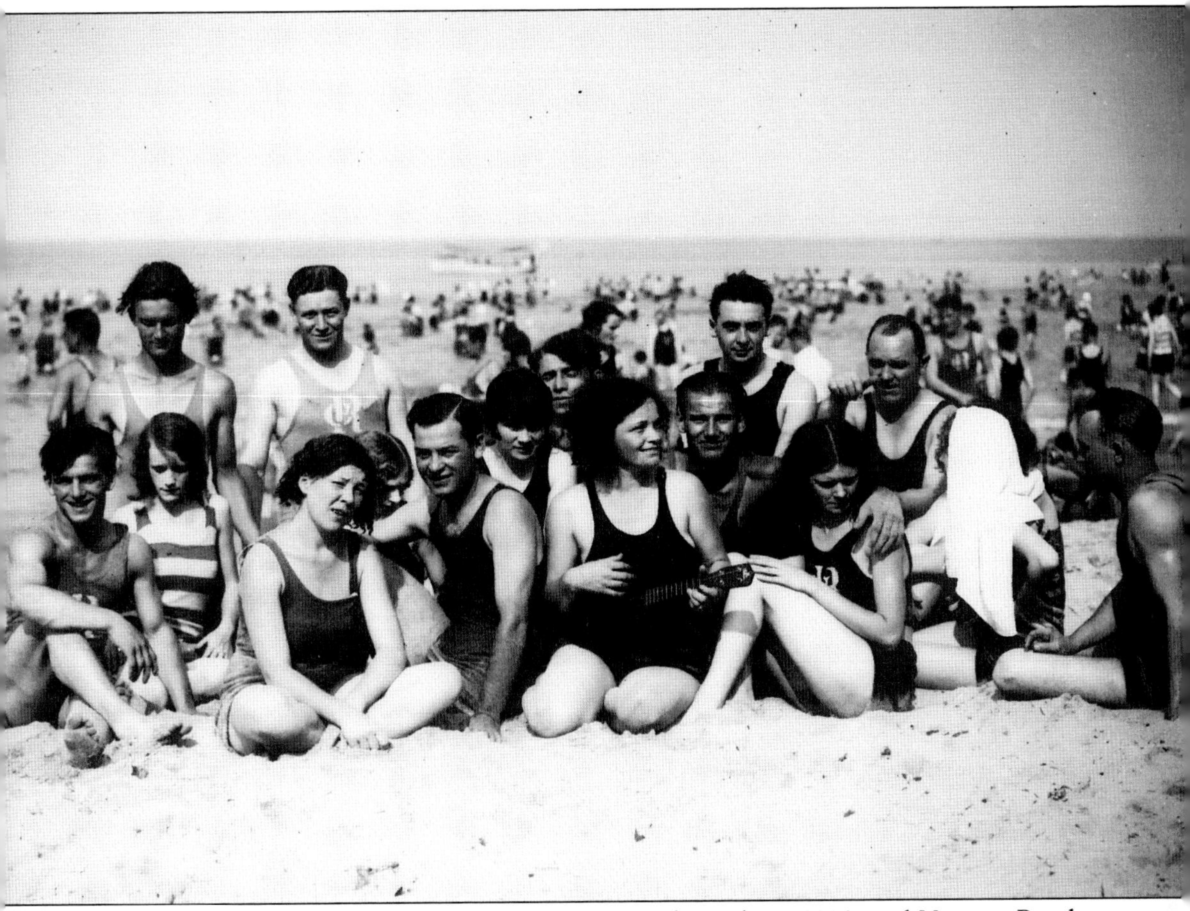

Ocean View had an all-year population of ten thousand people in 1928, and Virginia Beach claimed a population of permanent residents of equal size. There would be significant changes to the offerings at Ocean View when the summer season started on May 28. The Nansemond Hotel would open its doors for the first time, welcoming hordes of visitors from all over the United States. Leases of cottages and houses at the beach were growing daily as the opening date approached. Hotel, restaurant, theater, and business owners would not be disappointed at the summer crowds flocking to Ocean View by the tens of thousands. This happy group of young people was photographed at Ocean View on July 4, 1928. (Charles S. Borjes, photographer.)

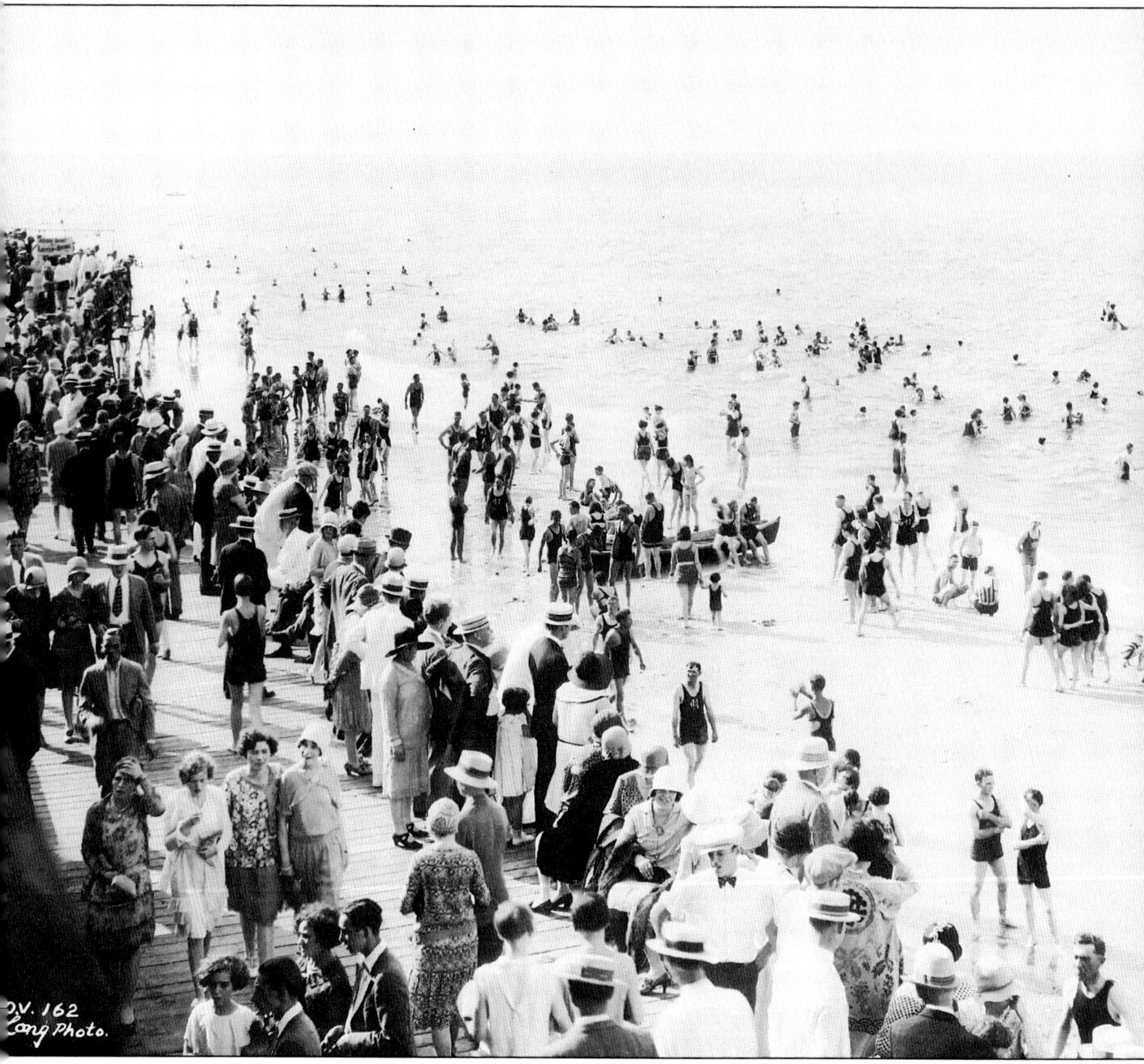

An immense throng of Fourth of July strollers and bathers went to Ocean View in search of a bit of saltwater, rest, and relaxation in 1929. Dressed in their best attire, families came to the beach to stroll along the boardwalk, and if they desired, take a dip in the cool waters of the Chesapeake Bay. The bathhouses at Ocean View were equipped with the most modern facilities available in the resort's heyday. (Photographer unknown.)

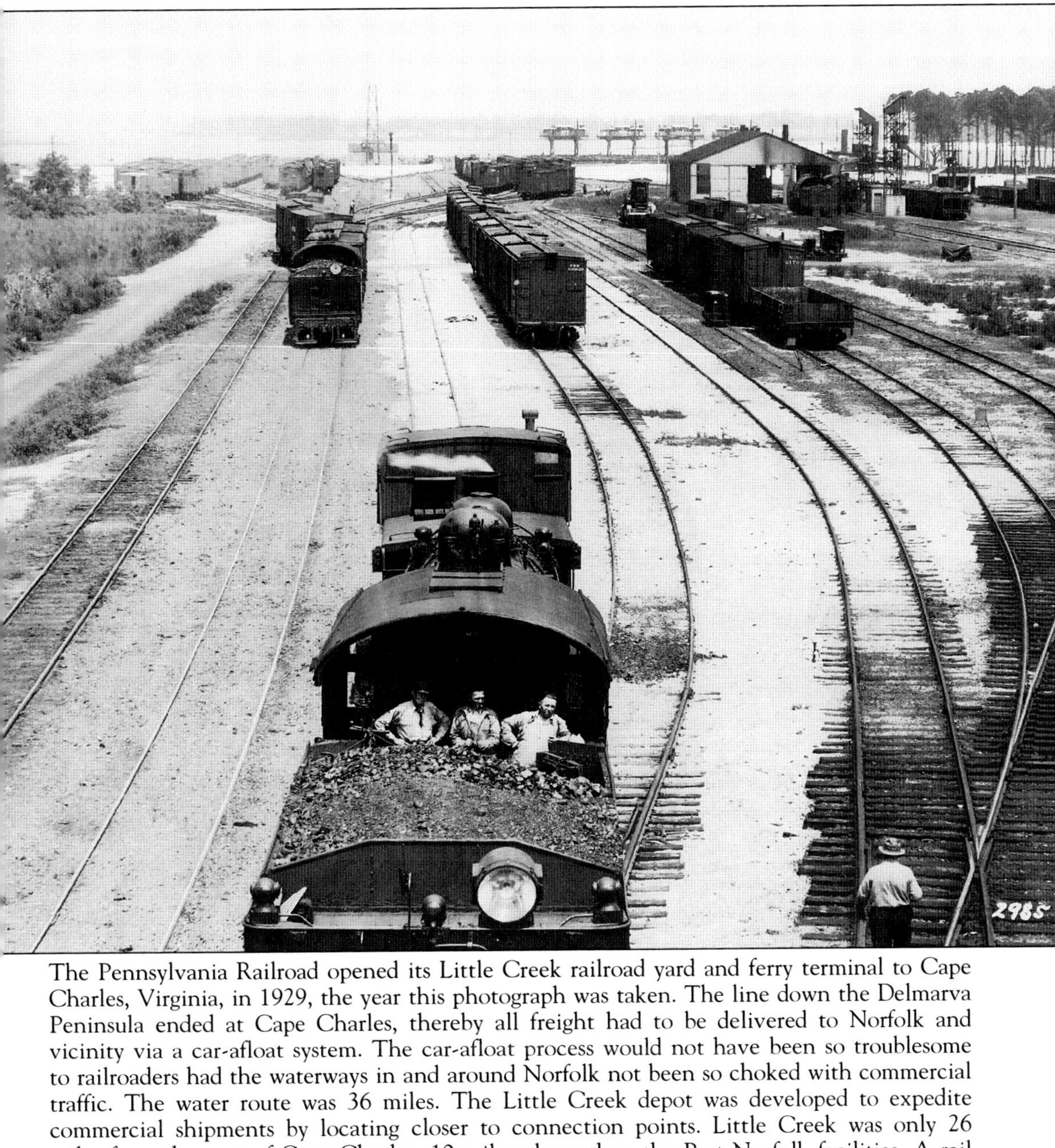

The Pennsylvania Railroad opened its Little Creek railroad yard and ferry terminal to Cape Charles, Virginia, in 1929, the year this photograph was taken. The line down the Delmarva Peninsula ended at Cape Charles, thereby all freight had to be delivered to Norfolk and vicinity via a car-afloat system. The car-afloat process would not have been so troublesome to railroaders had the waterways in and around Norfolk not been so choked with commercial traffic. The water route was 36 miles. The Little Creek depot was developed to expedite commercial shipments by locating closer to connection points. Little Creek was only 26 miles from the port of Cape Charles, 10 miles closer than the Port Norfolk facilities. A rail connection was established with Norfolk Southern Railway after Pennsylvania Railroad purchased trackage rights from the company's Electric Division. The Norfolk Southern track line ran to the Pennsylvania Railroad's St. Julian Creek freight station due east of the Norfolk & Western tracks in Norfolk. The new route saved as much as 12 miles across the Chesapeake Bay. The Norfolk Southern Corporation still owns and operates this facility, now surrounded on all sides by the Little Creek Naval Amphibious Base.

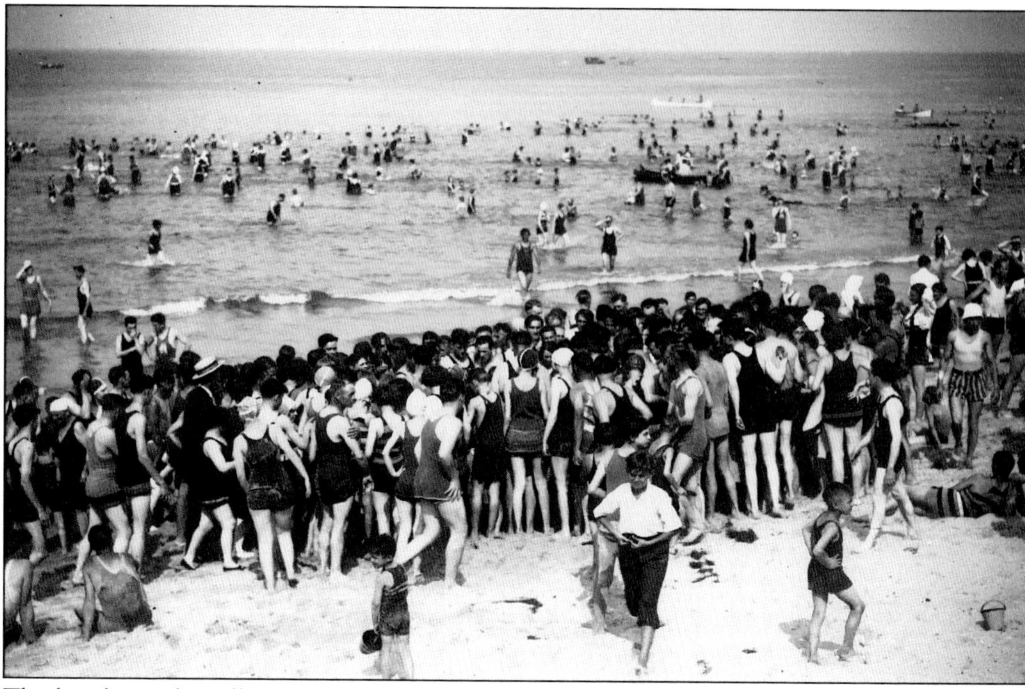

The beach was literally packed with bathers on July 4, 1929, as this delightful photograph by Charles S. Borjes so clearly demonstrates.

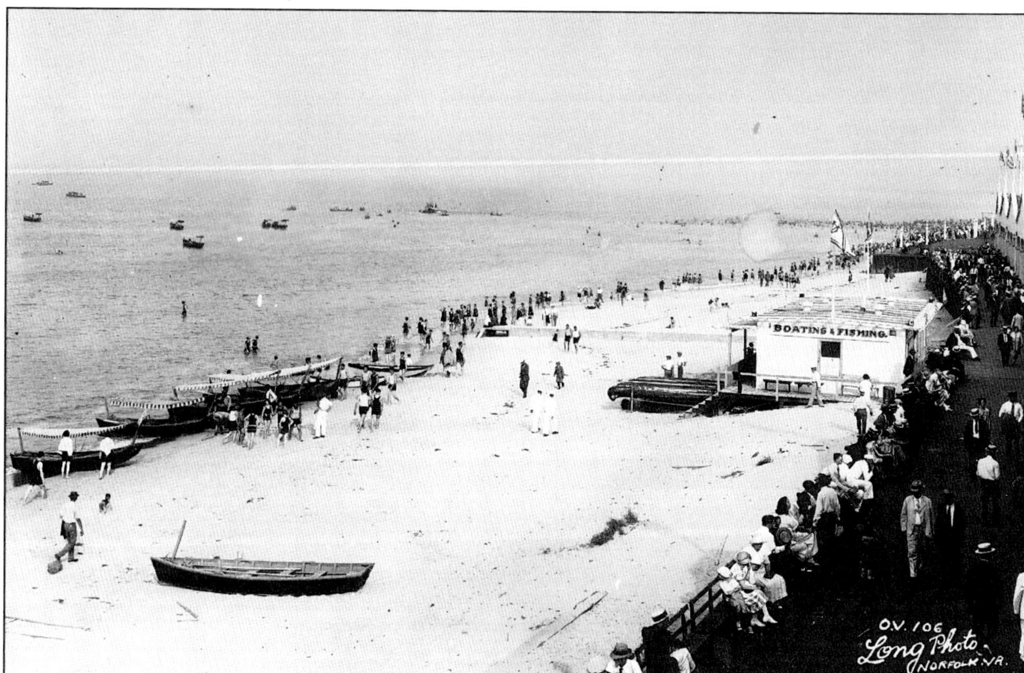

Fishing and excursion boats were readily available to Ocean View visitors. The boardwalk (on the right) was crowded with people going in and out of the amusement park and bathhouses. The beach east of the park (visible to the upper right of the photograph) was a sea of bathers and strollers. The picture was taken in July 1929 by an unnamed photographer.

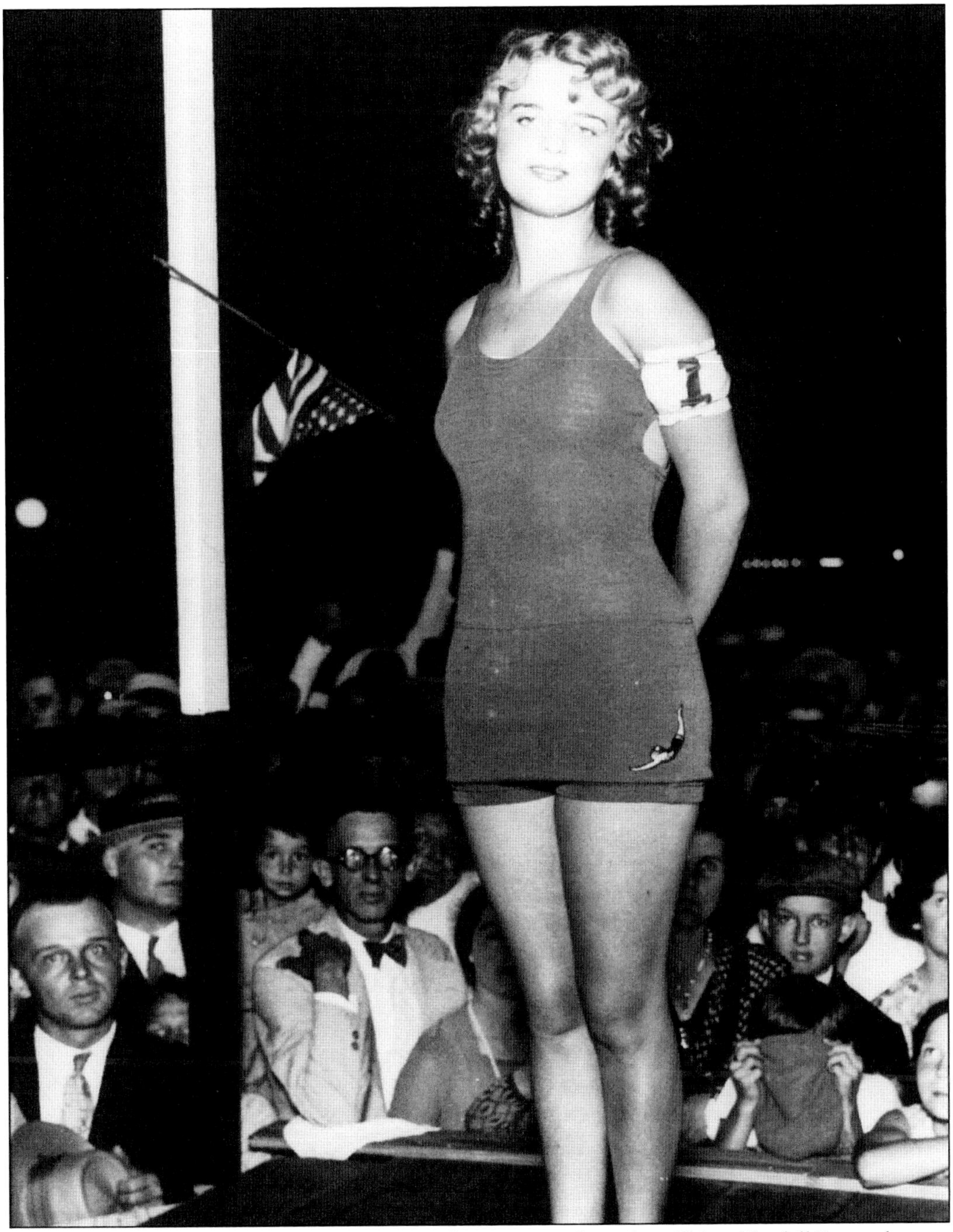

Virginia Carolyn Dowe, seventeen years of age, was selected as "Miss Norfolk" at a beauty contest held at Ocean View Park on August 23, 1929. A member of the junior class of Maury High School, the blonde, blue-eyed young woman was cheered by more than seven thousand people packed around the reviewing stand. Dowe was awarded $50, a sport suit, and a diamond ring by Herman Barr's. The Miss Norfolk pageant sent Virginia Dowe directly to the National Beauty Pageant, held in Baltimore, Maryland, where she unsuccessfully competed for top honors and a thousand-dollar wrist watch. (Charles S. Borjes, photographer.)

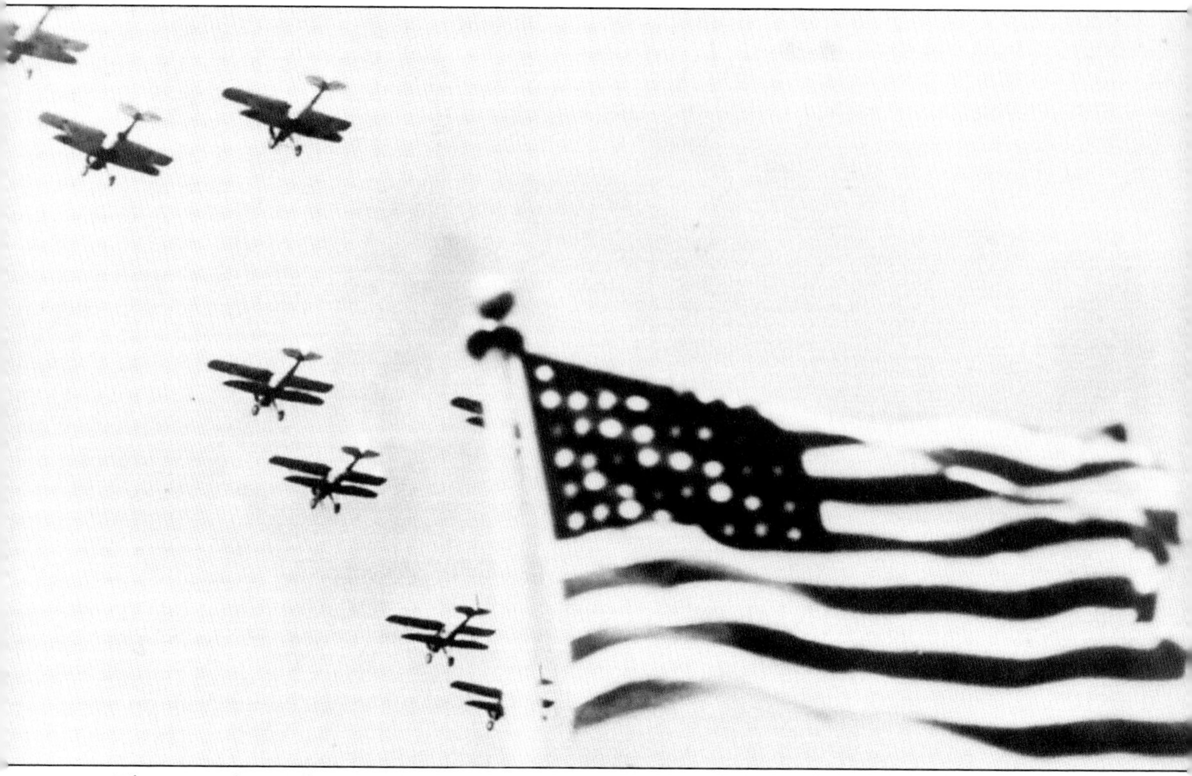

There are few sights as patriotic as this one of Boeing F4B-1 aircraft of VF-5B *Striking Eagles* inbound for Naval Air Station Hampton Roads on May 7, 1930. The squadron, stationed aboard the USS *Lexington* (CV-2), passed over Ocean View's large flag pole, and a lucky photographer captured the moment forever on film.

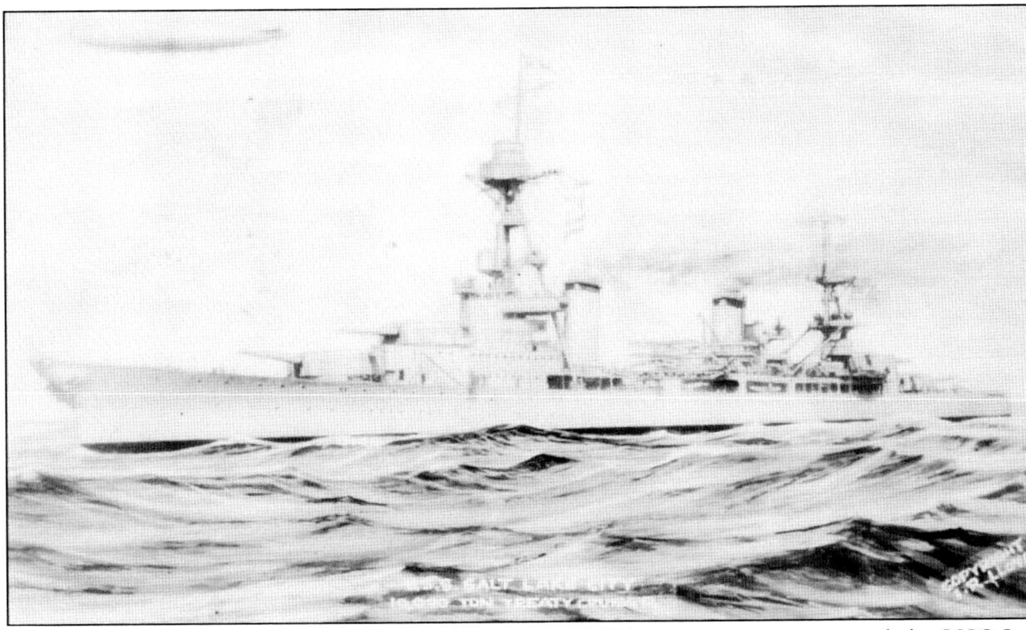

An artist's rendering of the USS *Salt Lake City*, a 10,000-ton treaty cruiser, and the USS *Los Angeles* (ZR-3), the grand dame of the U.S. Navy's airships, was produced as a postcard and became a popular souvenir of the airship era. The *Los Angeles* (visible in the top left corner), called the "Pride of the Navy," was America's most successful dirigible.

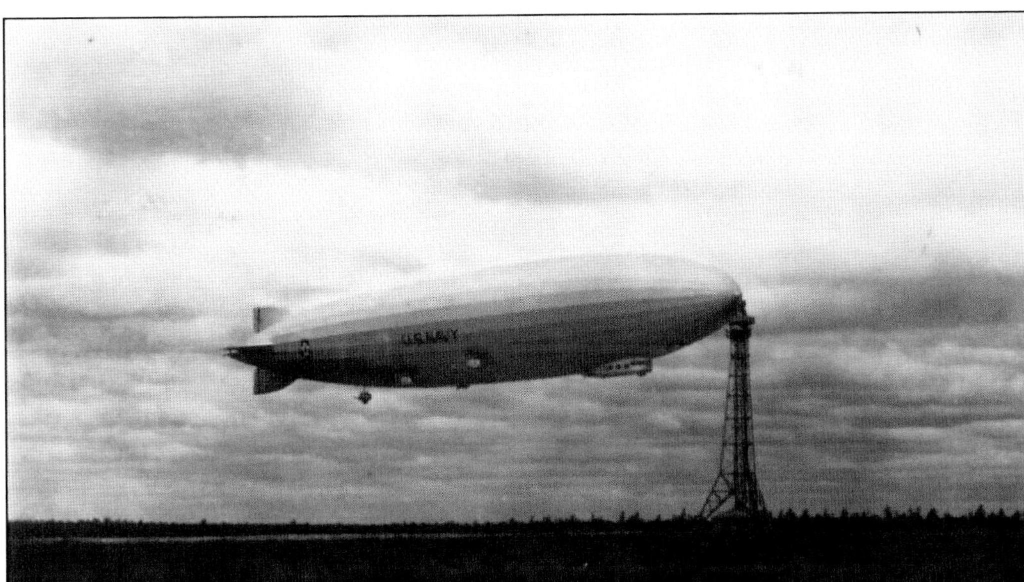

During 1931, *Los Angeles* flew over the lower Chesapeake Bay, crossing Ocean View and Willoughby before berthing at the mooring mast on Naval Air Station Hampton Roads. The great airship gave the throngs on the beach one of the most memorable thrills of their lives as she seemingly floated to earth.

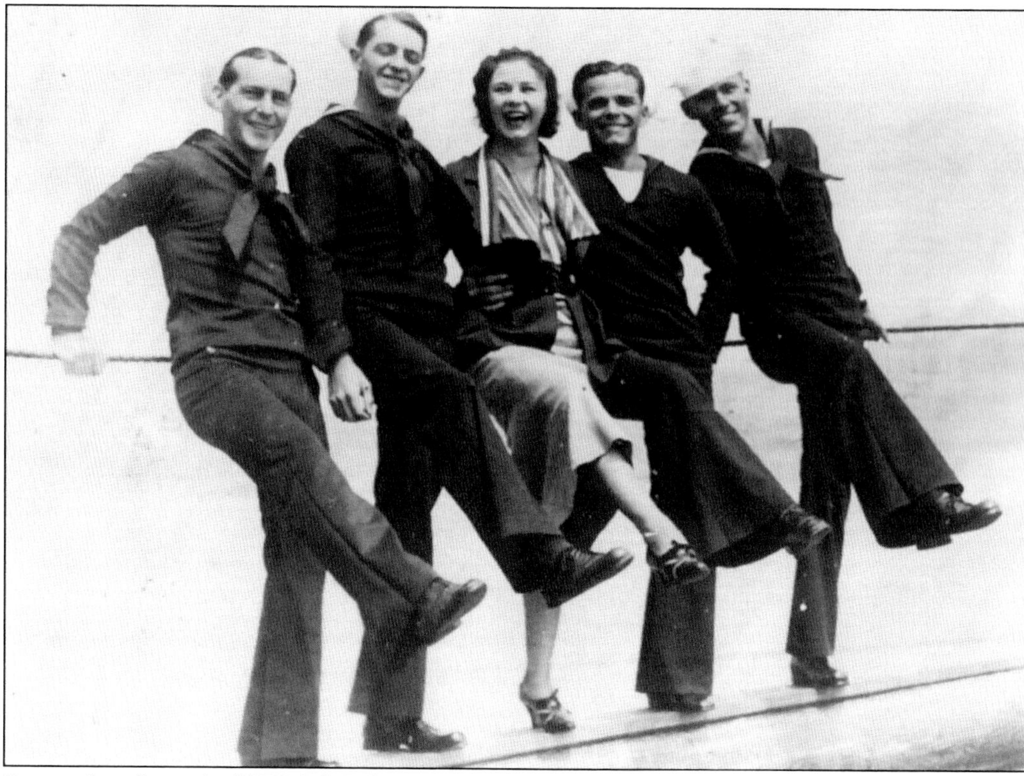

Four sailors from the USS *Salt Lake City* and a lucky date posed aboard ship before going out together for an evening of dinner and dancing at Ocean View Casino, 1931.

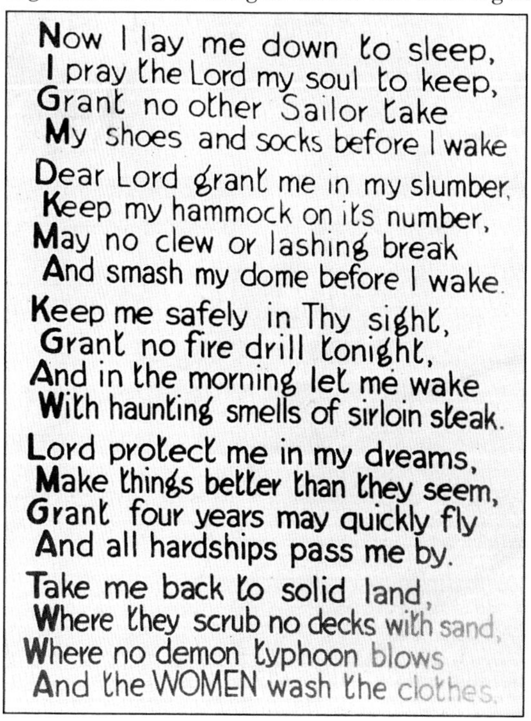

Now I lay me down to sleep,
I pray the Lord my soul to keep,
Grant no other Sailor take
My shoes and socks before I wake
Dear Lord grant me in my slumber,
Keep my hammock on its number,
May no clew or lashing break
And smash my dome before I wake.
Keep me safely in Thy sight,
Grant no fire drill tonight,
And in the morning let me wake
With haunting smells of sirloin steak.
Lord protect me in my dreams,
Make things better than they seem,
Grant four years may quickly fly
And all hardships pass me by.
Take me back to solid land,
Where they scrub no decks with sand,
Where no demon typhoon blows
And the WOMEN wash the clothes.

This card was carried in the wallet of a sailor on liberty who kept a journal of his experiences at sea and ashore. Times spent unwinding at Ocean View and Virginia Beach were invaluable to the morale and well-being of the sailor and his shipmates. The verse on the card certainly reflected the tone of the period in which it was wrought, *c.* 1930.

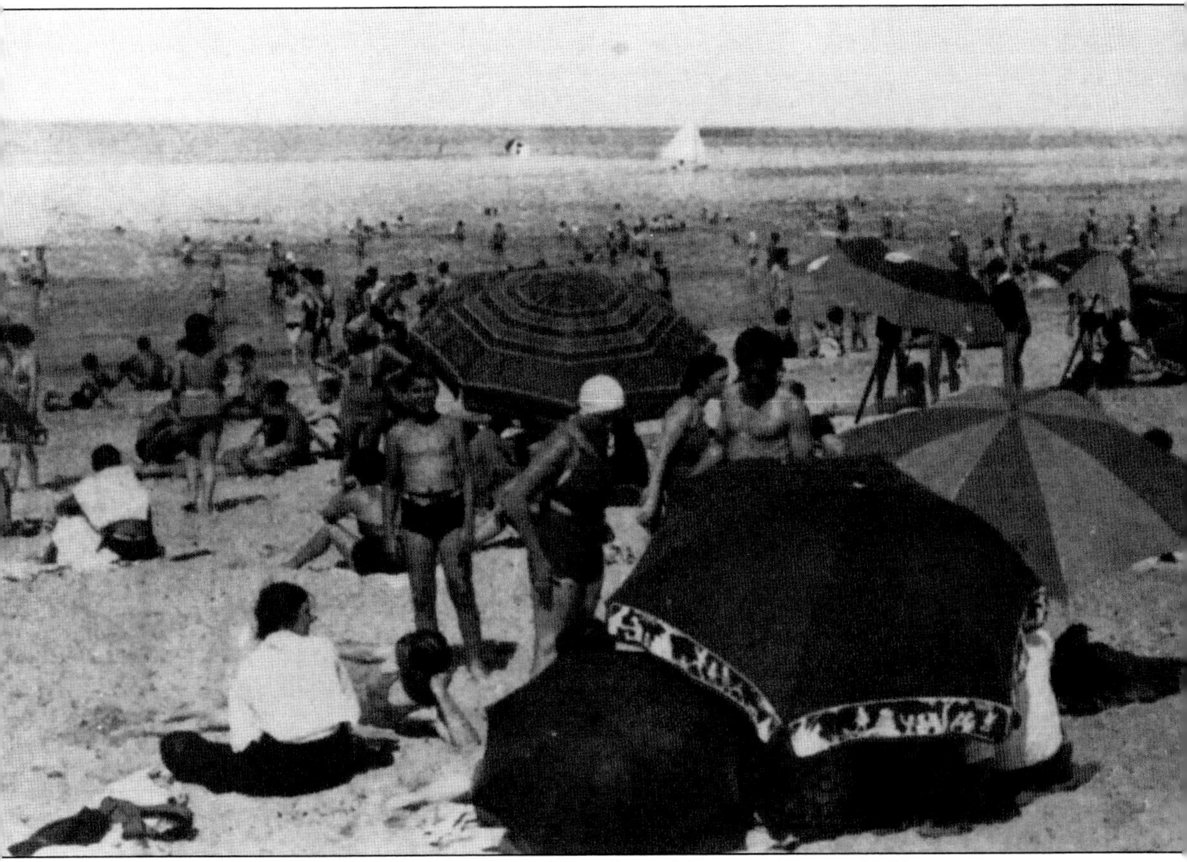

Bathers enjoy a splendid day on the sun-kissed beaches of Ocean View, *c.* 1931.

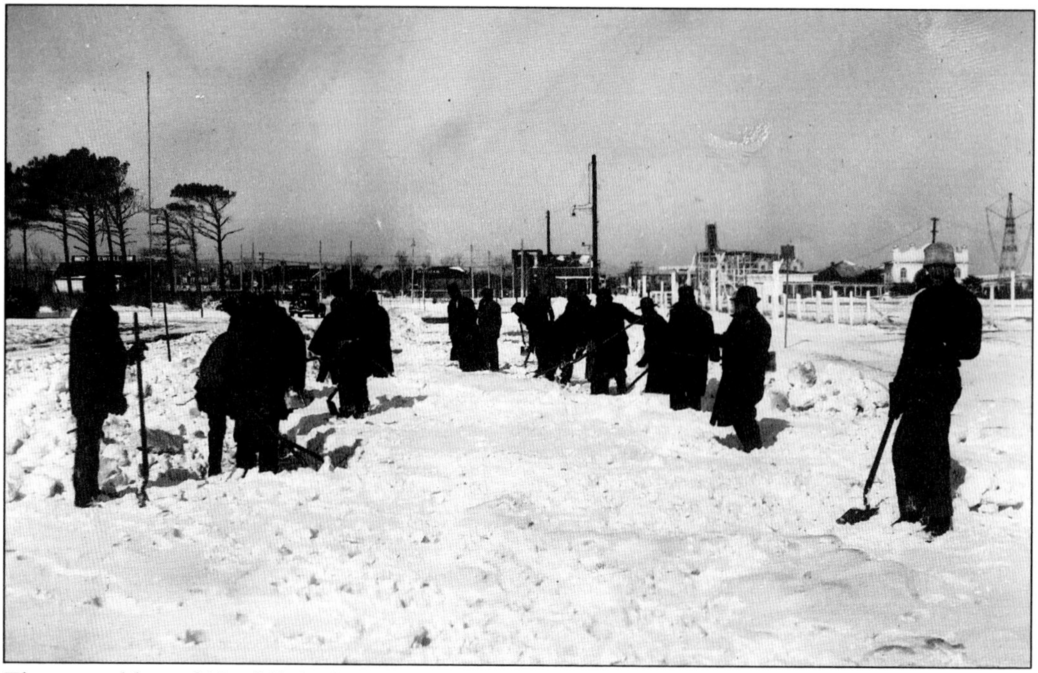

The worst blizzard Norfolk had seen in many years struck the first week of February 1936, and stayed. Crews worked feverishly to clear heavy snowdrifts along Ocean View Avenue near the amusement park (above) while Old Man Winter stared back at the cameraman from the Ocean View Casino (below). There was nothing but ice as far as the eye could see. The date of both pictures was February 8. (Charles S. Borjes, photographer.)

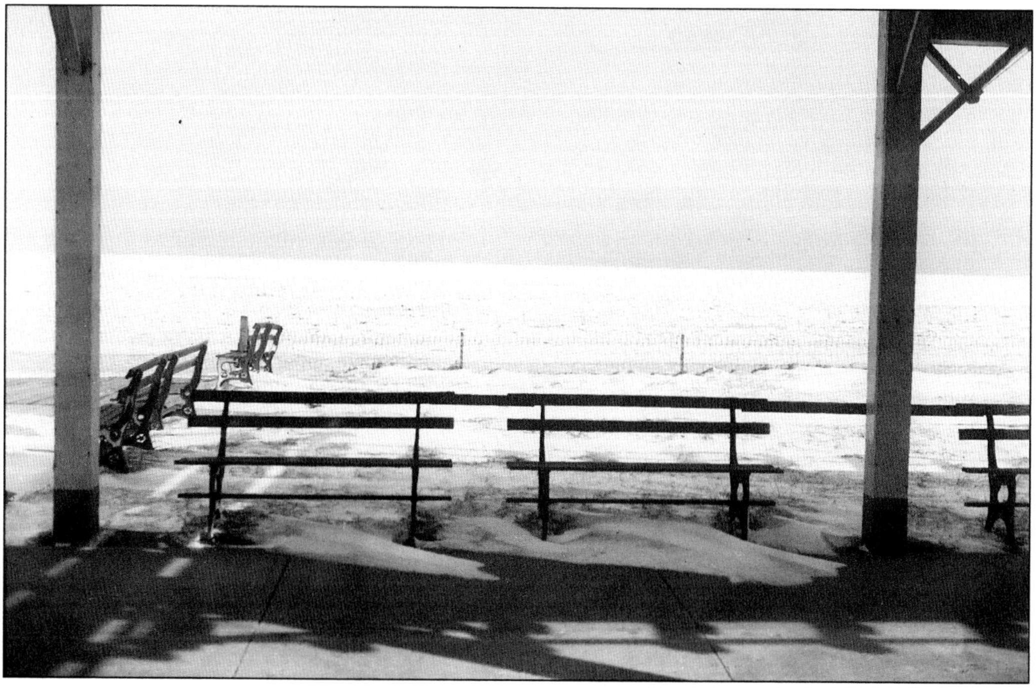

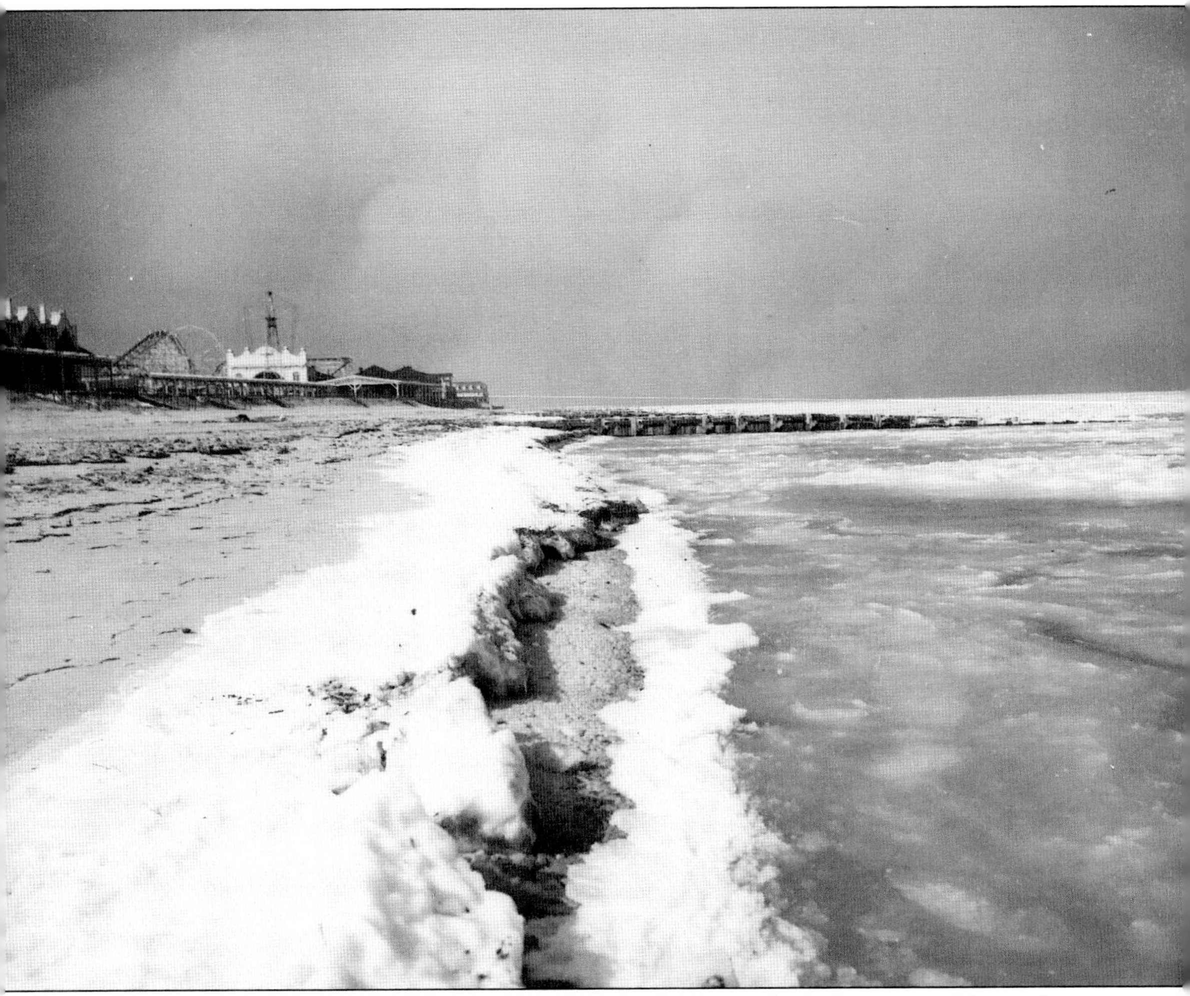

The shoreline at Ocean View was covered with ice and snow as far as the eye could see when Charles S. Borjes took this photograph on January 29, 1940. Light snow had fallen the morning the picture was taken, but temperatures finally moved above the freezing point that afternoon for the first time since January 24. While there was considerable ice in Norfolk's harbor, it did not impede boat traffic. The story on the Chesapeake Bay was different. Ice jams still blocked some points in the Chesapeake Bay, although vessels indicated a slight improvement from the previous week. Ice extended a considerable distance from the shore at Ocean View, evident in this picture.

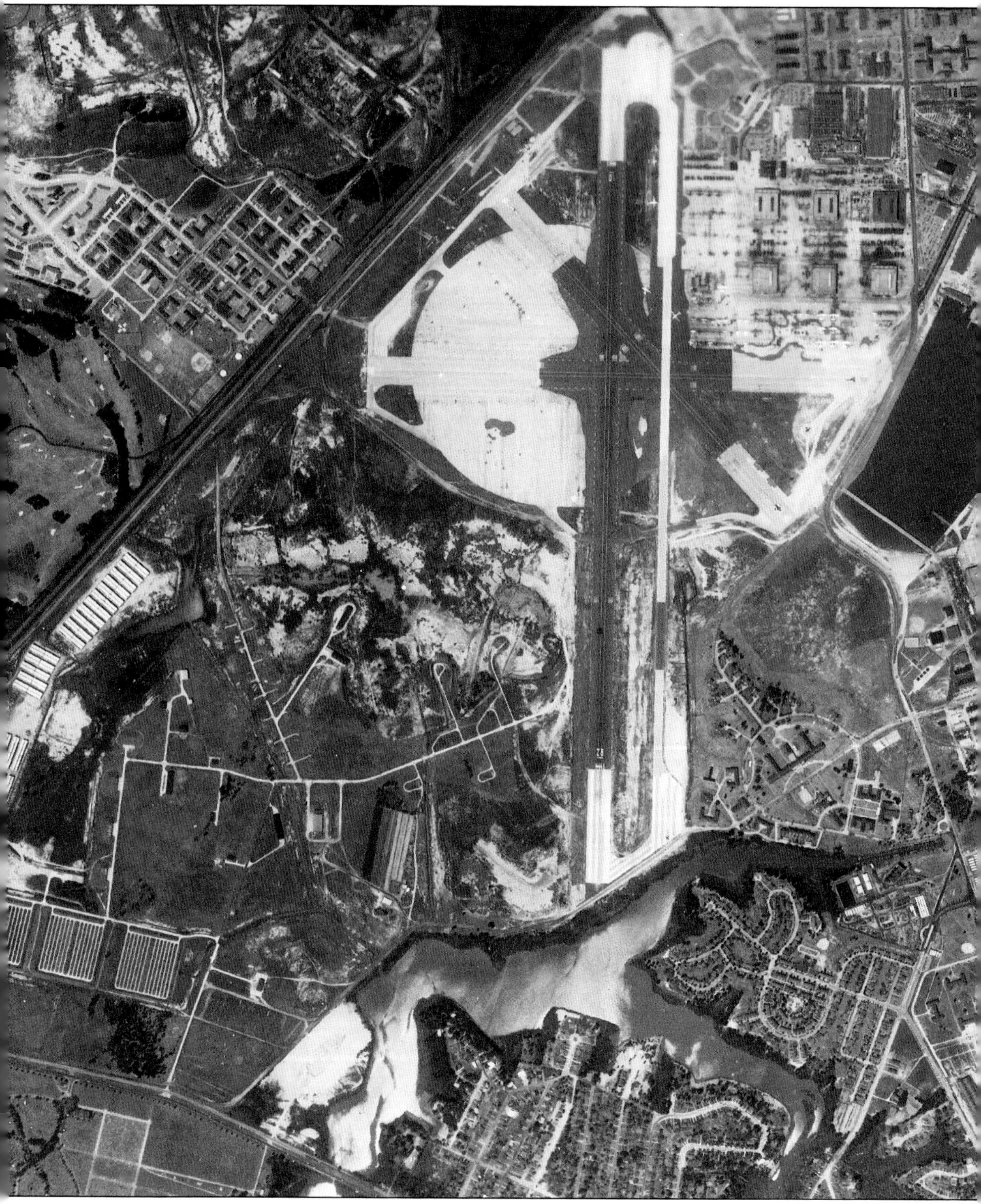

An aircraft from Naval Air Station Norfolk took this aerial photograph of Willoughby Bay from 25,800 feet on July 7, 1953. The air station rings the bay and adjoins Willoughby. Willoughby Spit is the finger of land to the far right of the photograph. The jetties of Willoughby and

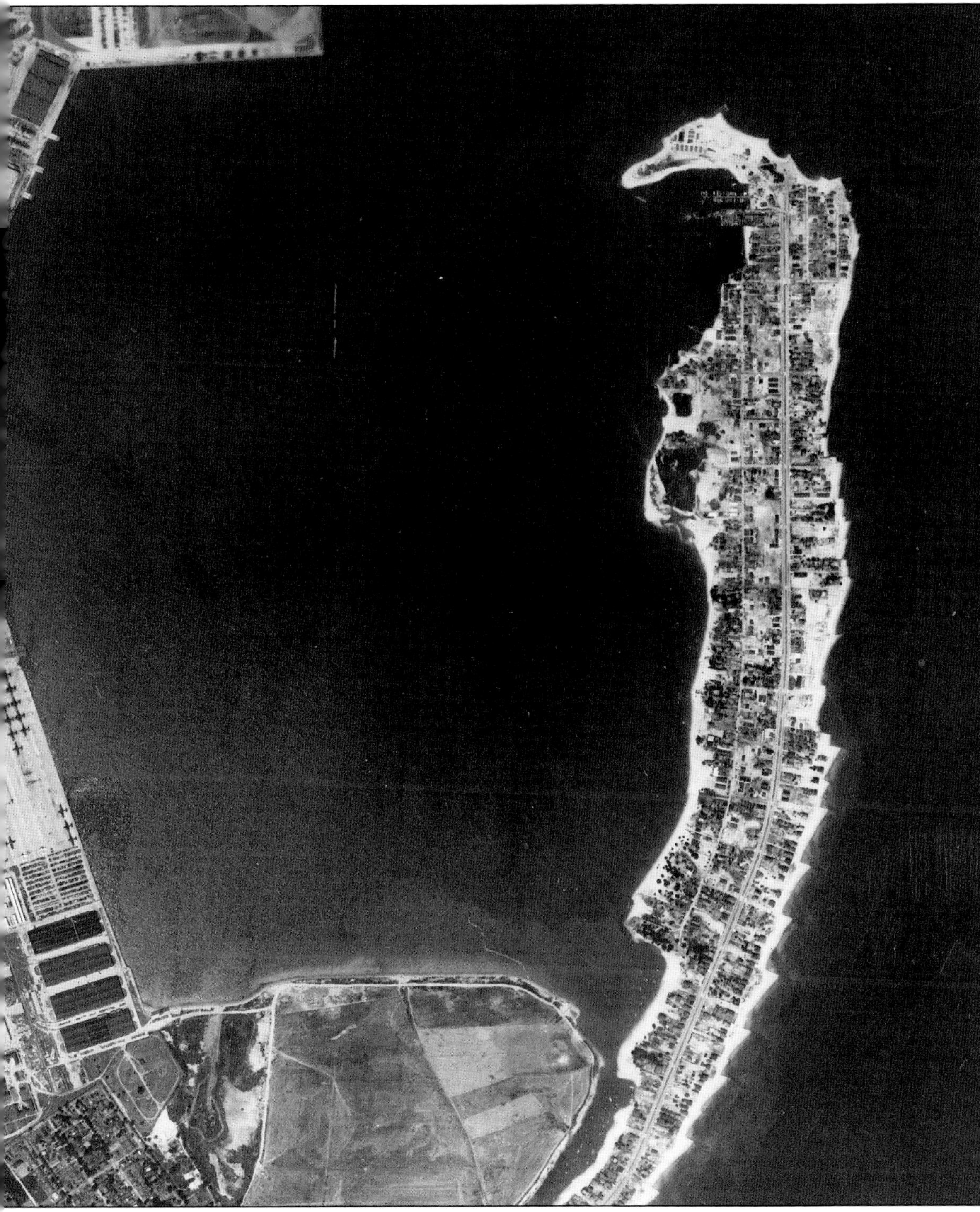

Ocean View created the jagged edges visible along the beachfront. The jetties were built down the length of Willoughby and part of Ocean View proper to protect the shore from erosion by the currents and tides offshore.

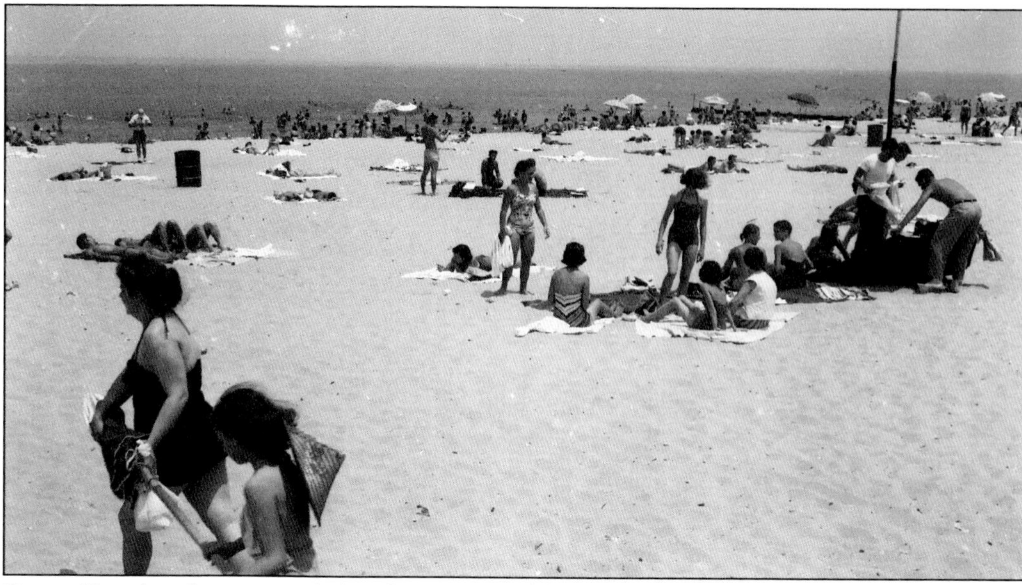

Ocean View beach was crowded with tourists and locals on July 2, 1954. Temperatures hovered around ninety-eight through the Fourth of July weekend as visitors headed straight for the beach for a cool swim. (Jim Mays, photographer.)

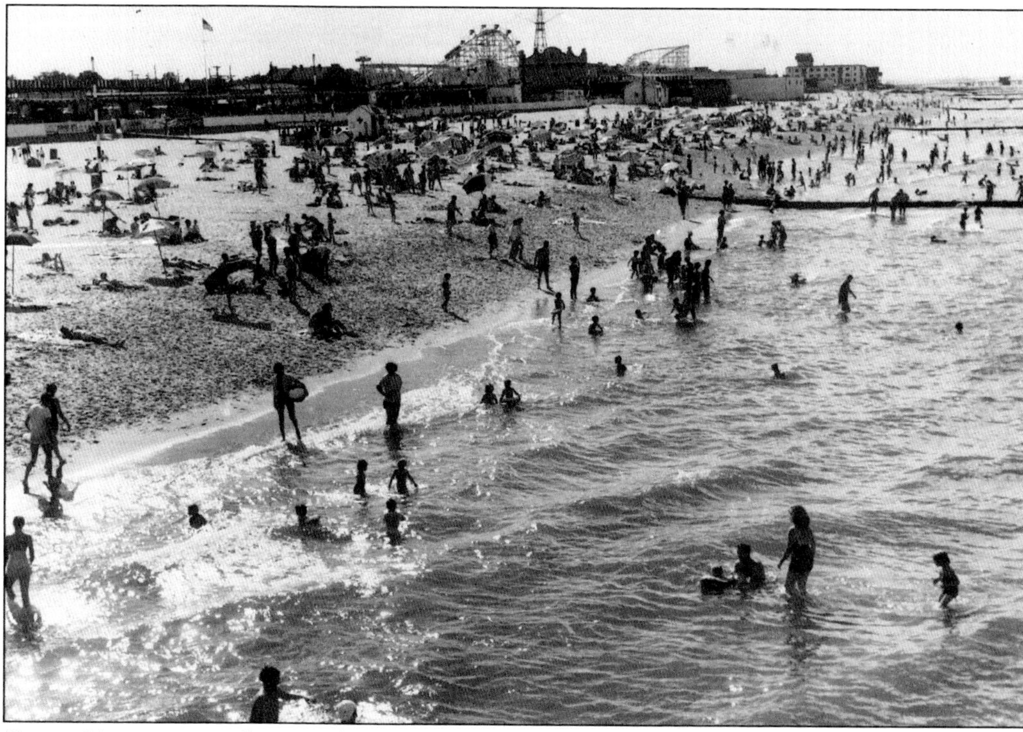

Ocean View remained a popular resort for tourists and area residents as this picture, taken on July 4, 1958, clearly shows. The beach and amusement park experienced record crowds throughout the day as tens of thousands of people brought their families to Ocean View for fun and relaxation. Not since the boom years of World War II had the beaches been so busy. (Photographer unknown.)

Four

HURRICANE!

"Now to their haunts the birds retreat,
   The squirrel seeks his hollow tree,
Wolves in their shaded caverns meet,
   All, all are blest but wretched we—
Foredoomed a stranger to repose,
No rest the unsettled ocean knows."
—From *The Hurricane*, 1784
Philip Freneau, American poet (1752–1832)

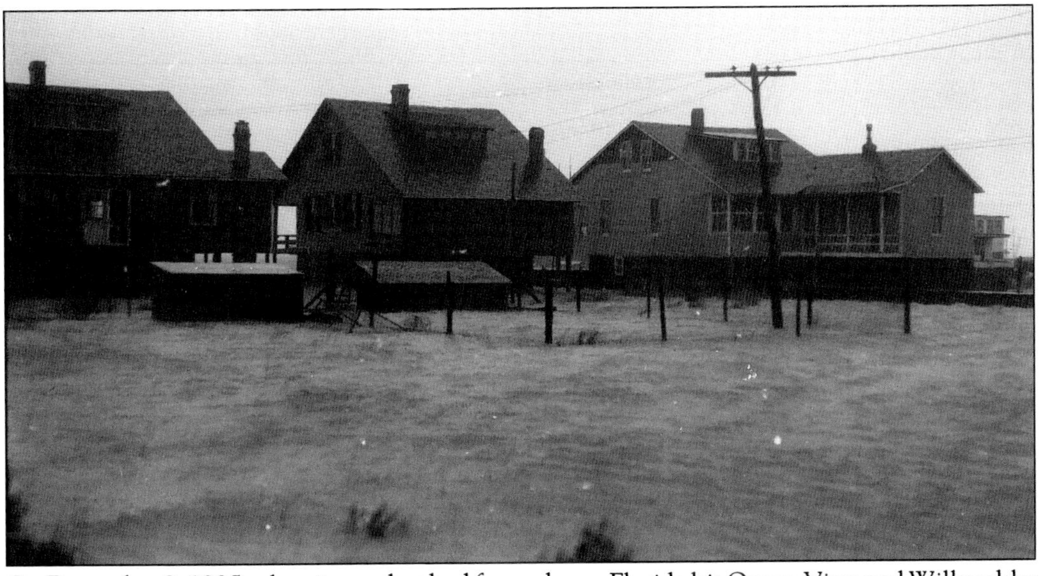

On December 2, 1925, a hurricane that had formed over Florida hit Ocean View and Willoughby from the northeast, dumping heavy winds and rain for several hours. Full gale warnings went out as the waters of the Chesapeake Bay took on an ominous greenish-yellow hue. The waves rolled in high, crashing against the beach with incredible force at Willoughby. Willoughby felt the storm the worst because it was the least protected. Ocean View, built up higher and farther from the water's edge, was hit hard, but nothing like Willoughby. At Fifth and Ninth Streets on Willoughby Spit, waves from the Chesapeake Bay crept over the boulevard and joined hands with the waters of Little Bay. Waves lapped the foundations of the cottages at Willoughby, enveloping some of them in water, but the area weathered the storm without major property damage. The tongues of the gale licked the cottages along the Cottage Line, and the storm reached into the Ocean View resort area with great gusts of wind. The winter population at Willoughby and Ocean View was not great, and many of the cottages, such as the ones shown here on the bayside, were vacant. (Charles S. Borjes, photographer.)

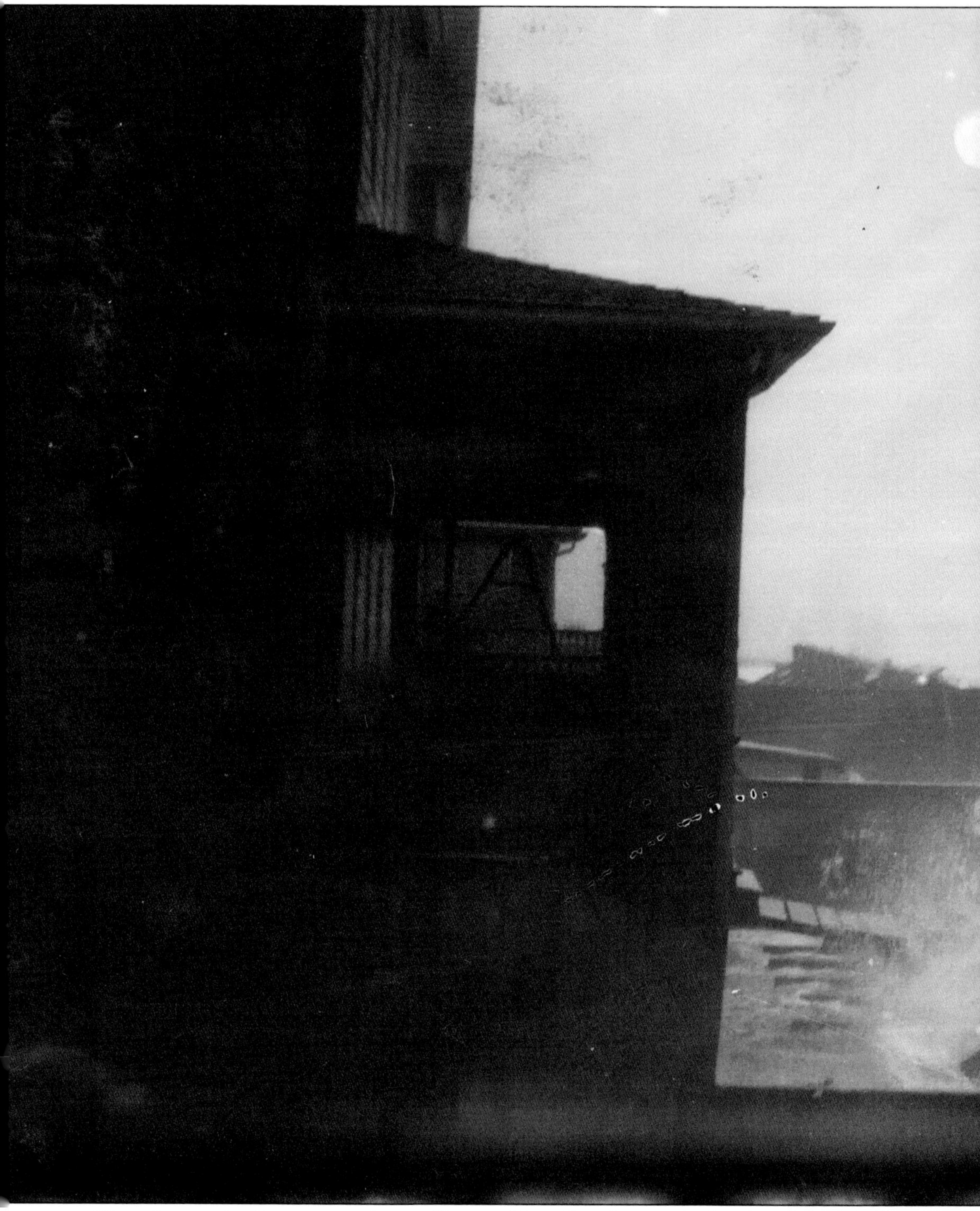

The Chesapeake Bay was caught on film in all her fury during the height of the big blow on August 23, 1933. The bay's water struck Ocean View and Willoughby so hard that cottages and business establishments were taken out to sea by the sheer force of water pounding the beach.

Parts of Willoughby Spit were completely underwater as Willoughby Bay, also called Little Bay, enjoined with the Chesapeake Bay and obliterated the land mass. (Charles S. Borjes, photographer.)

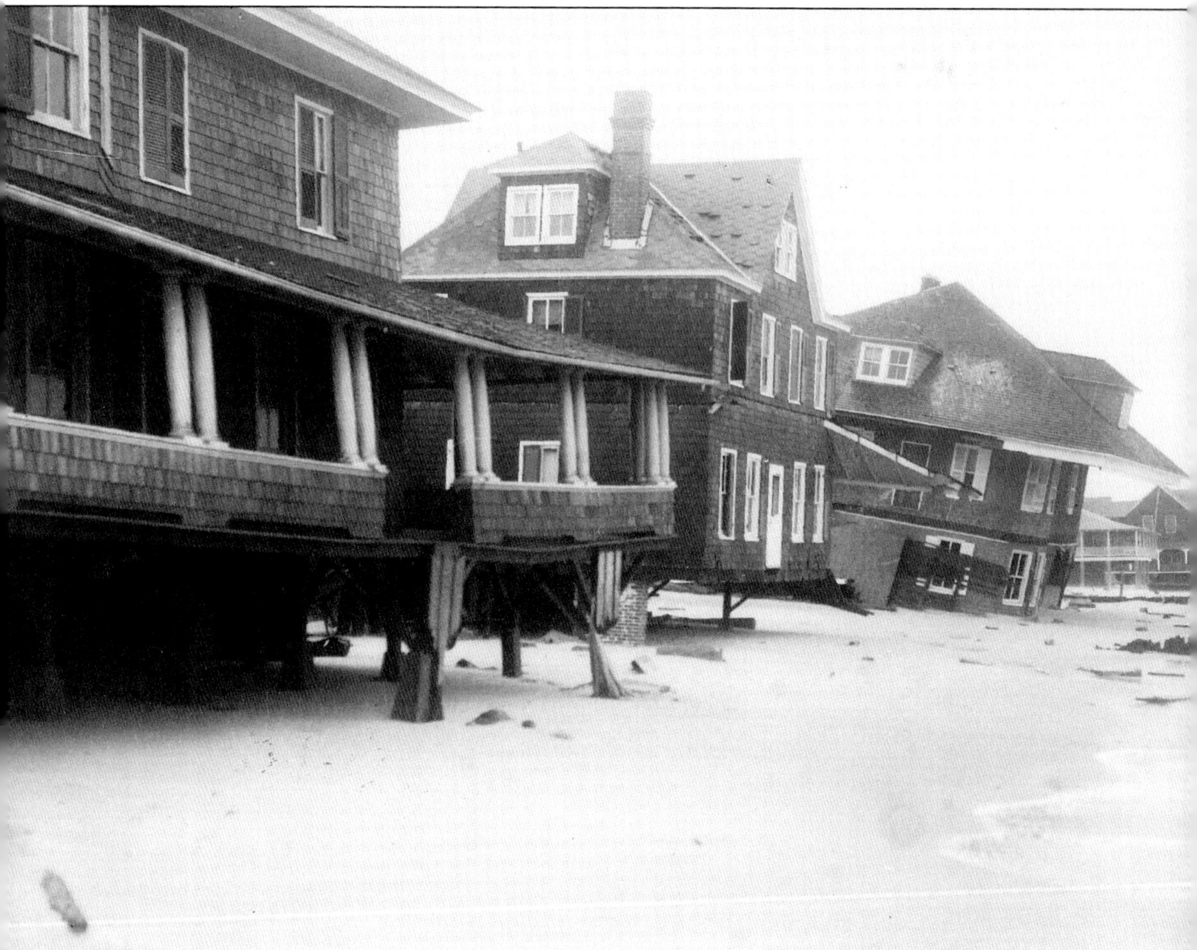

The storm destroyed many cottages along Ocean View while leaving others close to the brink of destruction. These cottages teetered precariously toward the sea on August 24, 1933. (Charles S. Borjes, photographer.)

THE BIG BLOW OF '33

The first hurricane to hit Ocean View and Willoughby, on August 23, 1933, was first spotted by a steamer east of the Windward Islands five days earlier. The National Weather Bureau issued a warning of a tropical disturbance located roughly 900 miles due east of Puerto Rico on August 18. The storm had reached a point only 150 miles southwest of Bermuda on August 21, and had attained a wind velocity of 64 miles per hour. Rain had begun to pelt Norfolk's bayfront community the day before the main body of the storm struck Ocean View's shores. Ocean View and Willoughby took the brunt of the hurricane's fury. Ocean View Amusement Park had at least $200,000 damage wrought by the storm. When Otto Wells was asked if the park would reopen for the remaining three weeks of the season, he remarked, "The Ocean View baths, at the other end of the park, are O.K. as are the scooter cars, coaster cars, Leaping Lena, Sky-Rocket and the Ferris wheel, Kiddyland, back from the beach, escaped severe damage. The decision to reopen is based partly on the desires of our patrons." Only one death occurred in Norfolk as a result of the hurricane. Property damage in the city was estimated at $2,850,000, most of which occurred in Ocean View and Willoughby. Of the two hundred six cottages and permanent residences on Willoughby, only five escaped damage.

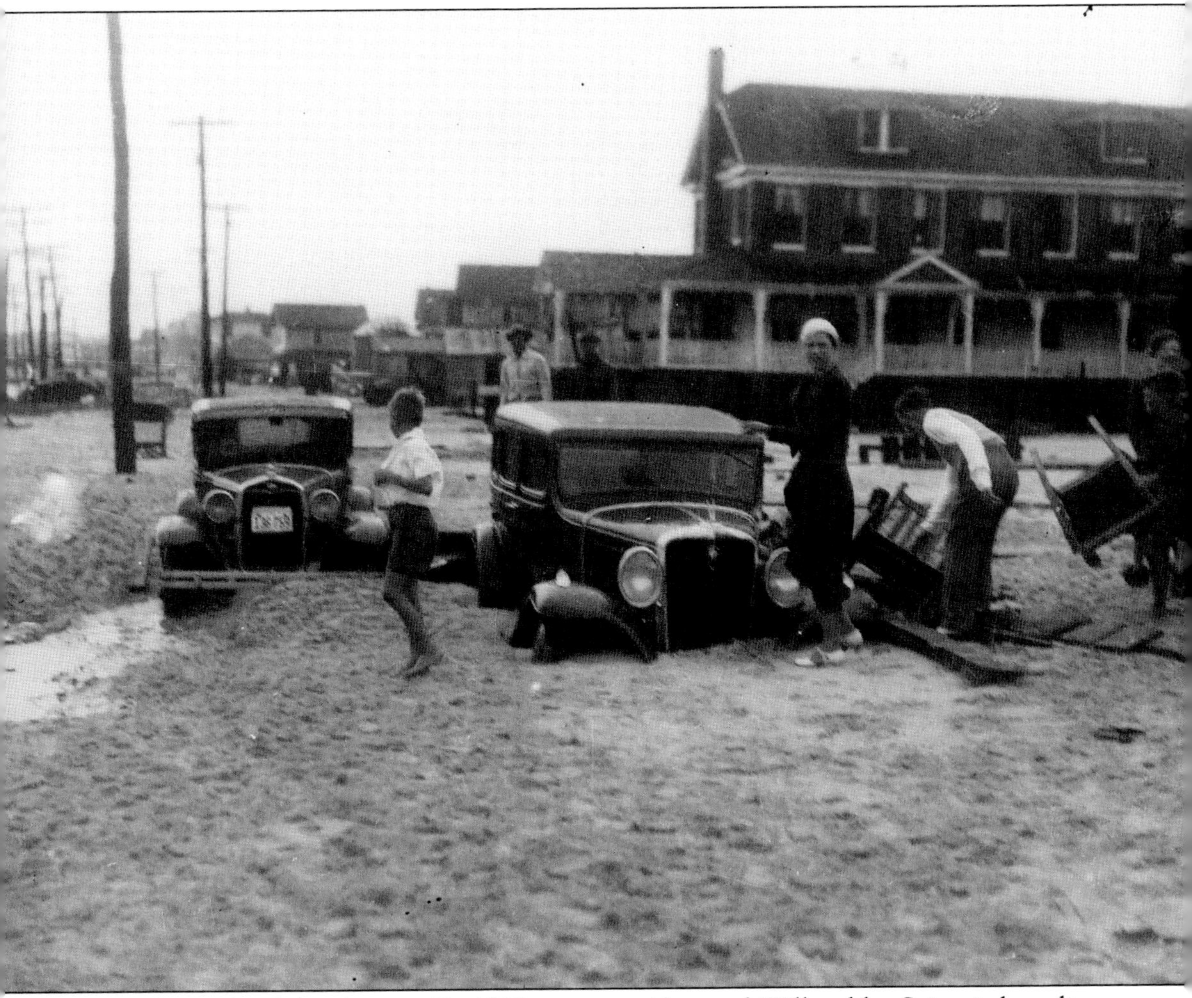

In the aftermath of the August 23, 1933 storm, residents of Willoughby Spit tried to dig out their cars and the street that once ran the length of the most exposed finger of land in Norfolk. Some automobiles were actually covered completely by sand. (Charles S. Borjes, photographer.)

FISH TALES

The hurricane that came through Hampton Roads on August 23, 1933, had its lighter moments. A fish normally found in profuse numbers at Ocean View swam into the Gross Bros. Shoe Repair Shop at 141 Atlantic Street. About 8 inches in length, the fish appeared to be a croaker, but it was not croaking. The fish's captors decided the excitement of the storm had rendered it dumb. Of course, over in the city courthouse, goldfish in the fountain found themselves in unrestricted waters as the storm peaked and drew river water up to the lip of their bowl. Smart goldfish made a wriggle for more spacious swimming accommodations. One of these was caught in the Royster Building, while the others made a clean getaway and were never seen again.

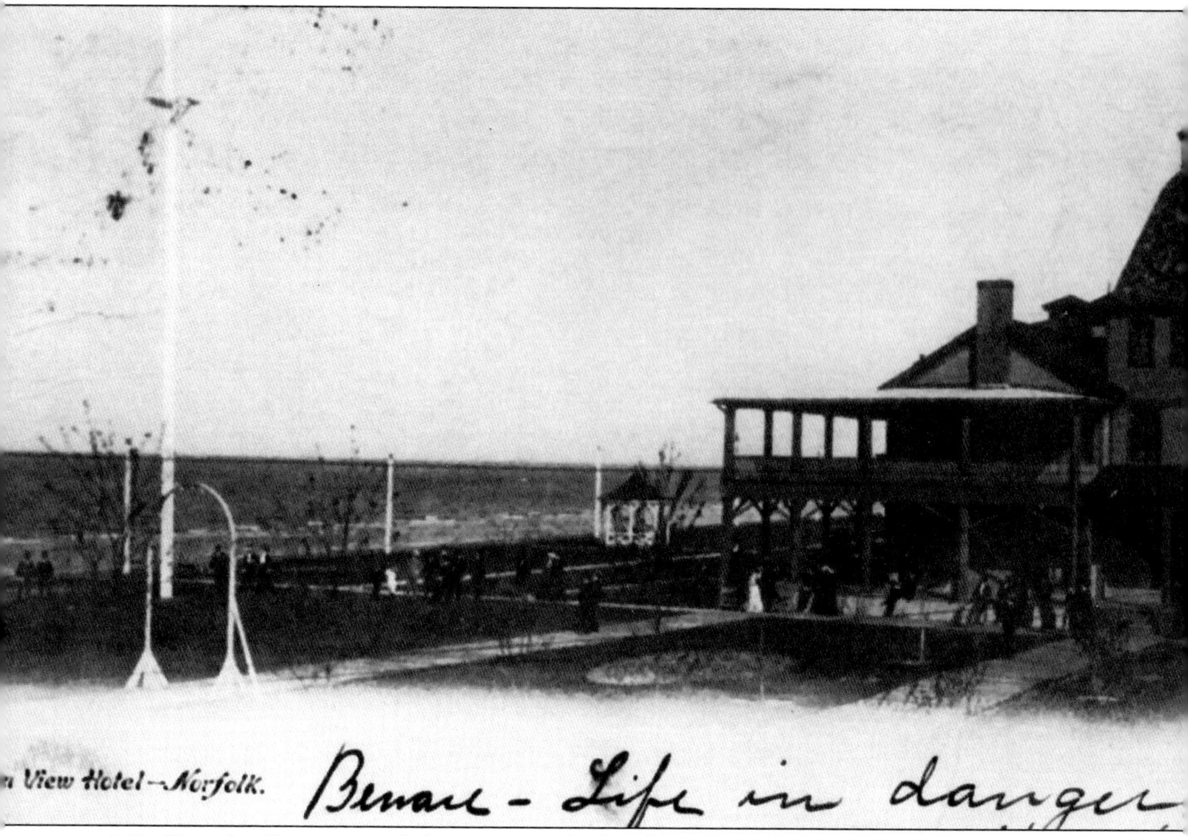

Miss Rosa Le Dareieux took her seat on the big flagpole at Ocean View Amusement Park on July 1, 1933, in an effort to remain aloft until Labor Day. Everyone in Norfolk followed the story of "Rosa Atop the Pole" for weeks, but public interest was truly peaked when news broke on August 23, that young Rosa had refused to come down from her perch 55 feet in the air during the height of the area's most devastating hurricane. Swaying to and fro at the top of the pole, she saw waves carry away many of the park's main attractions. Had she not been rescued by a fireman, La Dareieux may not have survived to make another attempt at the world-record for flagpole sitting. She was, without question, the only living person to witness much of the havoc wreaked by the big blow's fury. The fireman who saved La Dareieux performed one of the most daring acts of heroism of any firemen or policemen at the time of the storm. The flagpole at Ocean View, a precarious perch at best, is shown here as it appeared on a postcard cancelled August 8, 1904.

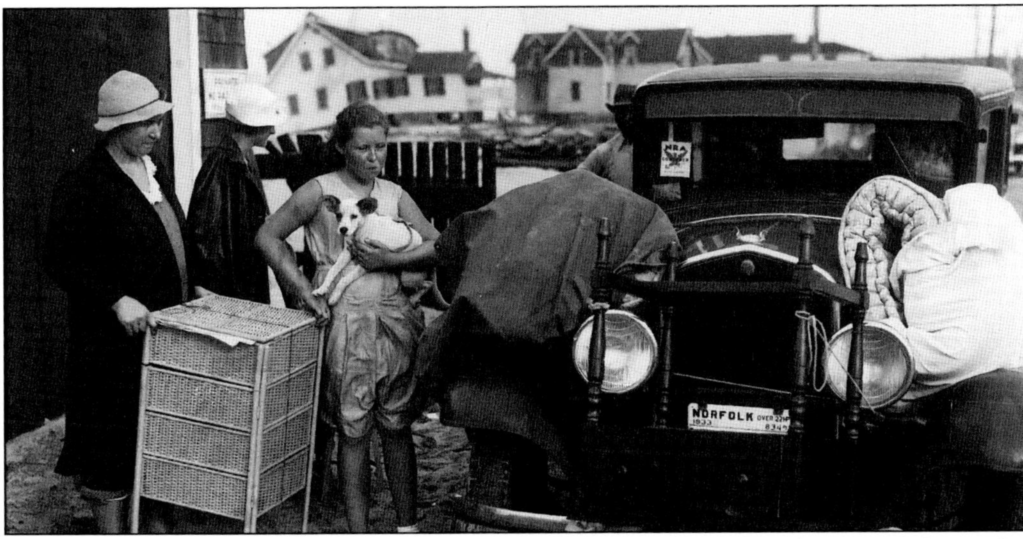

Presaging the storm to come, residents of Willoughby began evacuating the area on September 15, 1933. Those in the photograph (left to right) were Mrs. William Freeman Jr.; Constance Curtis, daughter of Mr. and Mrs. John Hughes Curtis; and Constance Freeman, holding her puppy dog, Skippy. As the surf rolled in, residents obligingly moved out or battened down in anticipation of a repeat of the August 23 hurricane. All along the Chesapeake Bay, residents of Willoughby and Ocean View took precautionary measures against the storm. (Charles S. Borjes, photographer.)

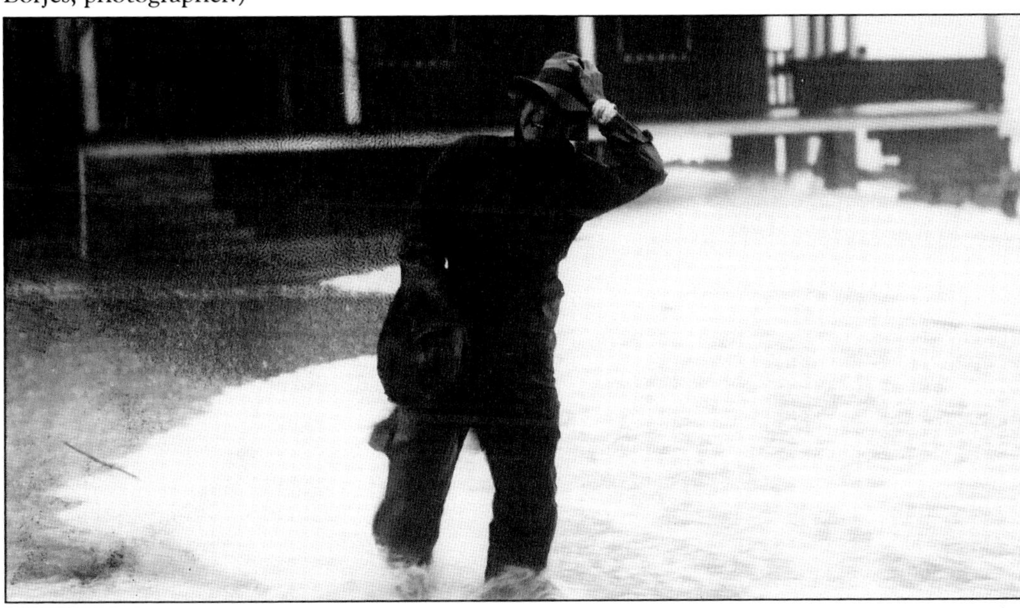

During the peak of the hurricane that passed over Ocean View and Willoughby on September 16, 1933, this gentleman clung to his hat and tried to make headway against the wind and surf. At its worst, the hurricane produced gusts of 70 miles per hour. Water undercut the foundations on cottages at Willoughby, and many were simply pulled into the sea without any warning. (Charles S. Borjes, photographer.)

"The man that is staggering by / Holds his hat to his head by the brim . . ." [From *The Storm-Wind*; William Barnes, English poet (1801–1886).]

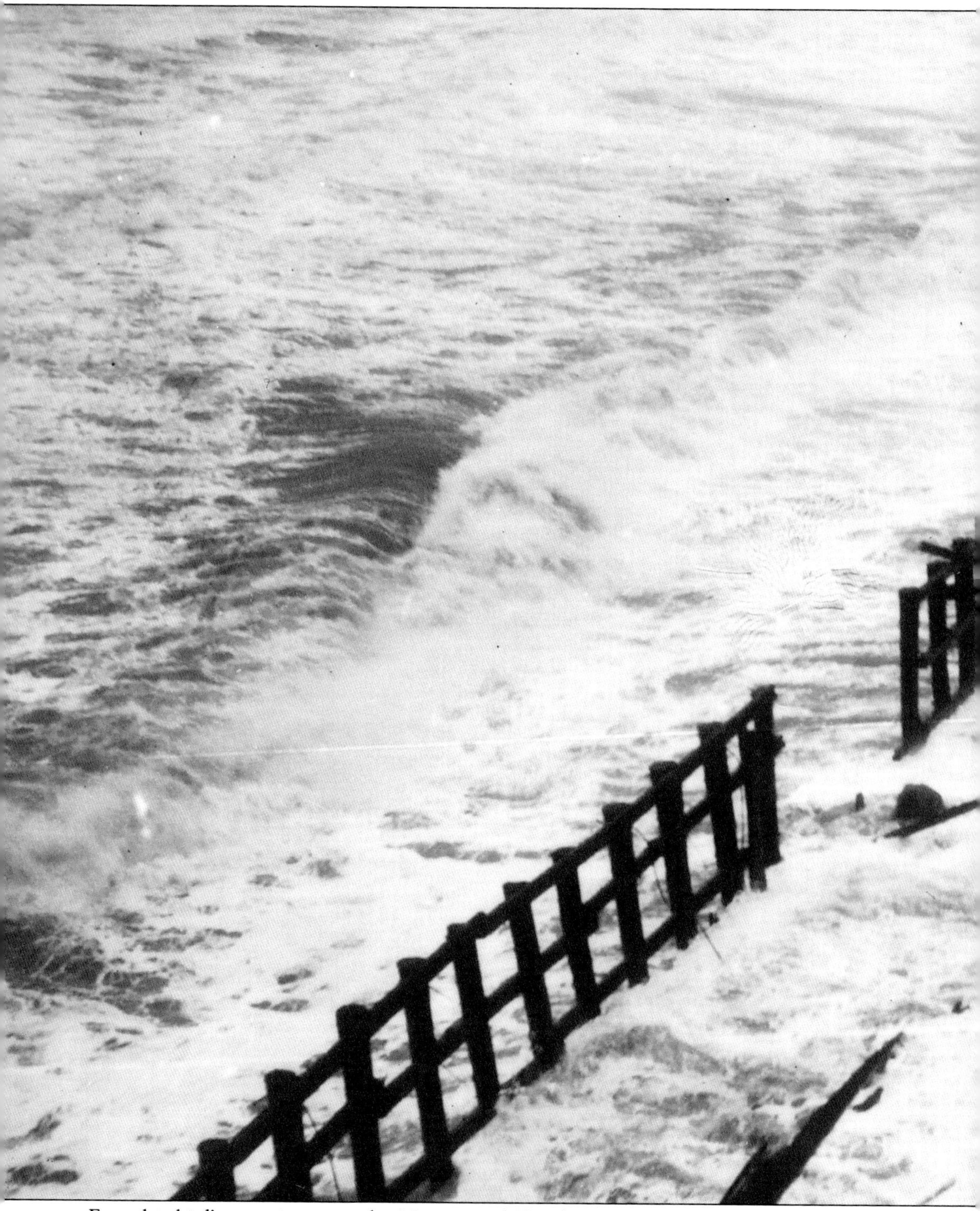

From his bird's eye view atop the Nansemond Hotel, *Virginian-Pilot* photographer Charles S. Borjes took this photograph of the heavy seas that piled into broken bulkheads and damaged buildings along the bayfront during the hurricane of September 16, 1933. Borjes took his

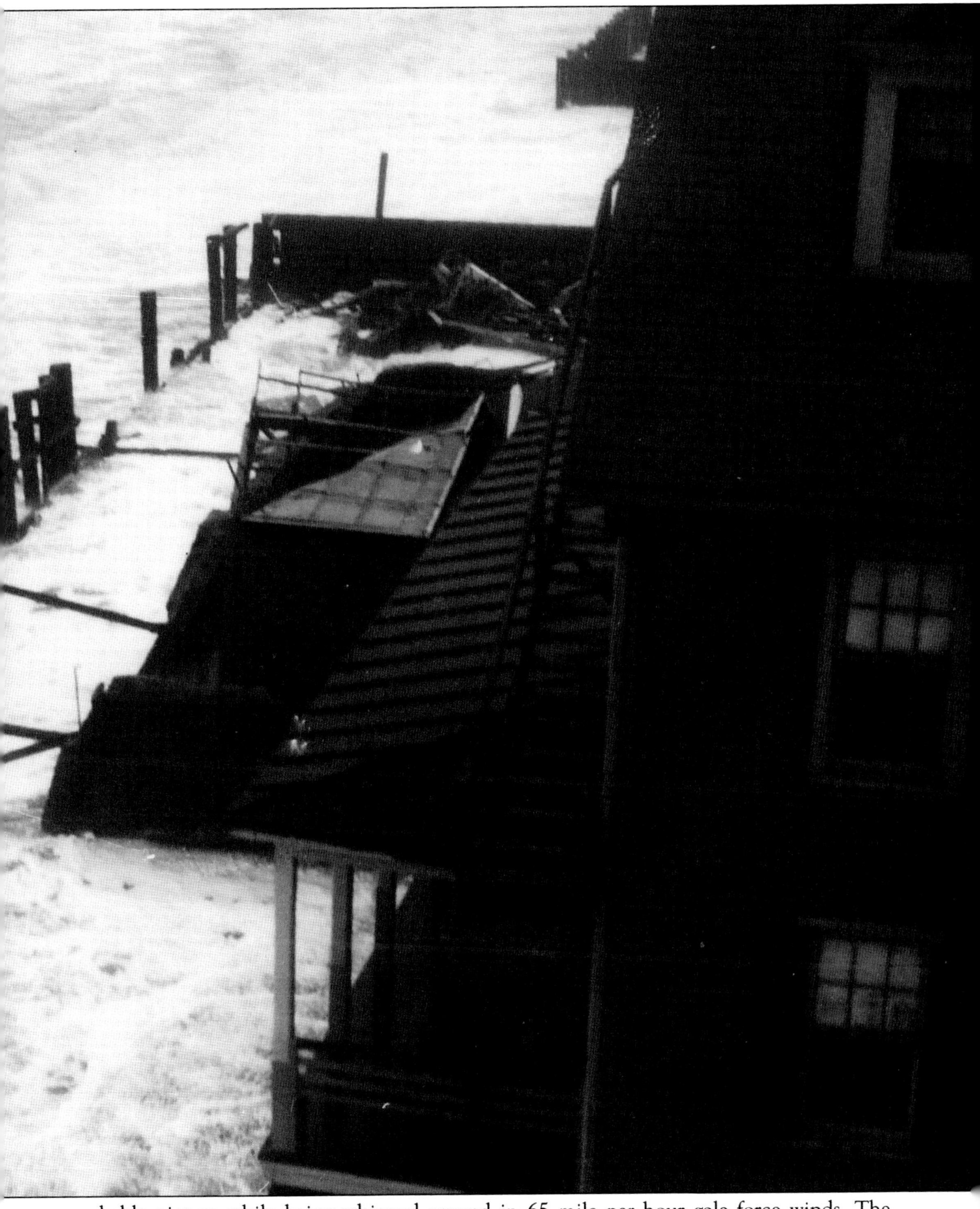

remarkable picture while being whipped around in 65 mile per hour gale force winds. The picture was taken looking in the direction of the amusement park at Ocean View proper.

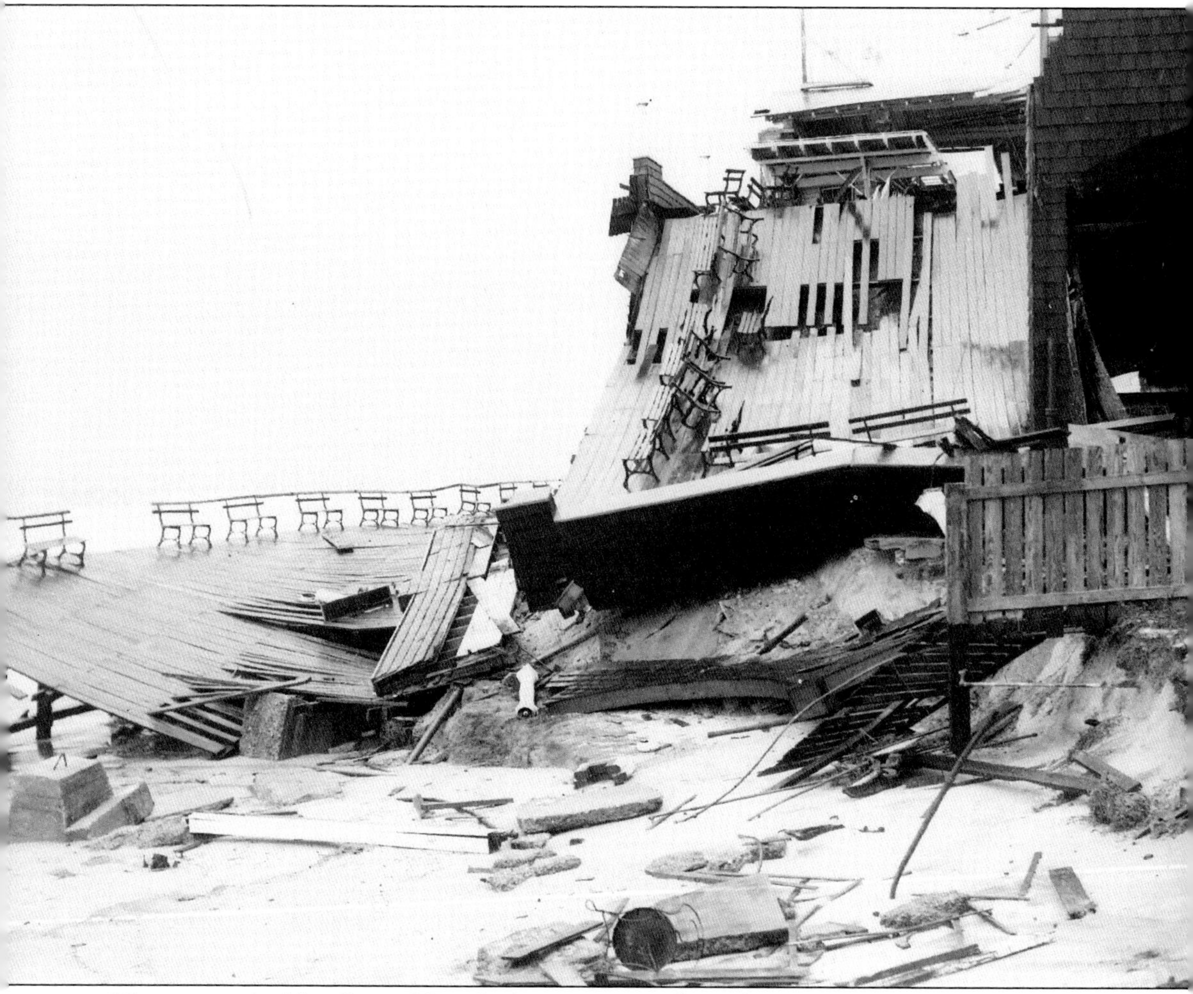

The west end of the Ocean View Park casino, as well as a large section of boardwalk, collapsed during the peak of a tropical hurricane that hit the Norfolk area on September 18, 1936. The hurricane inflicted only a fraction of the damage caused by the big blow of August 1933. Buffeted by winds upwards of 70 miles per hour and floodwaters 5 feet above the normal high, Ocean View was saved from more severe damage by two factors: a shift in the wind to the northwest held down the tide, and the center of the hurricane passed 20 miles east of Cape Henry instead of directly through the area. Ocean View residents and businessmen were given ample warning in advance of the storm, thus substantially reducing their risk to life and property as they evacuated to safer ground. (Charles S. Borjes, photographer.)

Five

Fisherman's Paradise and the Coney Island of the South

"The fish is swift, small-needing, vague yet clear,
A cold, sweet, silver life, wrapped in round waves,
Quickened with touches of transporting fear."
—From *The Fish, the Man, and the Spirit*, 1836
Leigh Hunt, English poet (1784–1859)

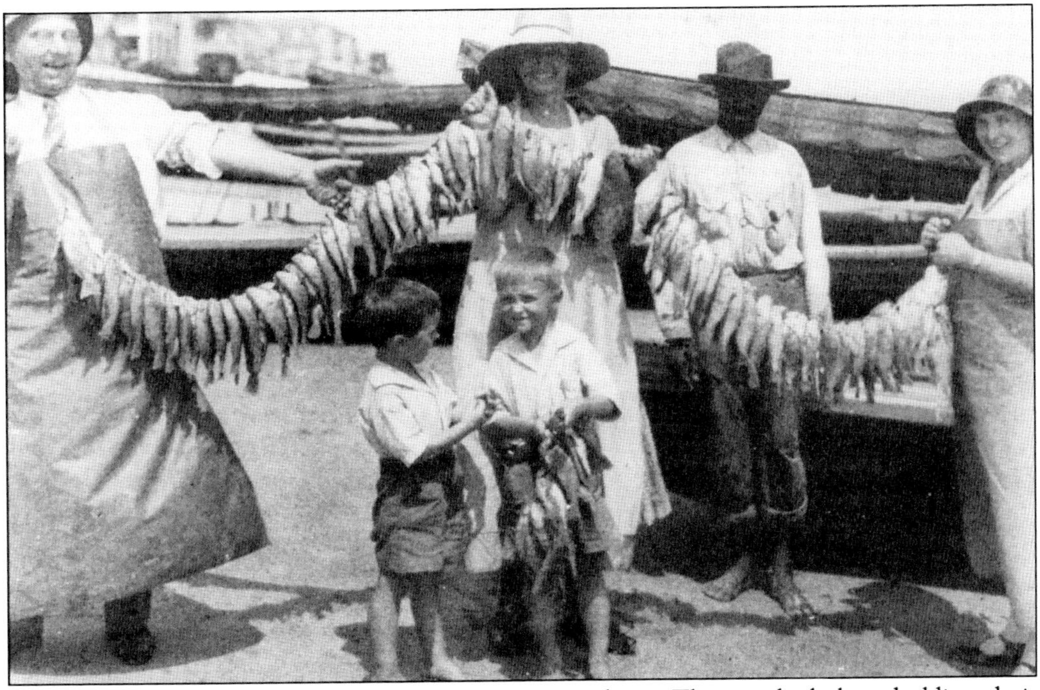

All of these fish were caught at Ocean View in one hour. The two little boys holding their catch look proud of the family's accomplishment. Fishing at Ocean View was considered a fisherman's dream come true. The photograph dates to c. 1910.

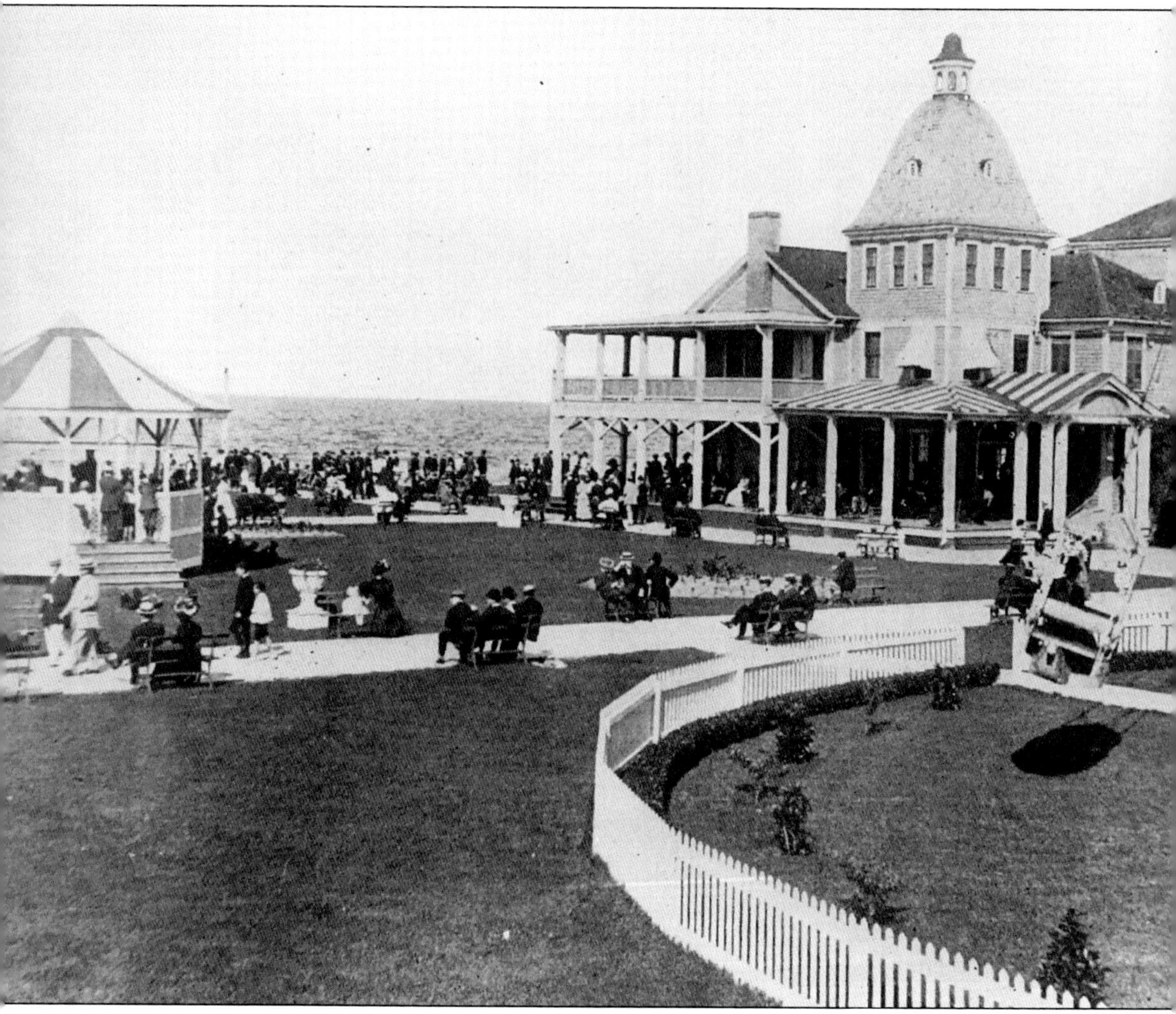

Ocean View had a lovely park and bandstand apart from its amusements. Shown as it appeared in 1908, the park was crowded and full of activity. (Photographer unknown.)

A Little Amusement Park History

The amusement park business goes back to the Middle Ages in Europe and the pleasure gardens that proliferated the purlieus of major cities. The gardens were the earliest antecedent of today's amusement parks since they featured the full gamut of human diversions from dancing, games, music, even rides, though these were quite simple, to fireworks. Europeans enjoyed the pleasure gardens through the early 1700s, but continual political upheaval led to their demise. The world's oldest, and continuously operated, amusement park is Bakken, opened in 1583 and located north of Copenhagen, Denmark.

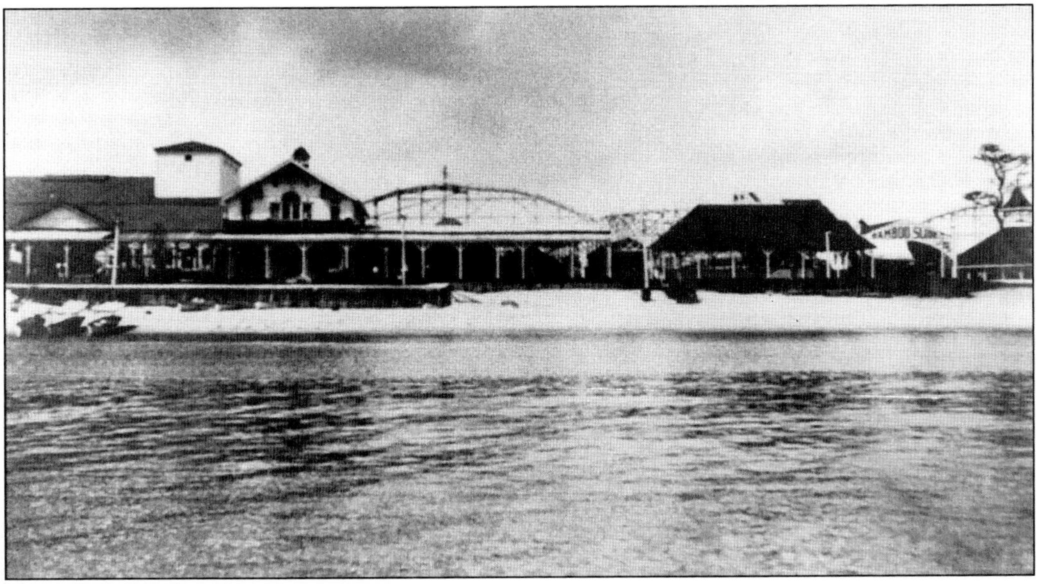

Ocean View was the bastion of bayfront resorts. The image pictured here provides a rarely seen look at the amusement park as it appeared from the water. The famous Bamboo Slide can be observed to the far right of the photograph, and the first Leap-the-Dips in the background. The scene was caught on film *c.* 1910.

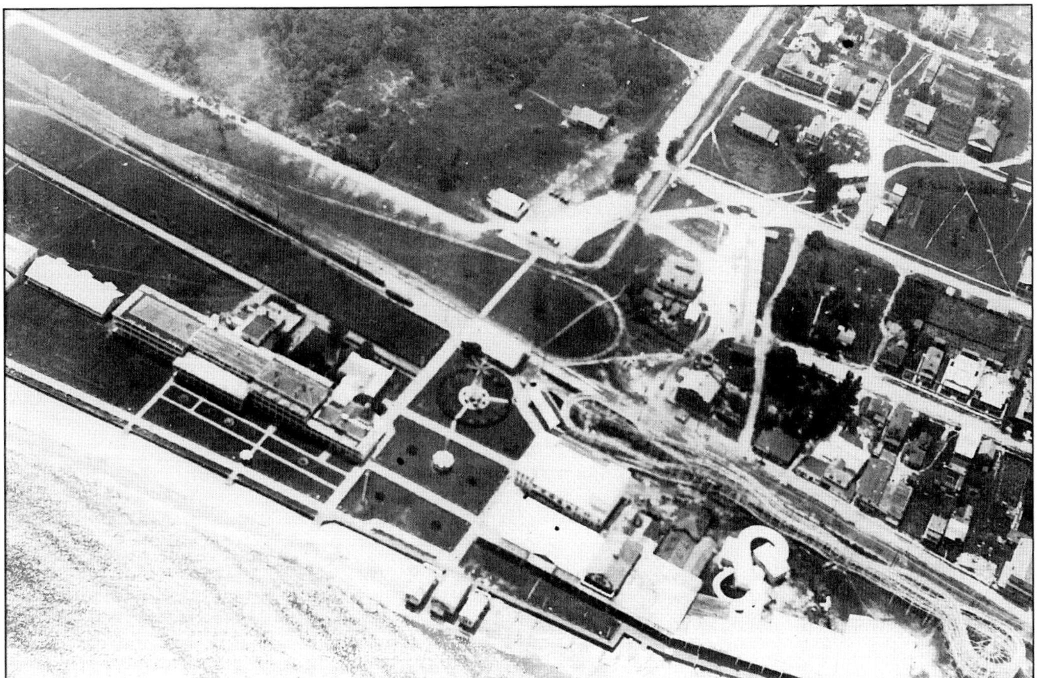

Frank J. Conway was a contract photographer for the Atlantic Coast Aeronautical Station, an experimental facility and aviation school in Newport News, Virginia, which was operated by the Curtiss Aeroplane Company of Hammondsport, New York. Conway took this aerial perspective of the old Ocean View Amusement Park *c.* 1916. He was being flown in a Curtiss JN-4 Jenny biplane piloted by one of Glenn H. Curtiss' test pilots.

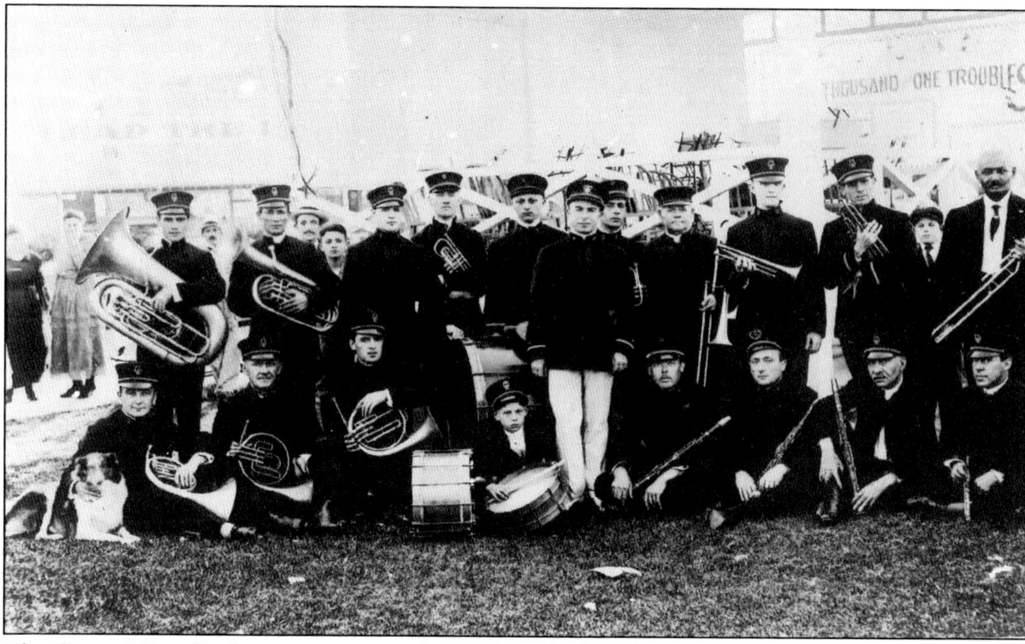

The Ocean View Orchestra entertained crowds in the bandstand of the park season after season. This photograph of the orchestra was taken about 1920.

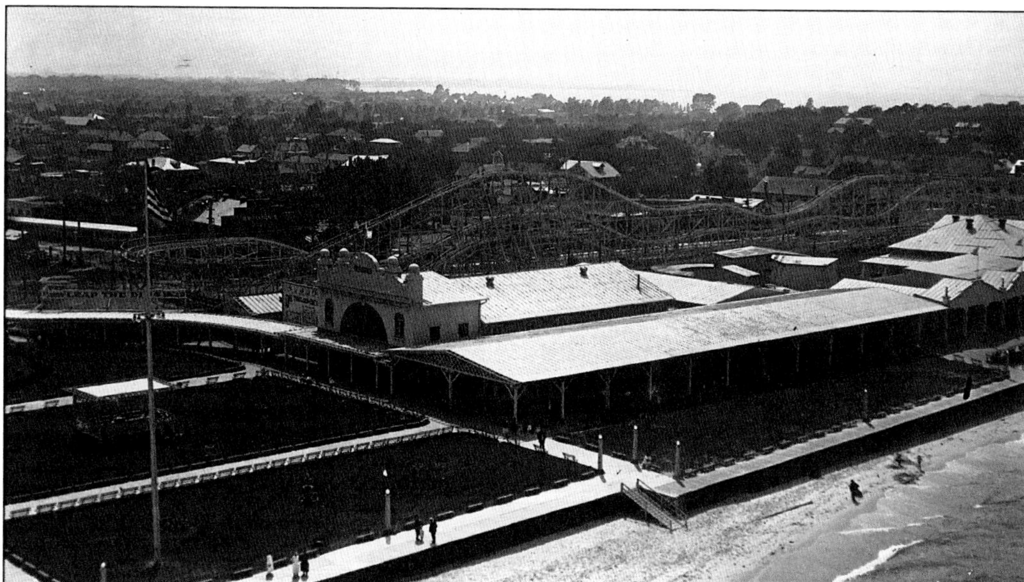

Ocean View had begun to grow as a tourist destination and as a community. Two years prior to being annexed by Norfolk in 1923, Frank J. Conway flew over the old amusement park again. At low altitude, Conway's photograph clearly shows the bandstand, casino, boardwalk, Leap-the-Dips, and other attractions at the park. Large, beautiful homes surround the park to the south and southwest. Naval Air Station Hampton Roads and Naval Base Norfolk are faintly visible across Willoughby Bay on the horizon.

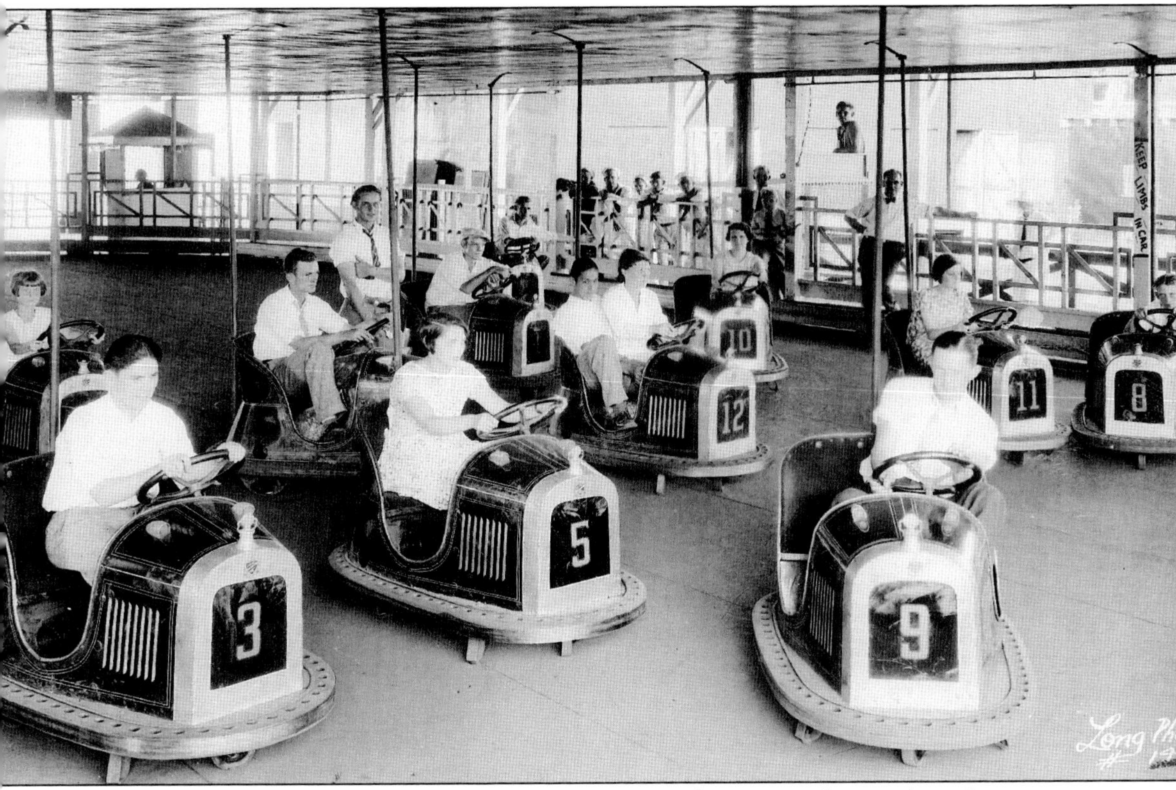

The bumper car ride was photographed in 1928. Notice the sign in the pavilion that warns, "Keep Limbs In Car."

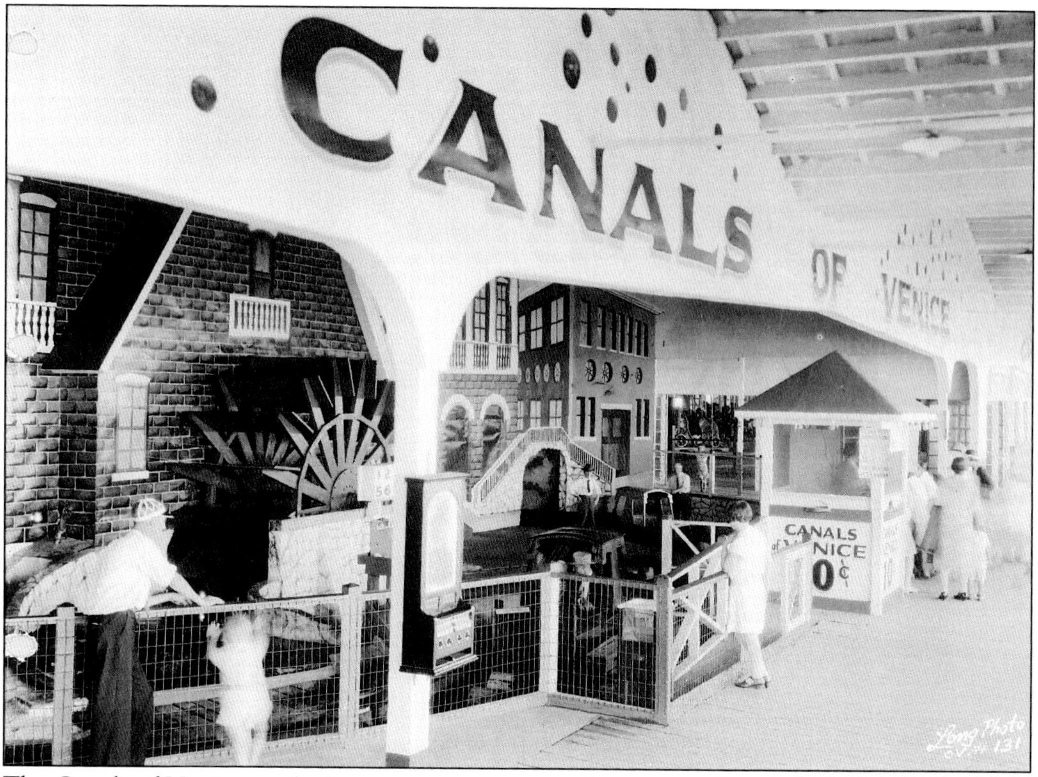

The Canals of Venice sparked many romances over the years and memories of fun-filled days gone by that will never be again. Photographed in 1928, the ride was at its peak of popularity.

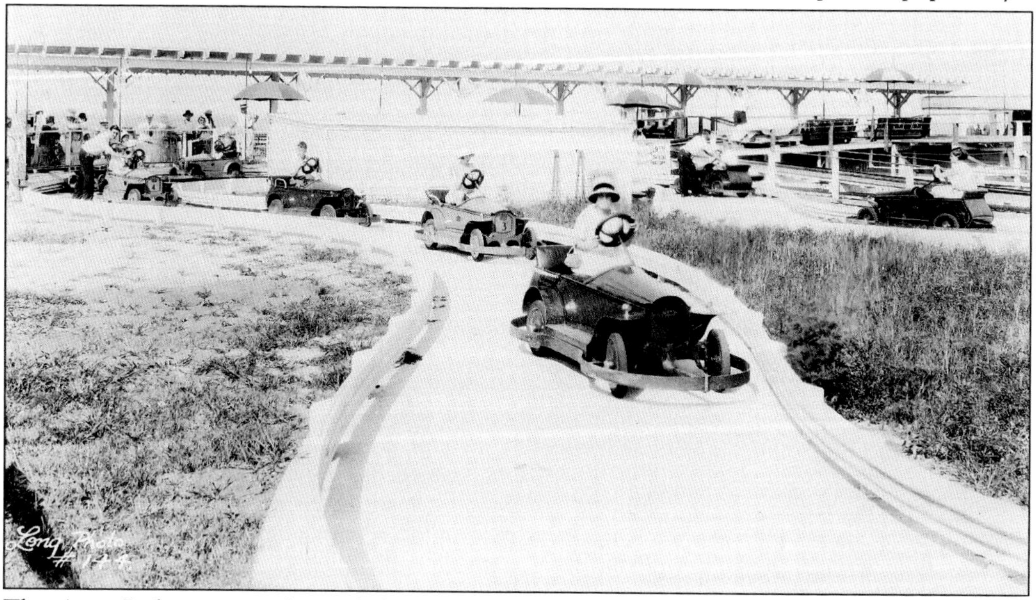

The Auto Ride was popular with boys and girls, and even adults, in 1929. These were the days before "speedy" automobiles were readily available to every household. The notion that one could leap into the car and presumably take a spin around town held great appeal to park visitors.

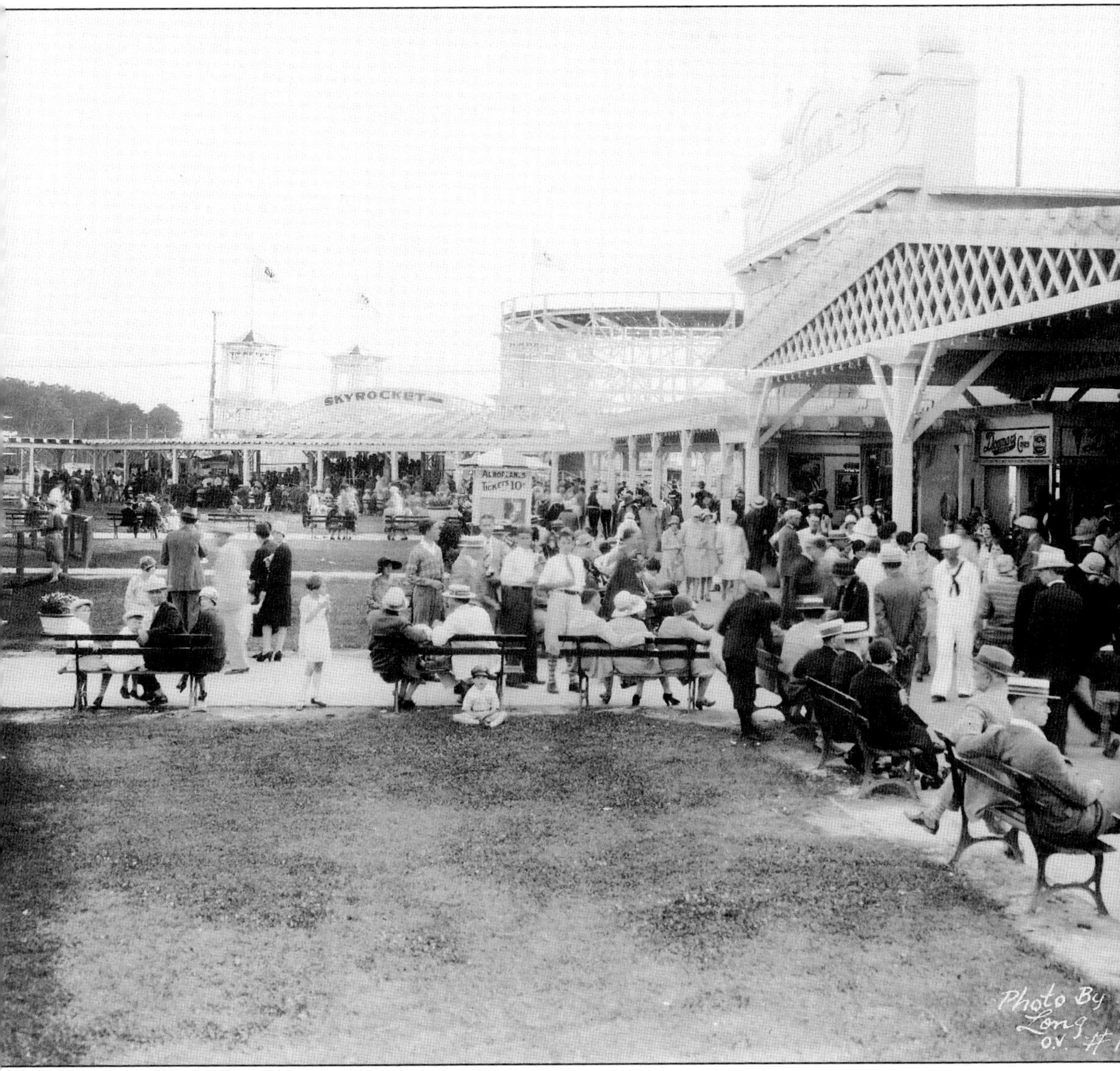

Visitors packed the area outside the Ocean View Casino on July 4, 1928. Amusement parks were experiencing the end of their golden era, an era that began with the 1893 Colombian Exposition in Chicago, Illinois, with the introduction of the amusement midway to the world. It was this event which prescribed the design of amusement parks for the next six decades. The first modern amusement park was opened by Captain Paul Boyton on Chicago's southside in 1894. The amusement park industry continued to grow by leaps and bounds over the next thirty years as crowds came to expect more diverse and exciting rides. There were well-over fifteen hundred amusement parks in the United States by 1919, but in 1929, the Great Depression came and the parks struggled to regain the crowds they had known in happier times. Only four hundred amusement parks were in operation by 1935, and those that weathered closure sought to stay open by offering special rates and rides to patrons.

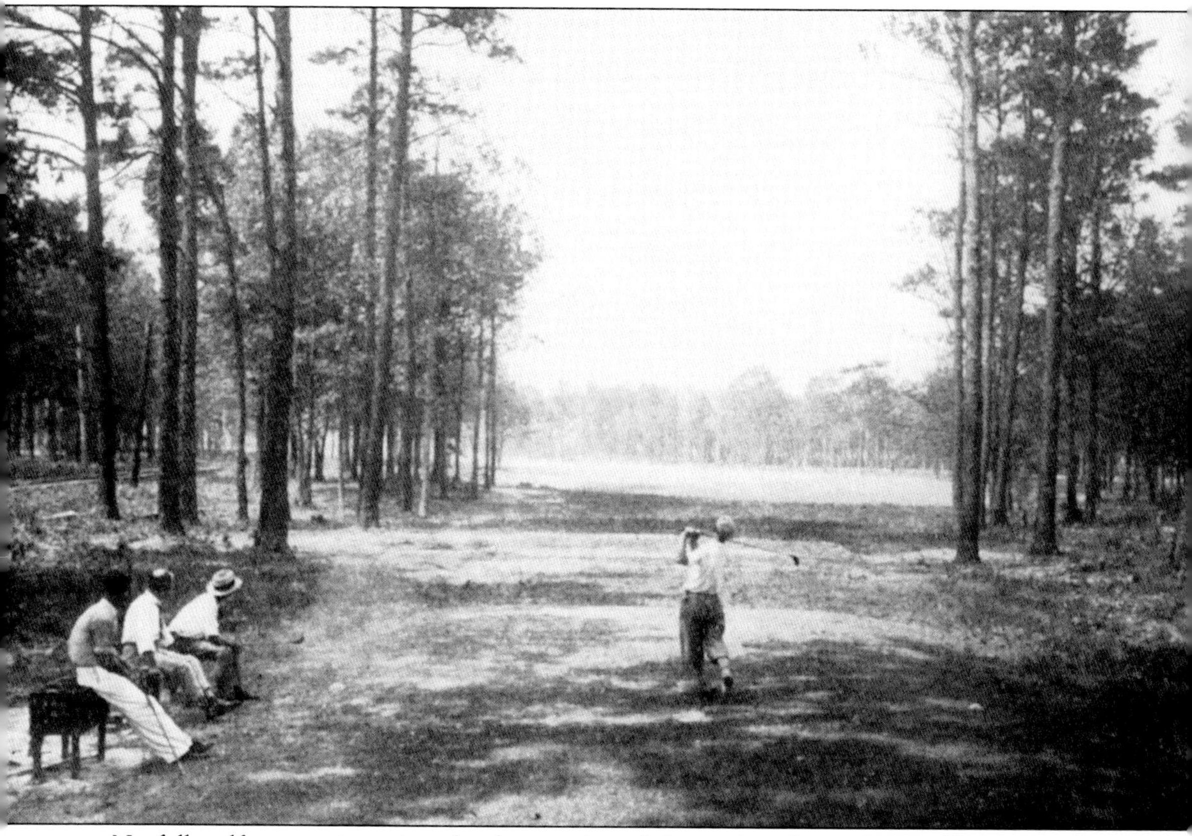

Norfolk golfers were impatient for the opening of the city's eighteen-hole golf course at Ocean View on August 24, 1929, but lack of rain to grow the grass had delayed play by professionals and amateurs lined up on Norfolk Avenue for an opportunity to christen the course. The Ocean View Golf Course was laid out by Walter Beckett, former Norfolk Country Club professional, and had a total length of 6,357 yards, for which the par held at 69. Beckett planned the course with no less than five three-par holes—one of those was 196 yards long, while another crossed a lake where the water was 10 feet deep. The course did not open until two months later because the grass on the fairways and greens needed to mature to guarantee good playing conditions. The first tee of the course was on Norfolk Avenue, a short distance south of Ocean View Avenue. Once the course was opened, it is interesting to note that golfers had to cross the Virginia Electric and Power Company tracks to get to the fourth tee and then drive straightaway to the west for 558 yards, the longest hole on the course, over alternate stretches of fairway and rough. There were not too many courses in the United States with streetcar tracks running through them, but the attraction to fitting the course into Ocean View was the resort draw of the amusement park and beach. The timing of its opening could not have been worse because the stock market crashed on October 24, 1929, and the amusement parks and resort areas took a heavy loss in business and revenues. The picture shown here was taken in 1936.

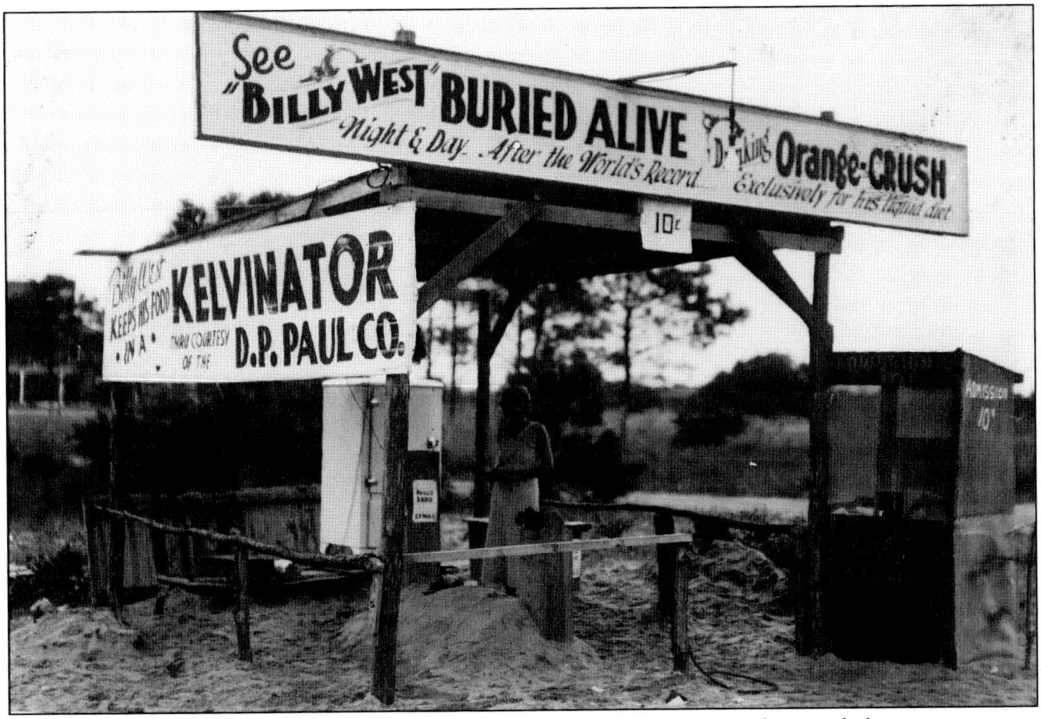

Ocean View was frequented throughout its history by exhibitionists who tried about every stunt known to mankind to make a dollar. "Billy West" was buried alive drinking Orange Crush night and day for his liquid diet. For 10¢, anyone could take a peek for themselves. Billy West was after the world's record in this attempt. The D.P. Paul Company, a popular Norfolk jewelry store, sponsored Billy's Kelvinator, the refrigerator visible under the sign. The picture was taken in July 1933. (Charles S. Borjes, photographer.)

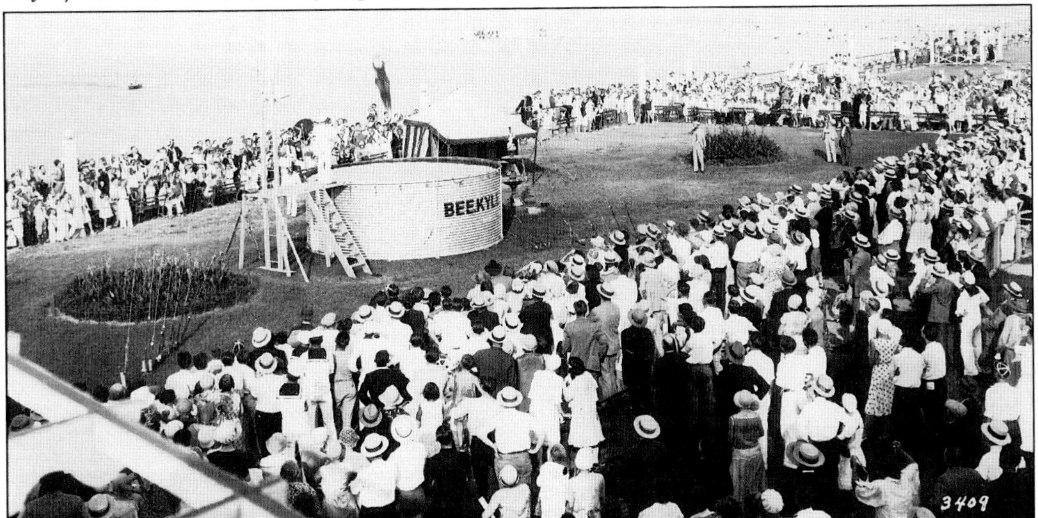

Bee Kyle was obviously a popular exhibitionist at Ocean View. On July 20, 1930, she captivated hundreds of beachgoers and park visitors with her thrilling platform dives into the tank below. Kyle had the complete attention of everyone in the crowd; all eyes were on her performance. (Photographer unknown.)

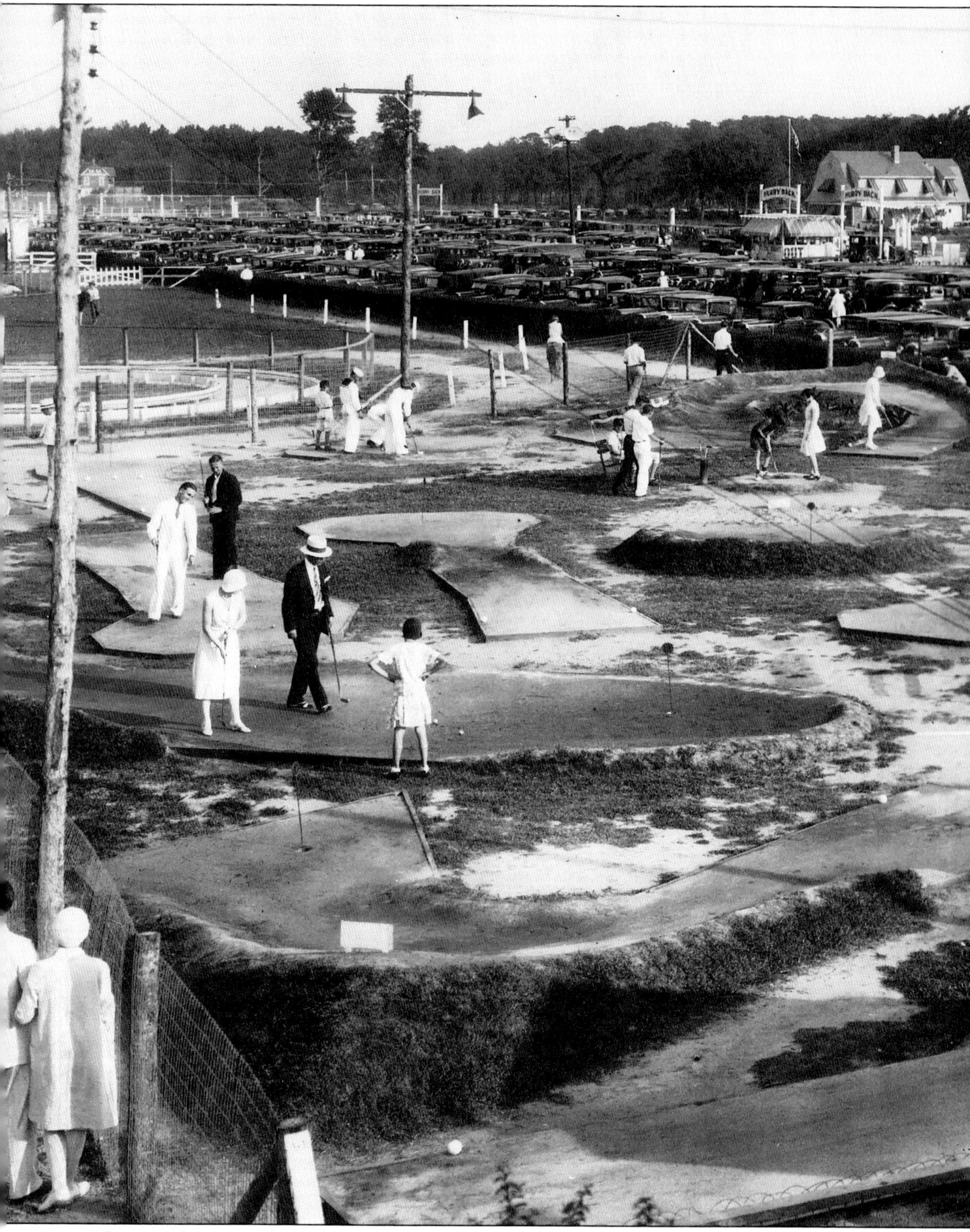

This was the Tom Thumb Golf Course at Ocean View Amusement Park. The photograph was taken on July 4, 1930, one of the busiest days of the year for the resort. The parking lots were

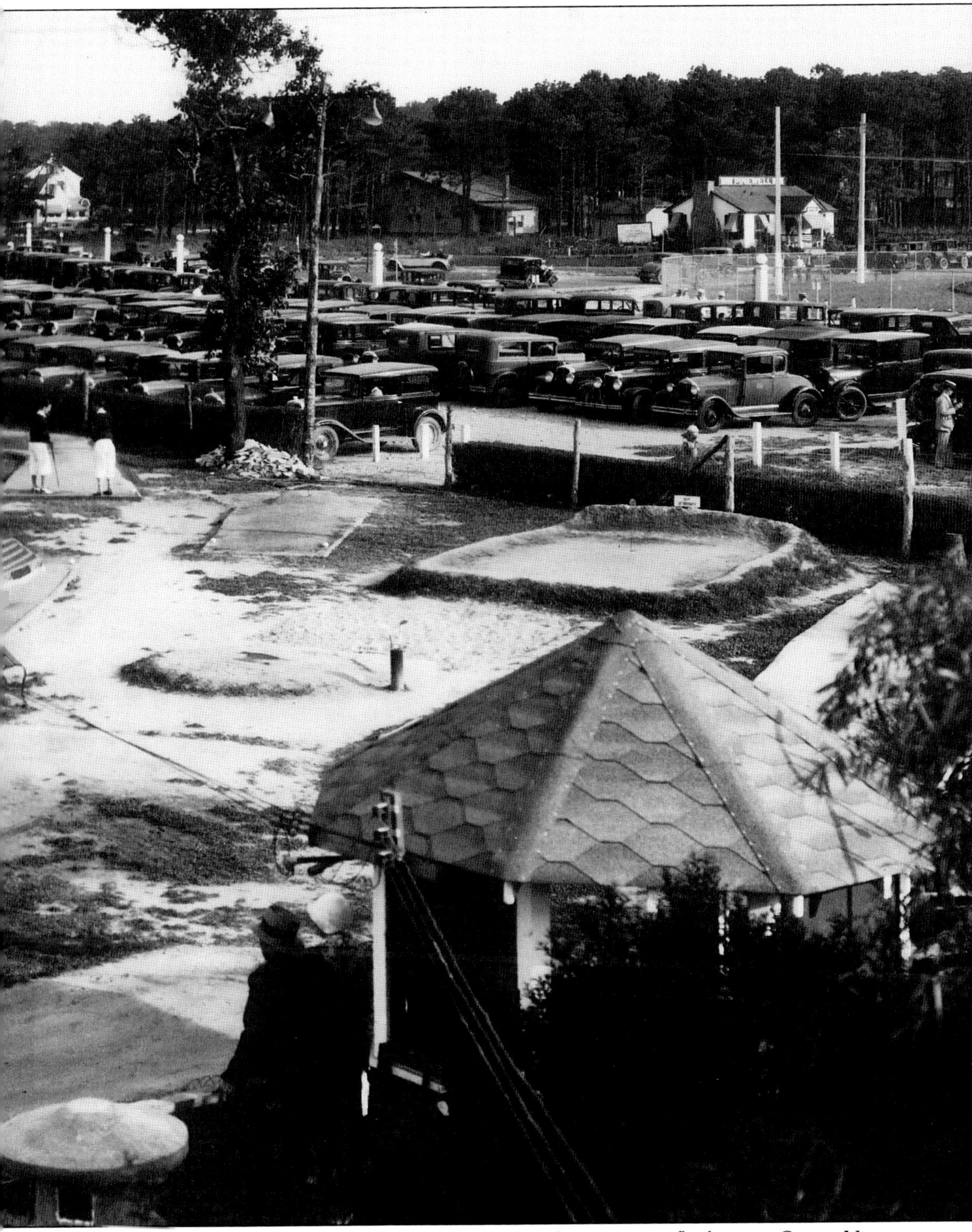

overflowing, and the electric car lines were deluged with passengers flocking to Ocean View. Beyond the Tom Thumb course was a track for pony rides. (Photographer unknown.)

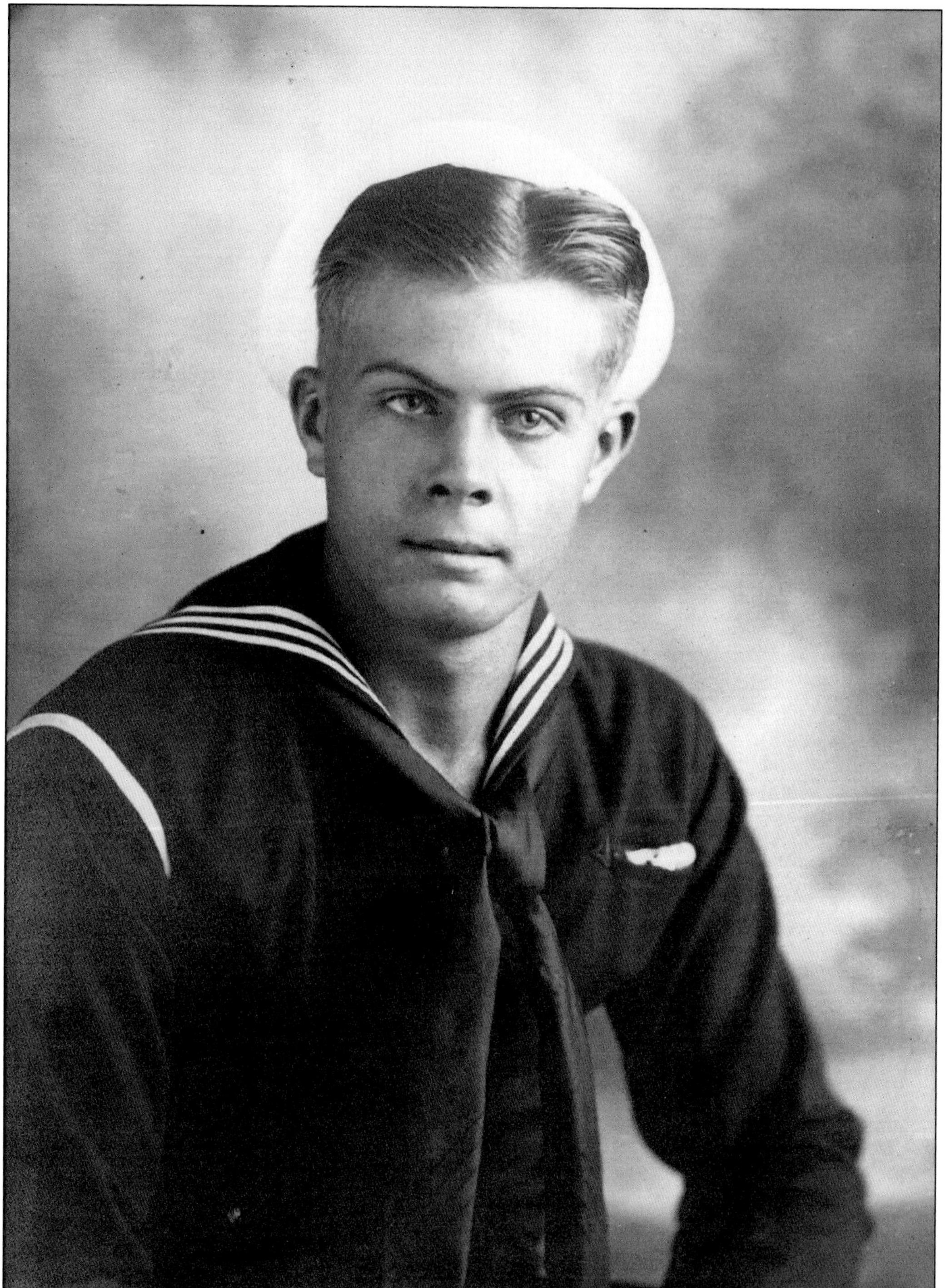

Ralph H. Scott had his picture taken at Long's Studio, Ocean View, on December 7, 1931. The picture of youth and strength, Scott was referred to by his friend and fellow sailor, Orbie White, as "a real pal." Scott was assigned to the treaty cruiser USS *Salt Lake City*.

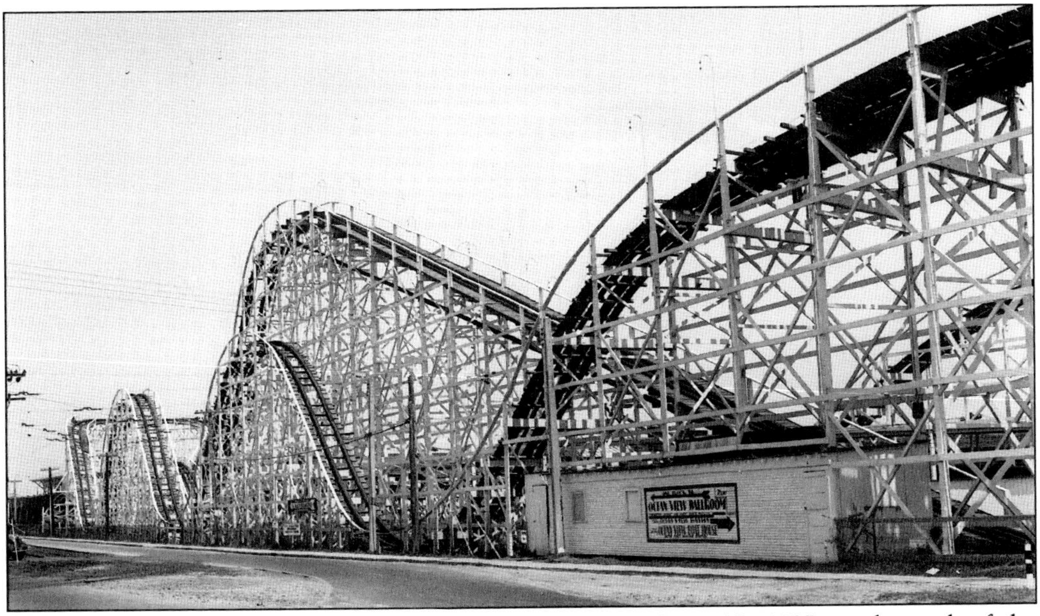

Leap-the-Dips was photographed by Charles S. Borjes on June 22, 1937, in the peak of the summer season. The park had grown substantially since the turn of the century. The famous roller coaster got its name from the local nomenclature. People who lived in Norfolk called roller coasters, "leap-the-dips."

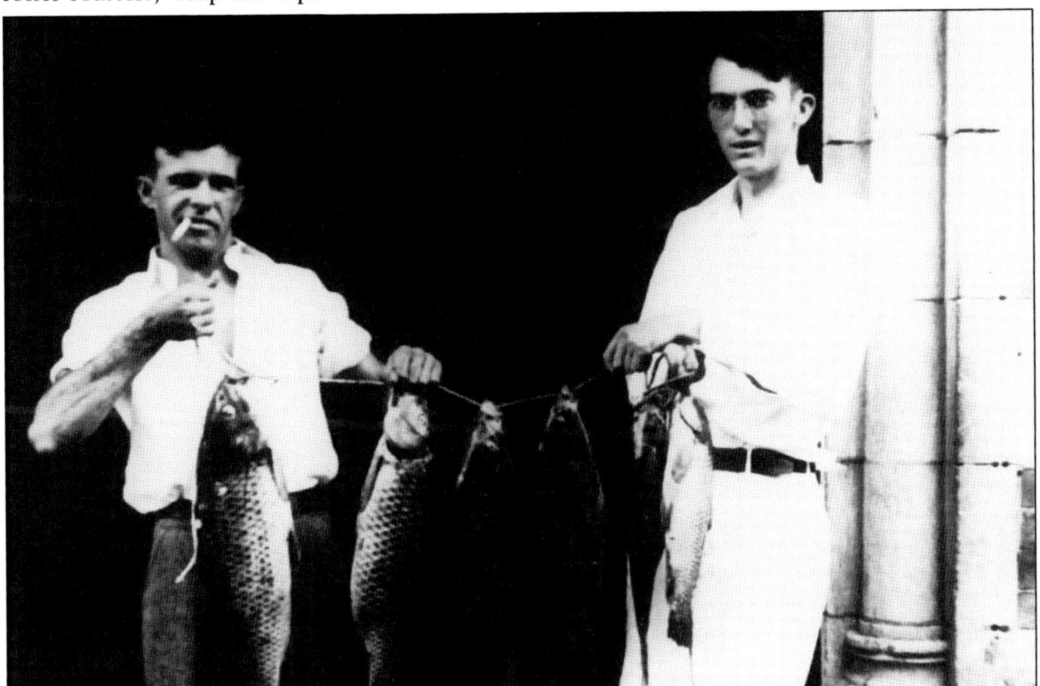

L.A. Lineberry (left) and "Stump" Stroud (right) displayed their catch on July 8, 1937. Ocean View was famous for its Ocean View spot, croakers, hog fish, trout, flounder, chub, sheephead, and many other varieties of fish caught in abundance. The most inexperienced fisherman could catch up to fifty fish in one hour. (H.D. Vollmer, photographer.)

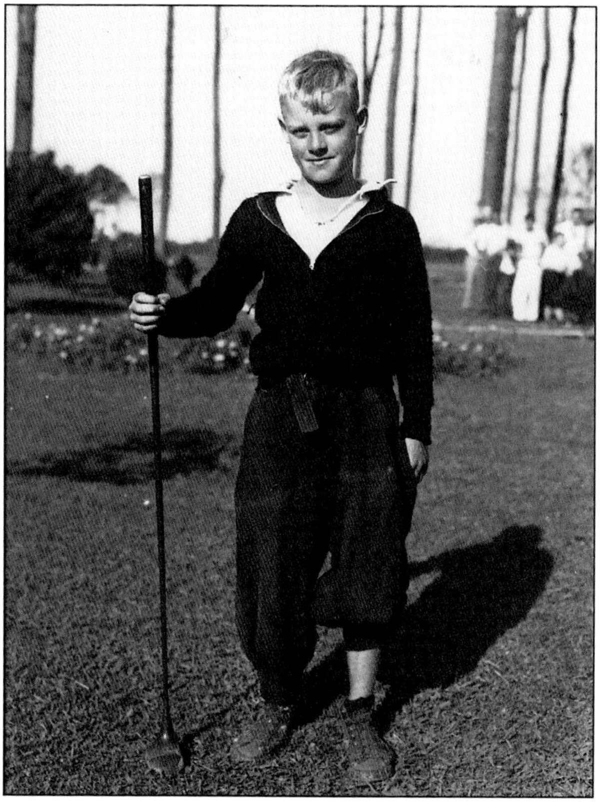

Young Philip Parnham shot a hole-in-one at Ocean View Golf Course on September 21, 1937. (Charles S. Borjes, photographer.)

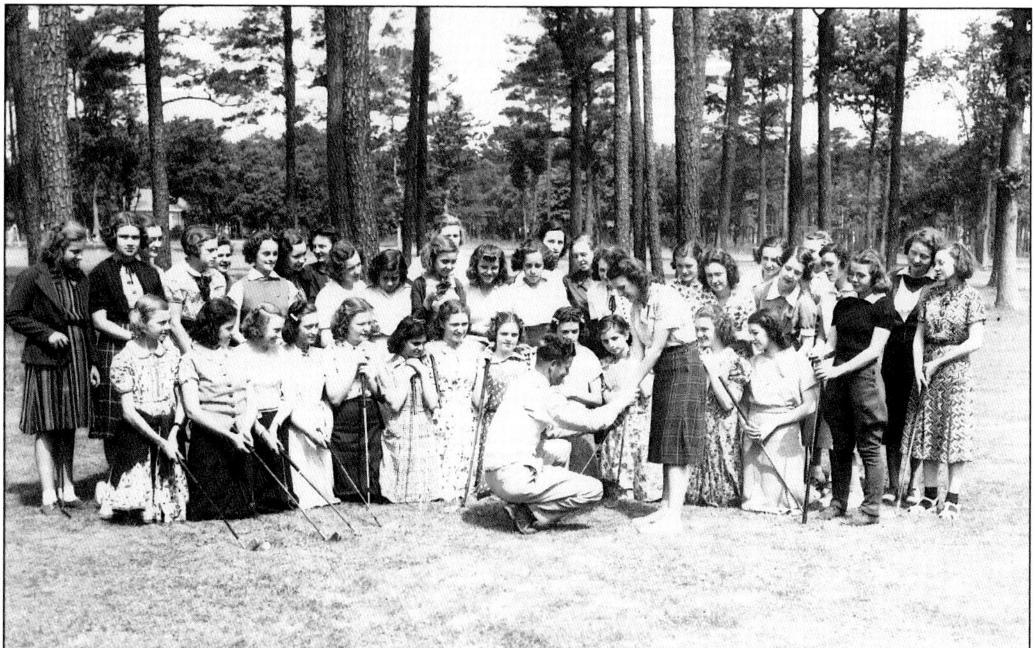

The Junior Chamber of Commerce sponsored classes at the Ocean View Golf Course to teach girls to play golf. H.D. Vollmer took this photograph on May 7, 1938.

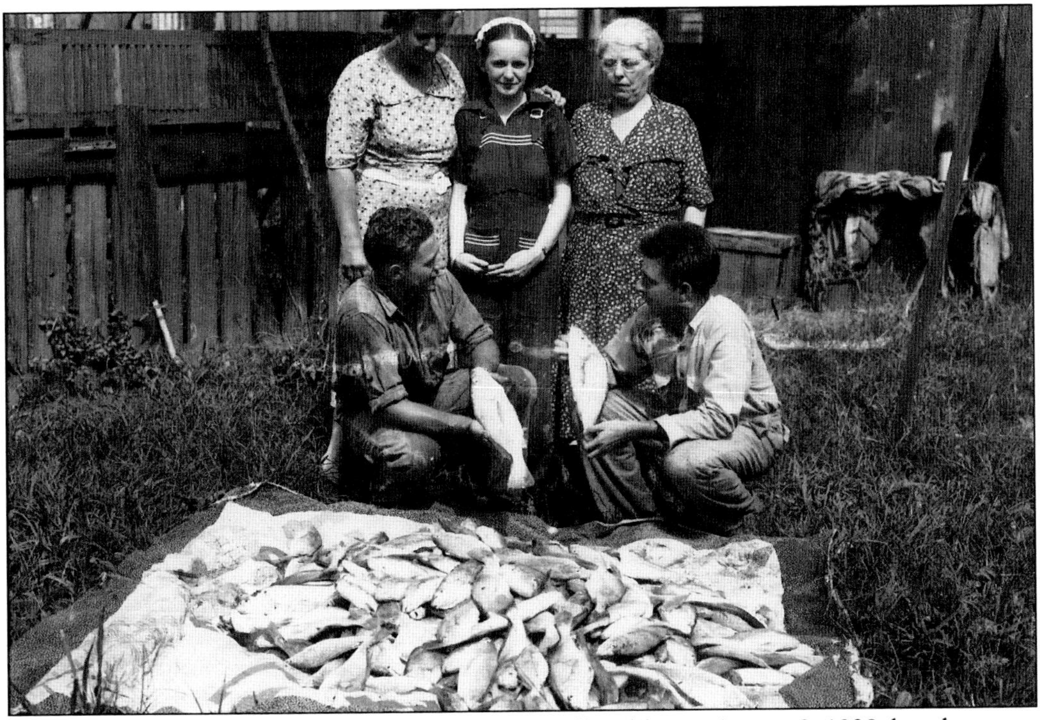

These enterprising fishermen caught 455 spot at Willoughby on August 8, 1938, but they were outdone by Dr. and Mrs. F.W. Manning and daughter, Lucille Manning, of 4801 Newport Avenue, and Dr. Vernon Brooks of Portsmouth, Virginia, who landed 586 spots in two hours and fifty-two minutes of fishing off Watkins' Boat Landing. Lucille Manning reeled in 162 of the 586 fish. Though the Manning party began their quest for croakers, the spot were biting. (Charles S. Borjes, photographer.)

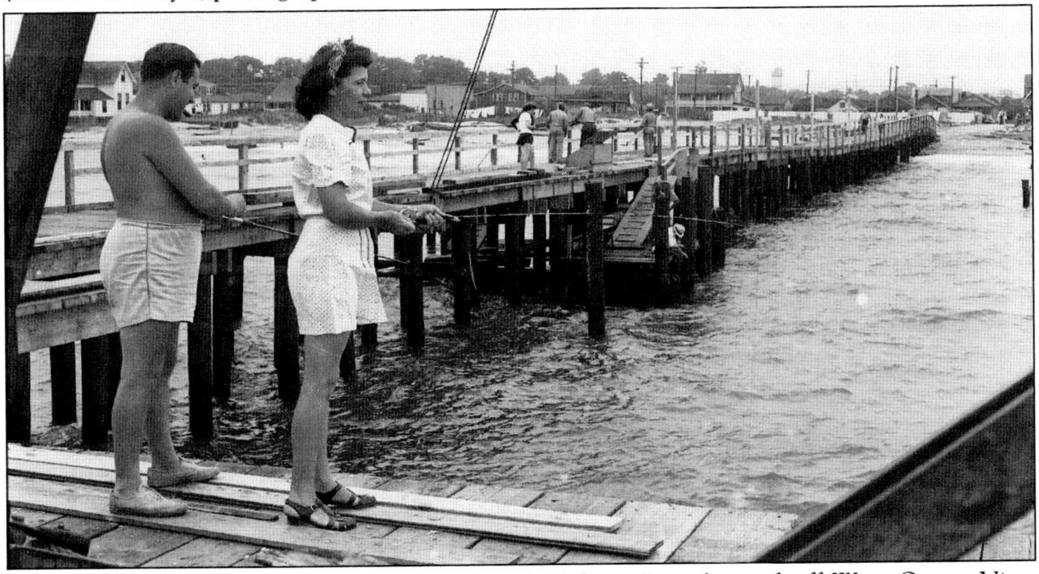

A couple enjoyed the day fishing at Harrison's Fishing Pier, located off West Ocean View Avenue. The date was August 6, 1947. The pier was being fitted with railing when Charles S. Borjes took the picture.

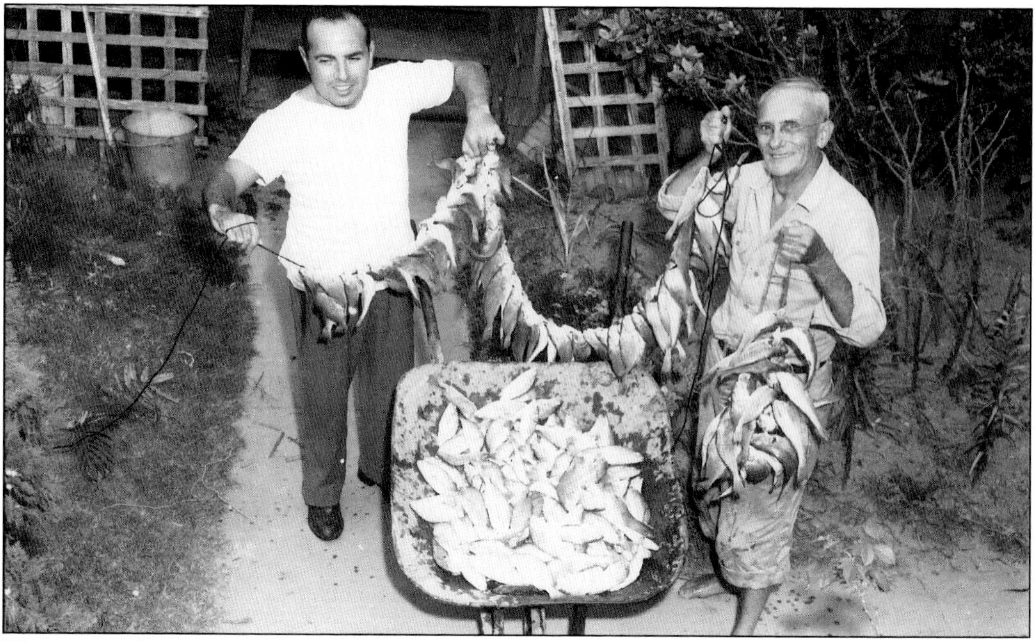

This was only a portion of the 360 spot, croaker, roundhead, and trout caught by John B. Lapetina (left) of 1032 East Ocean View Avenue, and Joseph Bihlman of Portsmouth, Ohio. The two lucky fishermen were a bit concerned about what to do with that many fish. The photograph was taken at Ocean View on August 8, 1948. (Charles S. Borjes, photographer.)

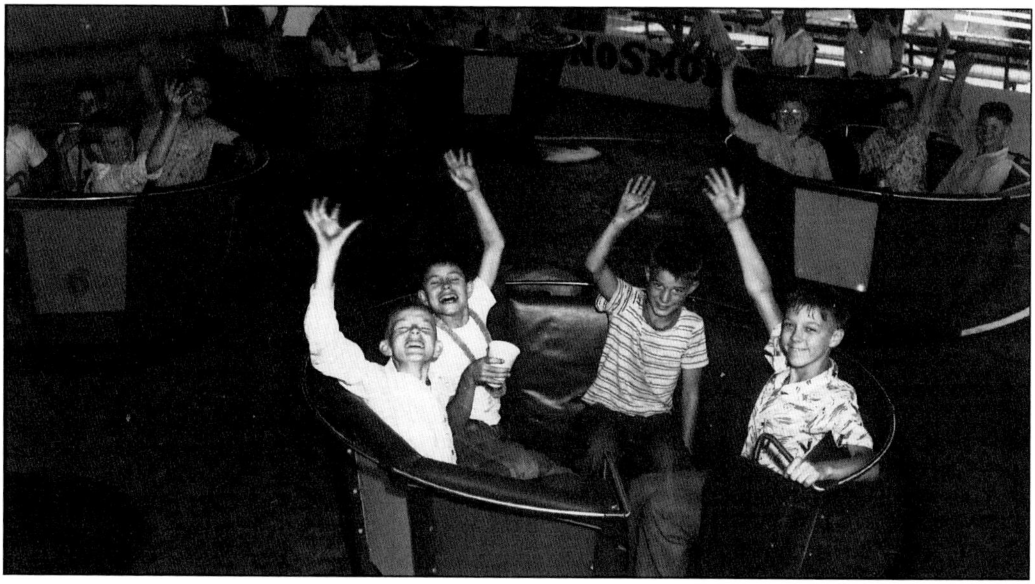

Youngsters from the Knothole Club wave enthusiastically from the teacup ride at Ocean View Amusement Park, where they were being entertained by the Norfolk Sports Club and park management on August 16, 1948. Members of this boys' club had earlier competed for extra books of tickets for free rides. Each had been asked to raise their hands if they knew the score of the previous day's Norfolk Tars' ballgame. The first ten were selected to come up and whisper the answer in the ear of Gus Meloni of the sports club. If the answer was correct, they got the tickets. Nobody missed. (Jim Mays, photographer.)

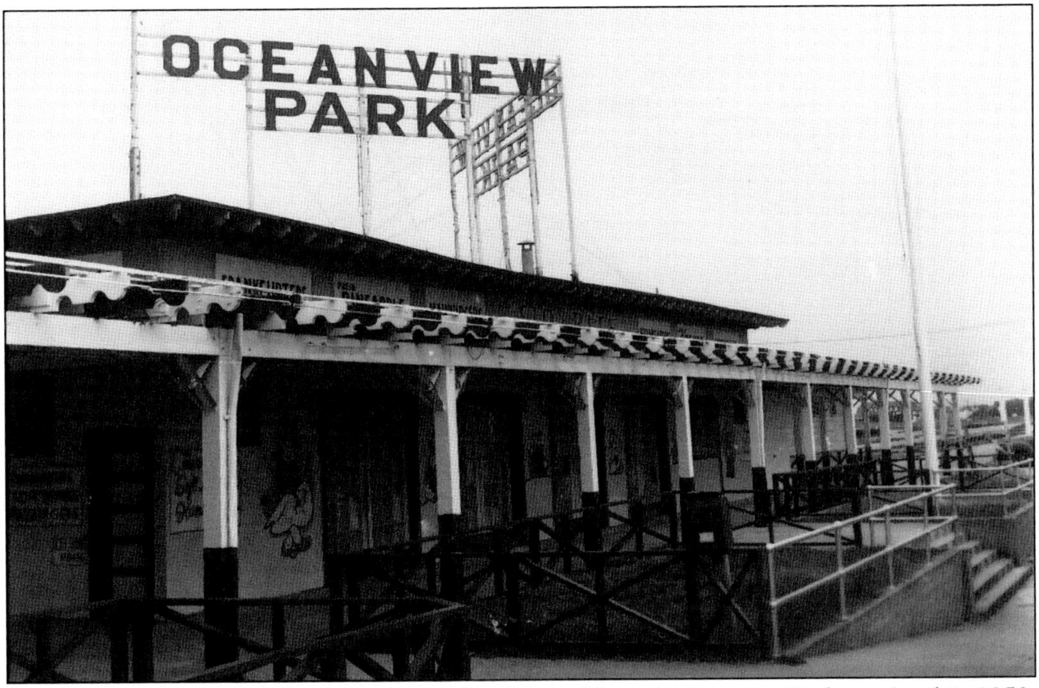

Jim Mays photographed the entrance to the Ocean View Amusement Park on April 1, 1950, the day the park opened its gates for the season.

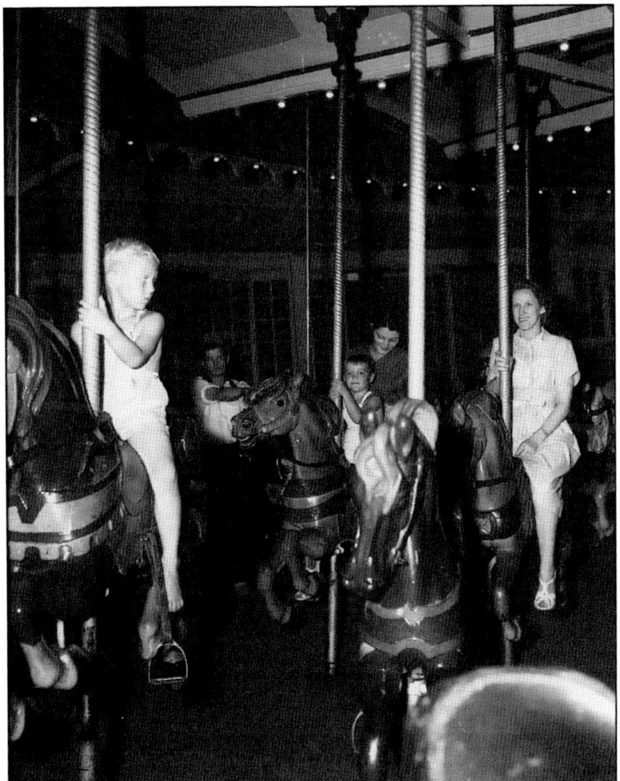
The carousel at Ocean View Amusement Park was the favorite ride of children for decades. Jim Mays photographed these happy children aboard their faithful steeds in July 1950.

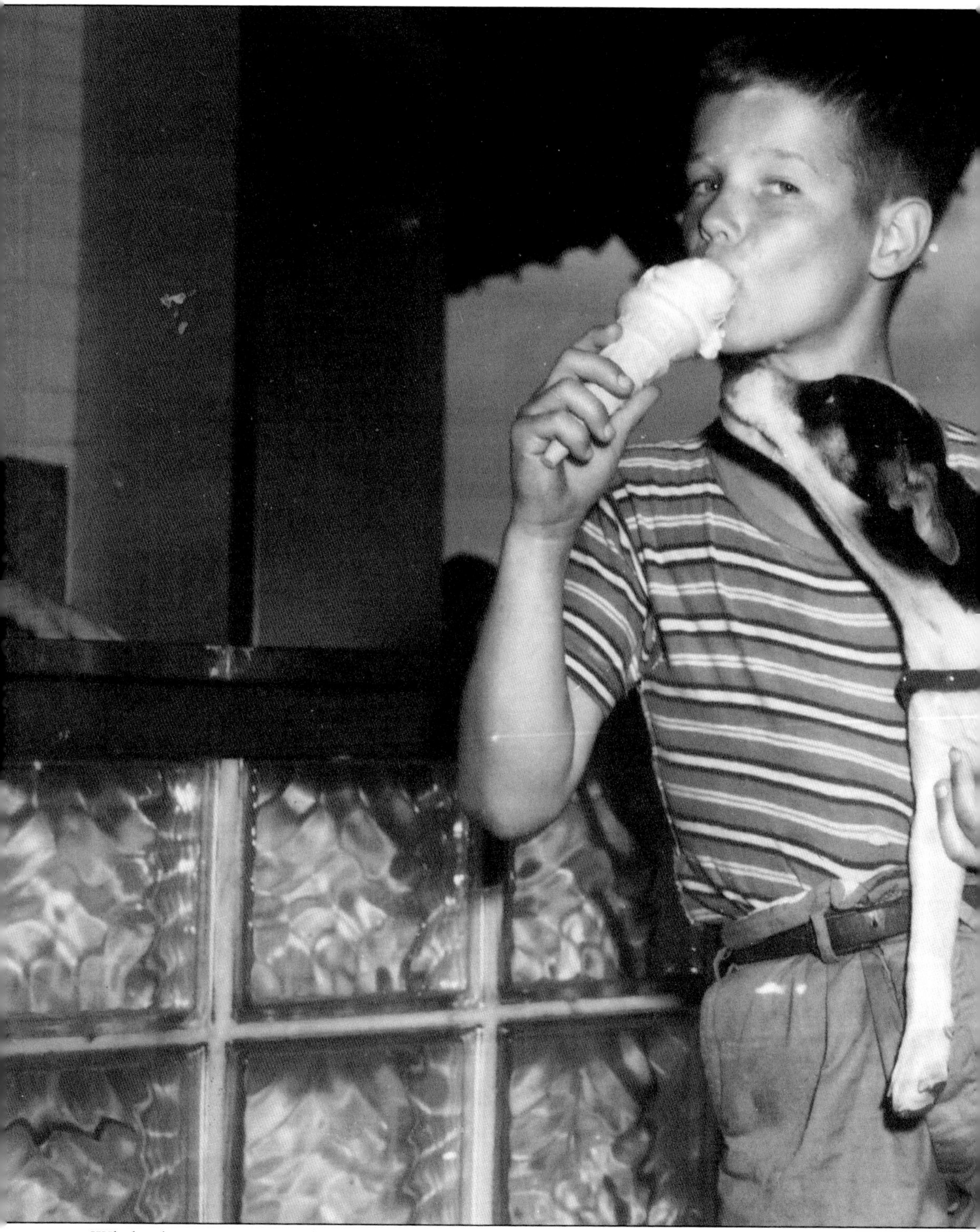

While the master partook of an ice cream cone, his best friend decided to go for a taste, too. The wide-eyed young ladies watching were enjoying candy apples. Jim Mays took this wonderful

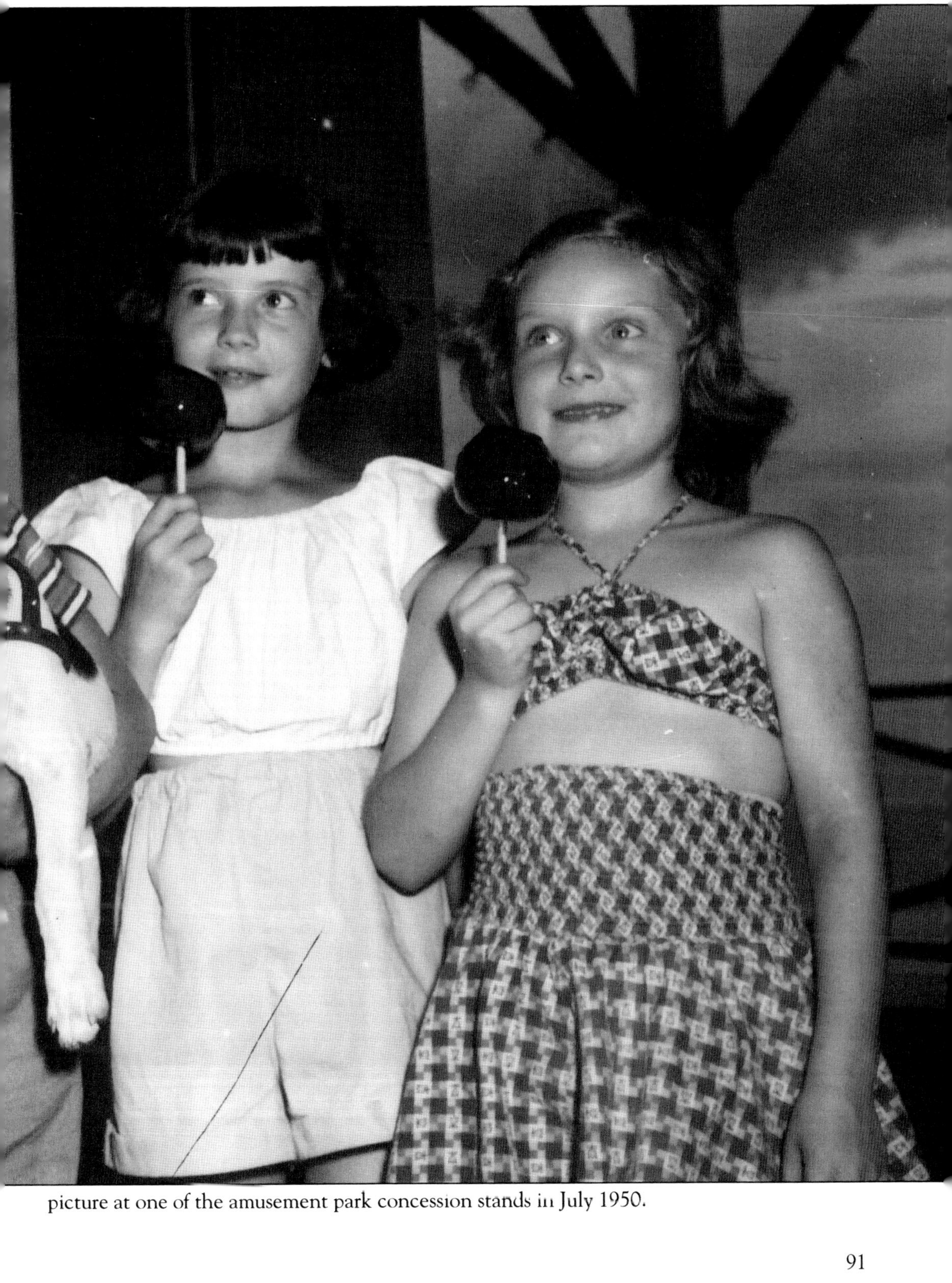

picture at one of the amusement park concession stands in July 1950.

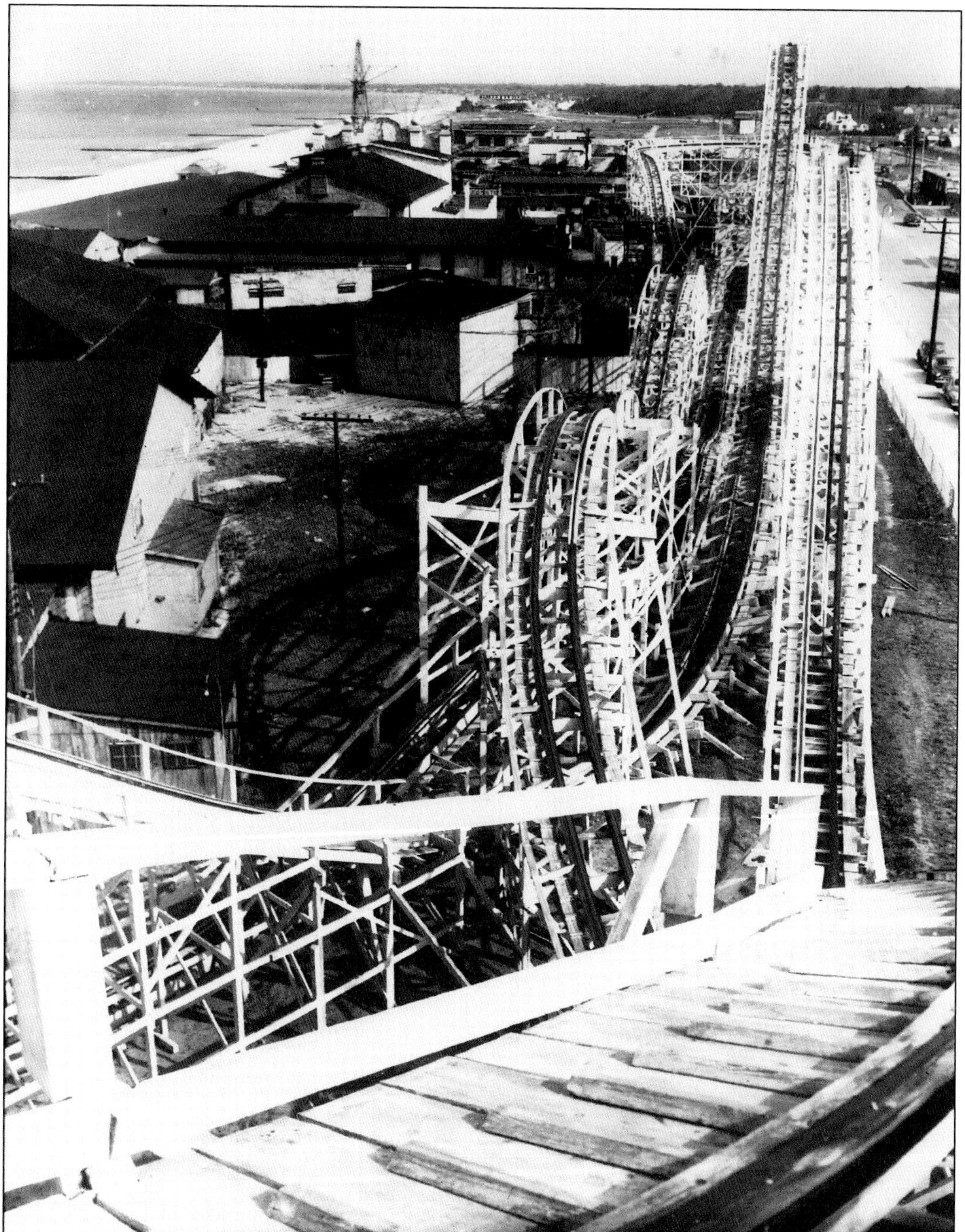

Leap-the-Dips was the star attraction of the amusement park, but by far the star attraction with children was Kiddyland, a little tots amusement park within the large amusement complex. For adults, the park offered exhilarating and laughter-producing diversions that were unique and enjoyable, from the Hilarious Fun House to the glorious Canals of Venice, where one could hold hands with a date, and the Sky-Ride, where everyone squealed with delight. This overhead shot of the roller coaster and grounds was taken by Jim Mays on April 1, 1950.

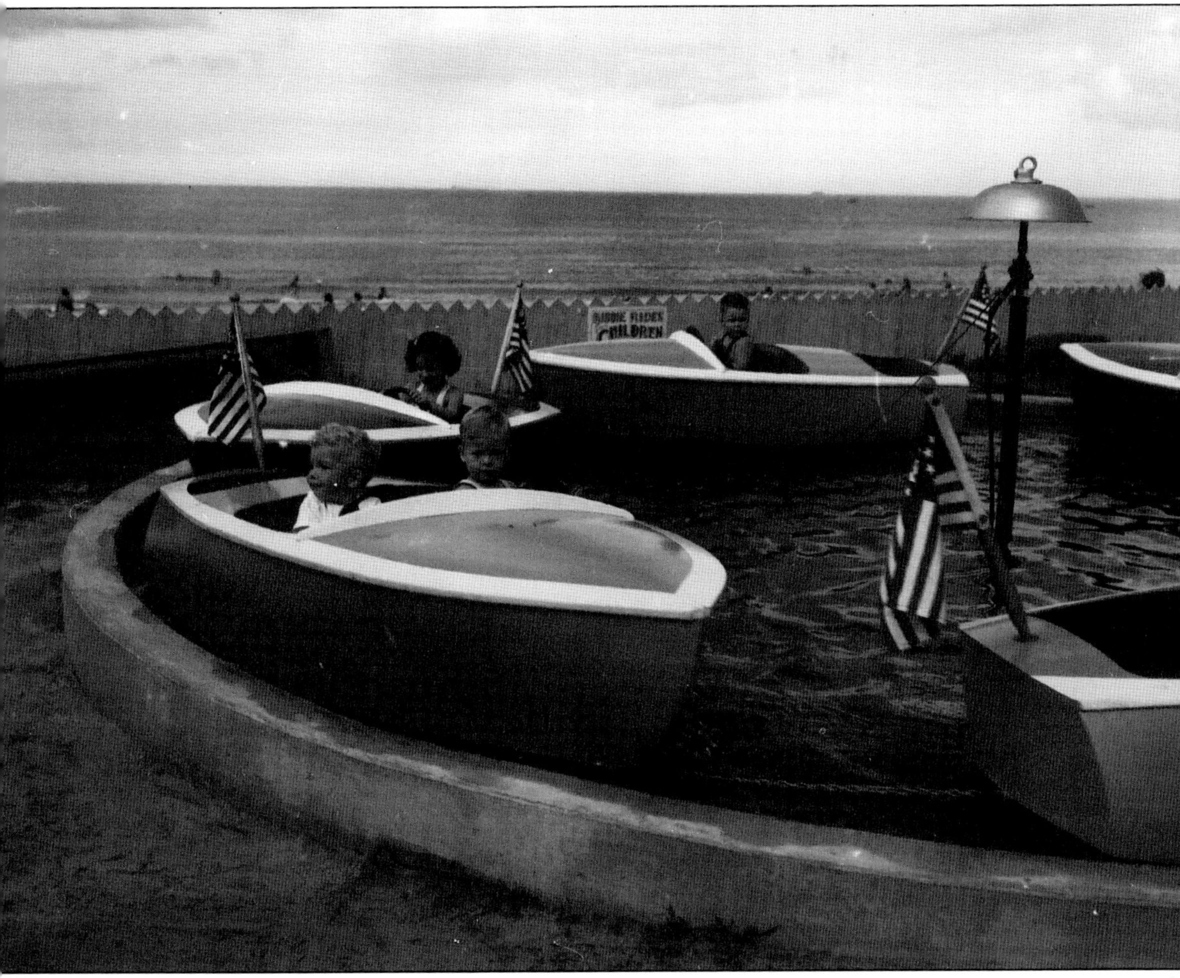

Kiddyland had this delightful boat ride for children, which could only have been the envy of their parents. The ride was situated on the north side of the park facing the Chesapeake Bay. Wystan Hugh Auden (1907–1973), an English poet who spoke eloquently in his poetry, prose, and drama of the underlying revolution of our culture in this century, wrote this line in his poem, *A Summer Night* (1933): "Whose river dreams long hid the size / And vigours of the sea." (Jim Mays, photographer.)

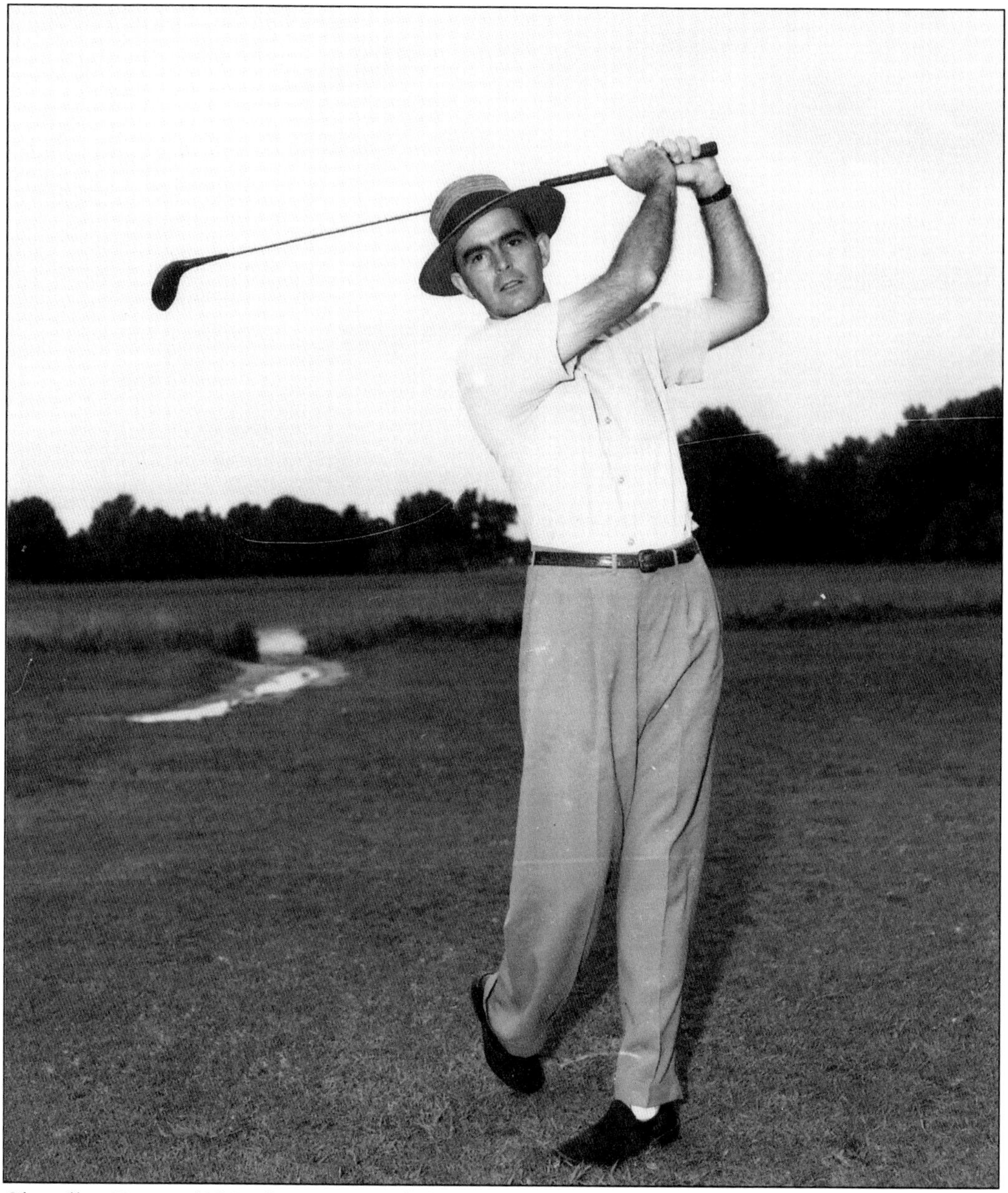

Chandler Harper (1914–), a native of the Port Norfolk section of Portsmouth, Virginia, was photographed at the Ocean View Golf Course on July 11, 1950. Harper won eleven Professional Golfers' Association (PGA) tournaments, including the National PGA Championship, the National Seniors Open, the World's Seniors, the National PGA Seniors, the Tucson Open, El Paso Open, Texas Open, Colonial Invitational, Virginia Beach Open, International Four-Ball, and PGA Quarter Century Championship. He was the Virginia State Open Champion ten times and a member of the highly prestigious American Ryder Cup Team. Harper was inducted into the PGA Hall of Fame in 1969. After playing in the Ryder Cup matches in 1955, he retired from competition and built the Bide-A-Wee Golf Club in Portsmouth, Virginia. Harper won the Tucson Open in 1950, the year the picture was taken. (Charles S. Borjes, photographer.)

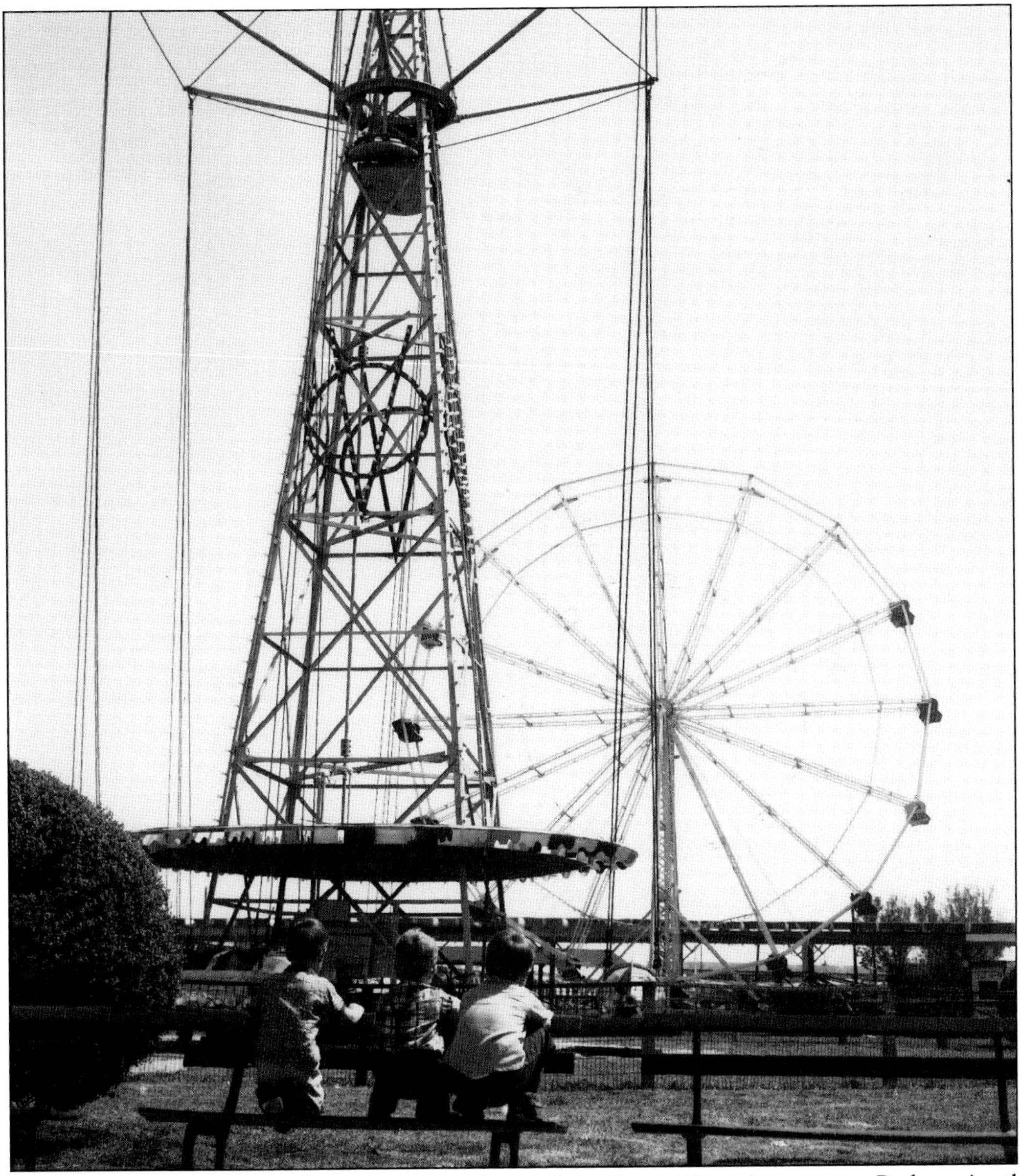

Three prospective patrons check out the airplane ride at Ocean View Amusement Park on April 8, 1954. The park opened for business the next day, but these little gentlemen decided to get a sneak-peek at the refurbished rides and park facilities. During the off-season, Dudley Cooper, owner and operator of the park, made several improvements, including the addition of a picnic shed and area to accommodate one thousand people at the east end of the park as well as new rides. Another section of the boardwalk had been replaced by a more permanent concrete area. The Ferris wheel in the photograph was not part of the original rides built by Otto Wells in the 1900s. George Washington Gale Ferris, a resident of Pittsburgh, Pennsylvania, invented the first Ferris wheel, a 264-foot-high ride, in 1893, but it was not until forty years later that anyone built another from his design. The first sky ride was seen at the Century of Progress fair in Chicago in 1933. Ocean View got its first Ferris wheel shortly thereafter. (Jim Mays, photographer.)

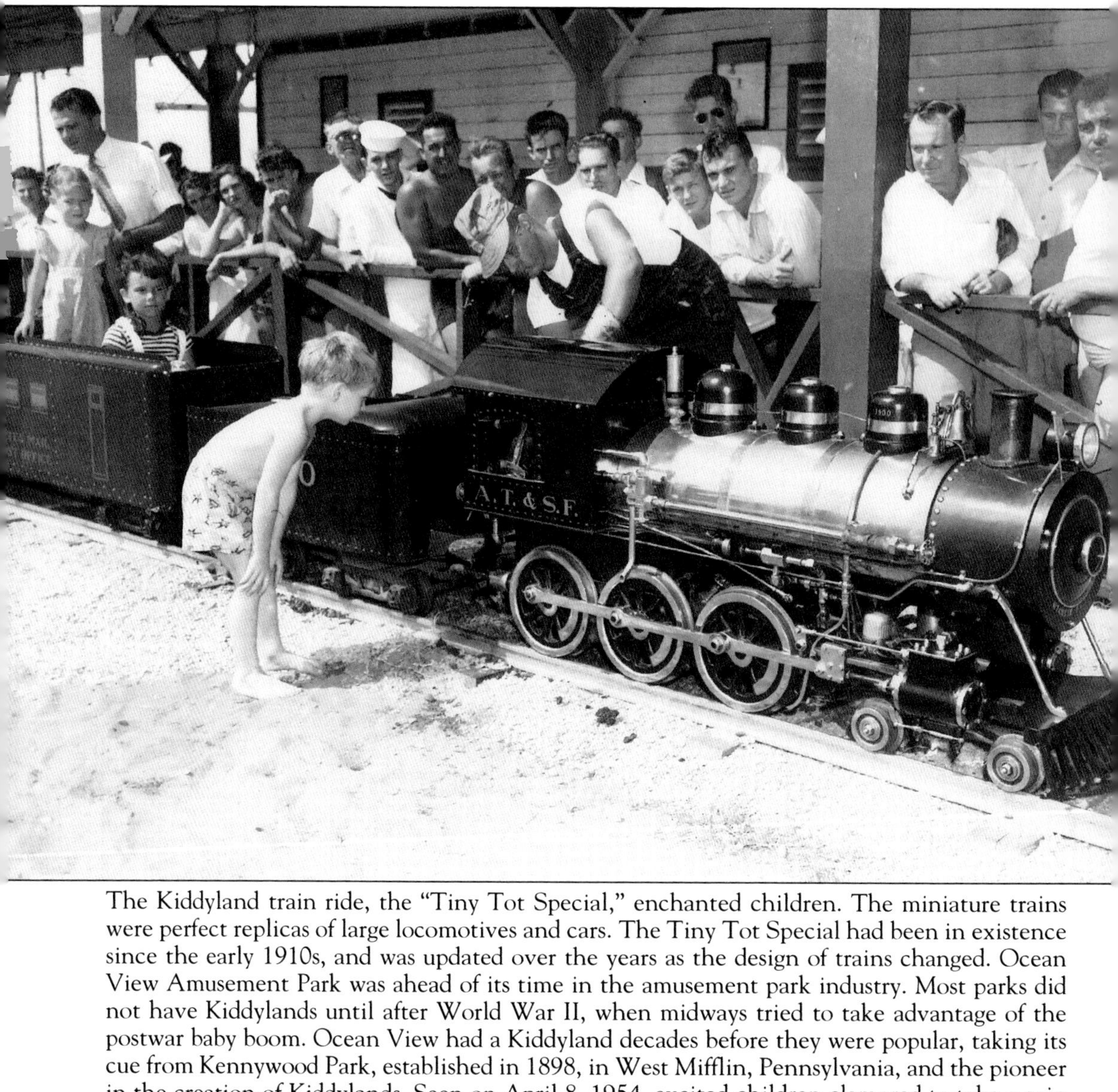

The Kiddyland train ride, the "Tiny Tot Special," enchanted children. The miniature trains were perfect replicas of large locomotives and cars. The Tiny Tot Special had been in existence since the early 1910s, and was updated over the years as the design of trains changed. Ocean View Amusement Park was ahead of its time in the amusement park industry. Most parks did not have Kiddylands until after World War II, when midways tried to take advantage of the postwar baby boom. Ocean View had a Kiddyland decades before they were popular, taking its cue from Kennywood Park, established in 1898, in West Mifflin, Pennsylvania, and the pioneer in the creation of Kiddylands. Seen on April 8, 1954, excited children clamored to take a spin on the "Ocean View Special." (Jim Mays, photographer.)

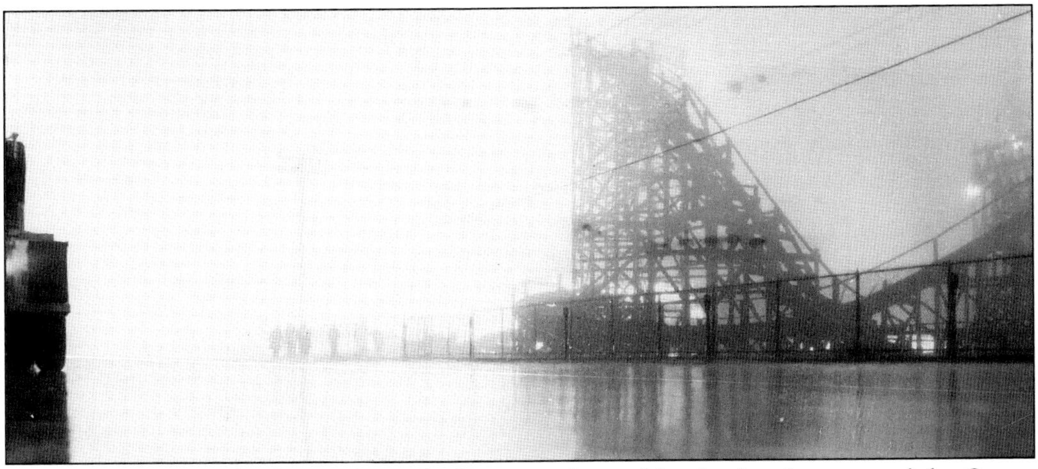

Silhouetted against the flames, Leap-the-Dips was doomed by the fire that ravaged the Ocean View Amusement Park the evening of February 26, 1958. Driving rain, heavy winds, and fallen power lines impeded firemen as they tried to subdue the fire that razed two-thirds of the park in less than two hours. The park sustained $500,000 damage, and stores, restaurants, and taverns on the south side of Ocean View Avenue and a bank adjoining the park had extensive heat and smoke damage. The three-alarm blaze drew assistance from three neighboring cities and the Naval Base Norfolk Fire Department. The fire had started in a storage shed near the roller coaster. (Jim Mays, photographer.)

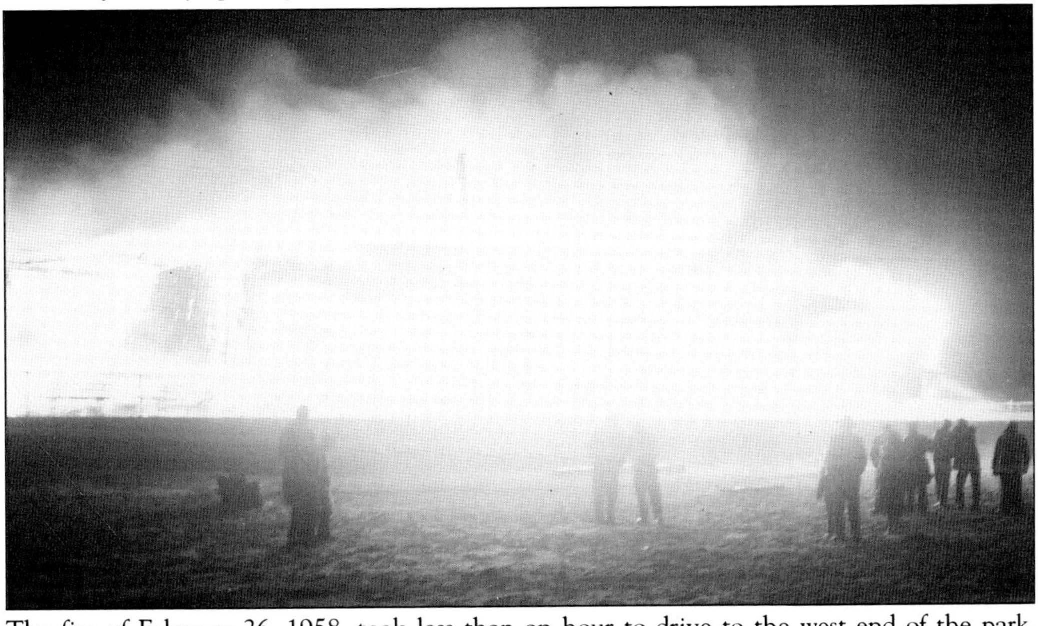

The fire of February 26, 1958, took less than an hour to drive to the west end of the park, burning the dance hall (pictured here), the beloved merry-go-round, the Moon Rocket, and a number of other concessions. The beginning of many a summer romance was housed in the Ocean View Amusement Park dance hall. As the dance hall exploded into flames, firefighters gathered in a close group to protect a branch of the Southern Bank of Norfolk. Everything from the boardwalk to Ocean View Avenue was razed, but the physical damage to the park could not match the anguish of children who wept demonstratively as their source of summer rides and memories went up in flames. (Jim Mays, photographer.)

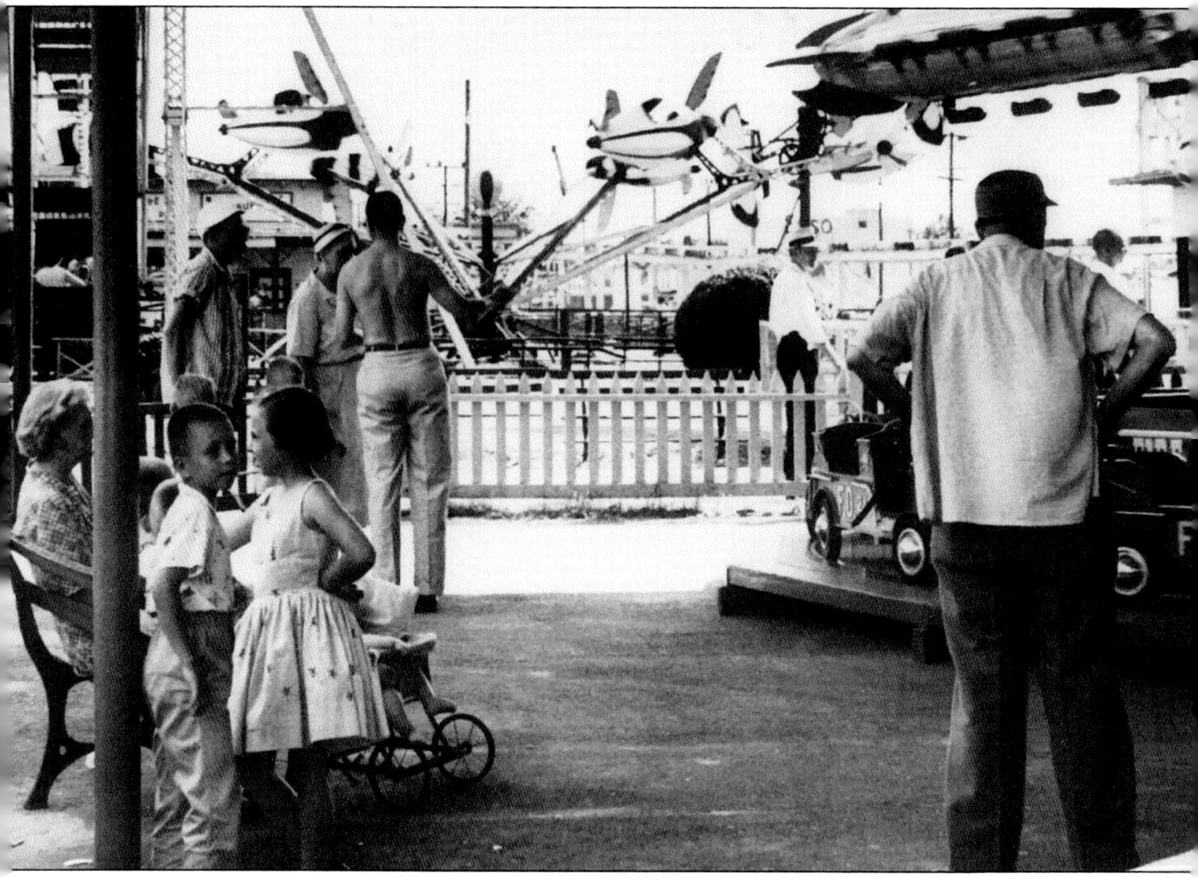

The airplane ride at Ocean View Amusement Park had come to reflect the popular aircraft of the day (center), and rocket ships carried screaming children on a circle ride sure to thrill. The date was July 4, 1958, less than six months after the devastating February fire that destroyed two-thirds of the park. (S.H. Ringo, photographer.)

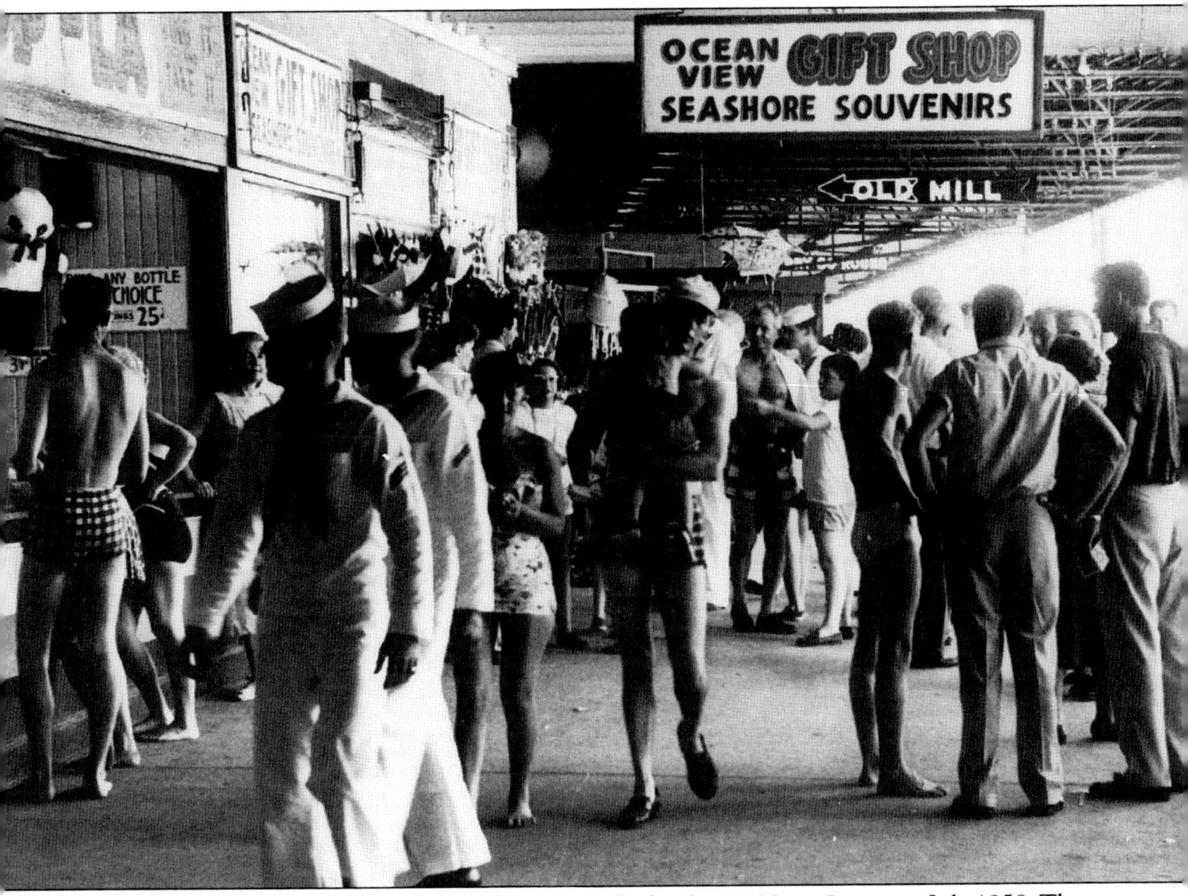

Sailors mingled in the sea of tourists and locals outside the Ocean View Casino in July 1958. The park experienced a post–World War II boom in business that would fade away by the end of the 1950s. The birth of television, white flight from the urban core, desegregation, and the pangs of suburban development drew people away from places of the past. Ocean View's resurgence in the 1950s was short-lived because more people were drawn to an entirely new concept in the amusement industry—the theme park. In 1955, Disneyland opened in Anaheim, California, as a theme park, drawn upon Disney's knowledge of film sets and characters and the translation of those elements into a family-oriented vacation destination. (S.H. Ringo, photographer.)

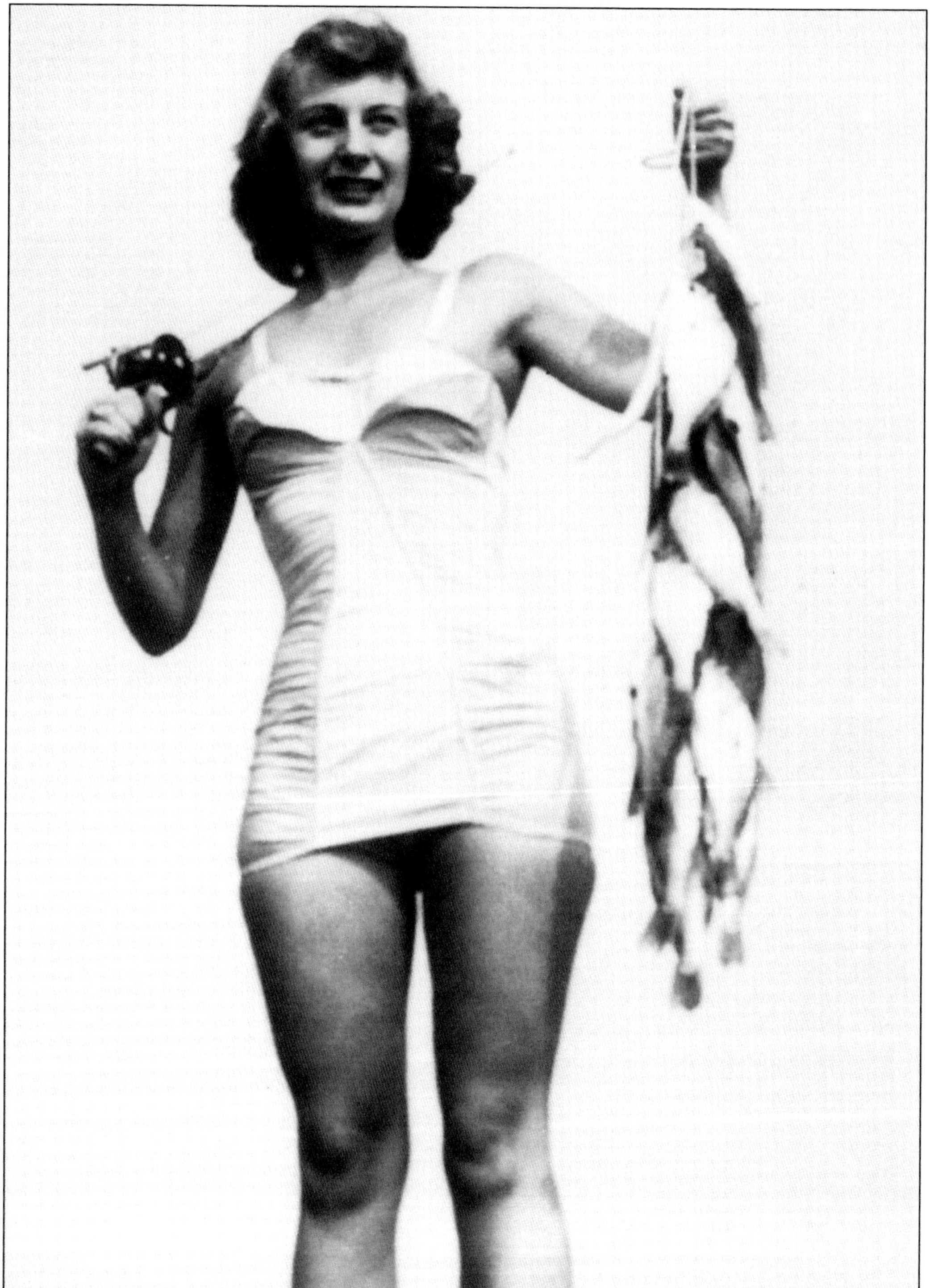

Fishing was still good at Ocean View as evidenced by this impressive catch of fish in 1960. (Photographer unknown.)

Six

WORLD WAR II AND THE BIG BAND ERA

"Who is the happy Warrior?"
 It is he who:
"Finds comfort in himself and in his cause;
 And, while the mortal mist is gathering, draws
 His breath in confidence of Heaven's applause.
 This is the happy Warrior; this is He
 That every Man in arms should wish to be."
 —From *Character of a Happy Warrior*, 1805
 William Wordsworth, English poet (1770–1850)

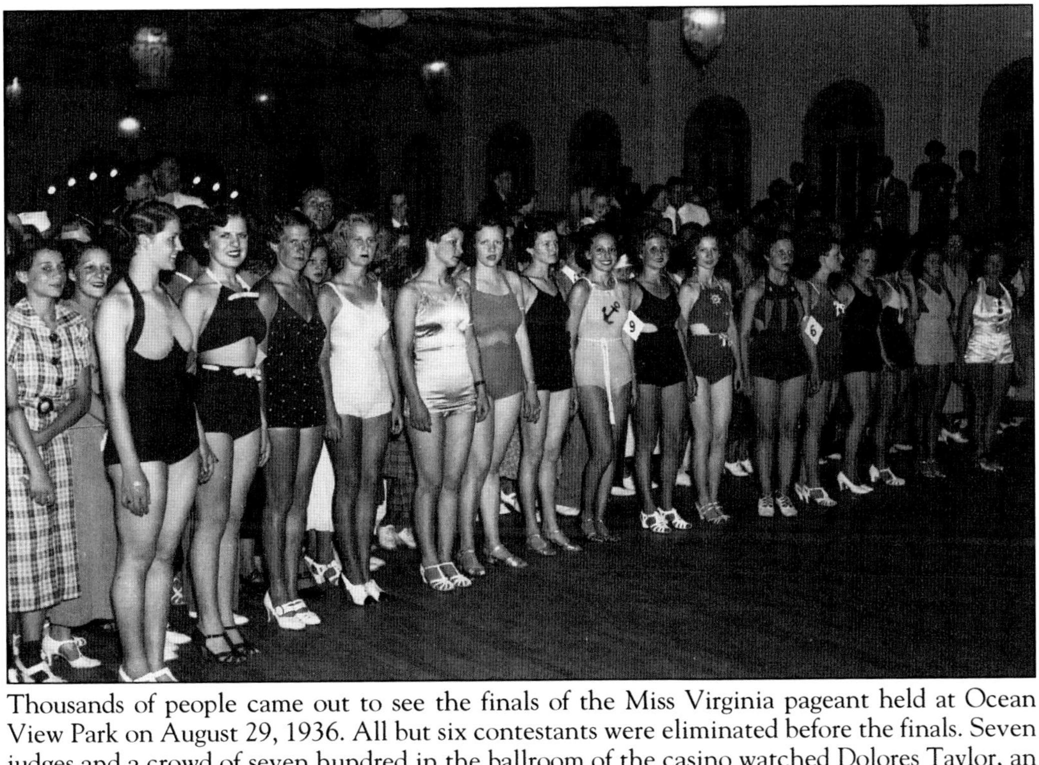

Thousands of people came out to see the finals of the Miss Virginia pageant held at Ocean View Park on August 29, 1936. All but six contestants were eliminated before the finals. Seven judges and a crowd of seven hundred in the ballroom of the casino watched Dolores Taylor, an eighteen-year-old blonde of Chesapeake Street in Ocean View, win the title of Miss Virginia. Taylor went on to represent the state in the national contest at Atlantic City, New Jersey, beginning the week of Labor Day. Lillian Warr of Norfolk won second place in the Miss Virginia contest. A thunderstorm broke just as the finals began, driving thousands of eager spectators away. (Charles S. Borjes, photographer.)

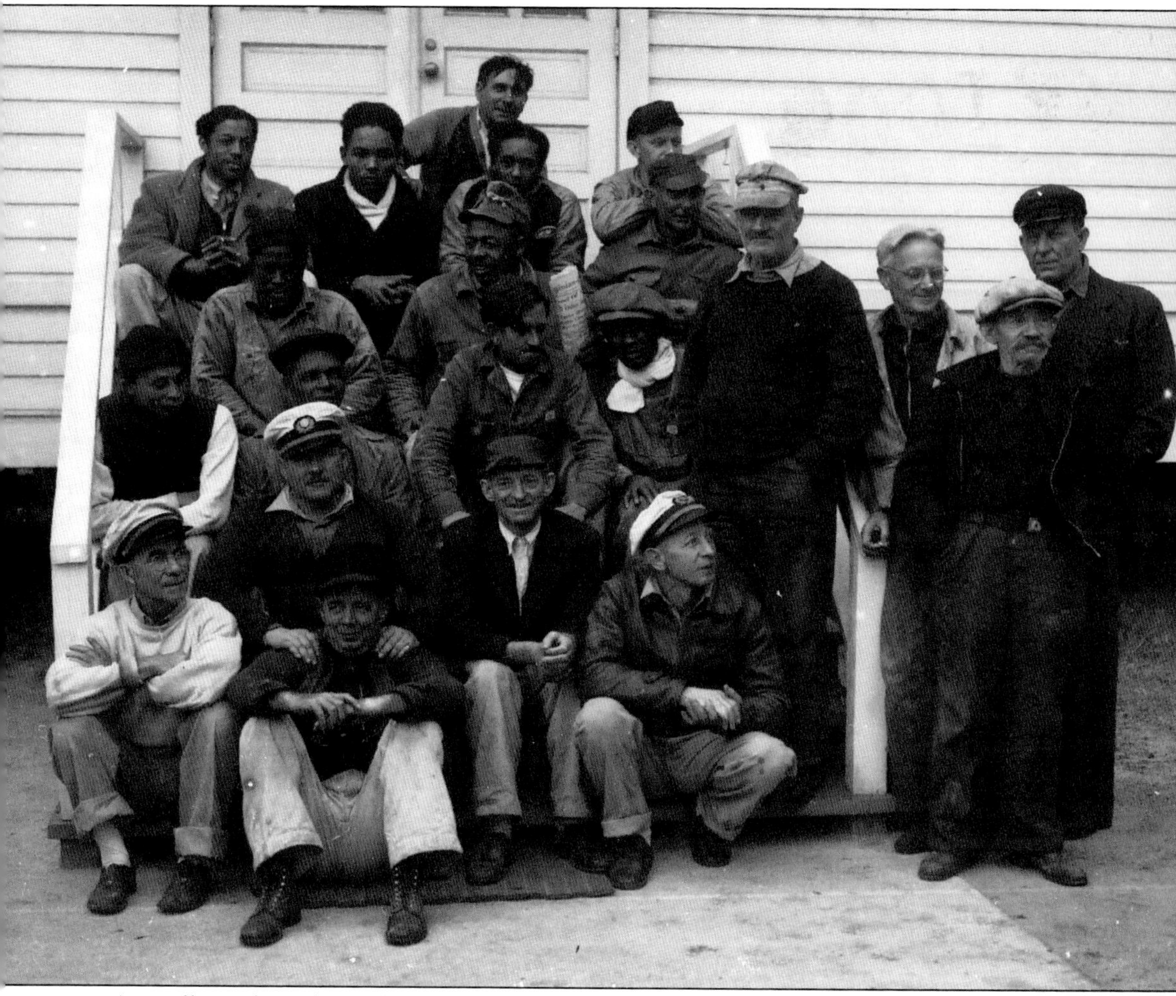

A small number of merchant seamen aboard the SS *Venore*, an American-owned ore and oil carrier, survived the sinking of their vessel by a German U-boat on January 23, 1942. The battle for supremacy of the seas in the Atlantic was fierce in the early days of the war. The *Venore* became part of the saga later dubbed the Battle of Torpedo Junction, a battle in which German U-boats torpedoed merchant vessels at will and sent many seamen to watery graves off the coast of North Carolina and Virginia. Twenty-one survivors were eventually returned to Naval Operating Base Norfolk, where this photograph was taken on January 26. They recounted the *Venore*'s sinking southeast of Diamond Shoals near Creeds Hill in compelling fashion. Two of *Venore*'s crewmen—Samuel Lynwood Mitchell of Wilmington, North Carolina, second assistant engineer; and Cecil James Bird of Baltimore, Maryland—had been aboard ships torpedoed during World War I. Mitchell remarked that his previous experience with enemy submarines did not make the *Venore* incident "any less harrowing." (Charles S. Borjes, photographer.)

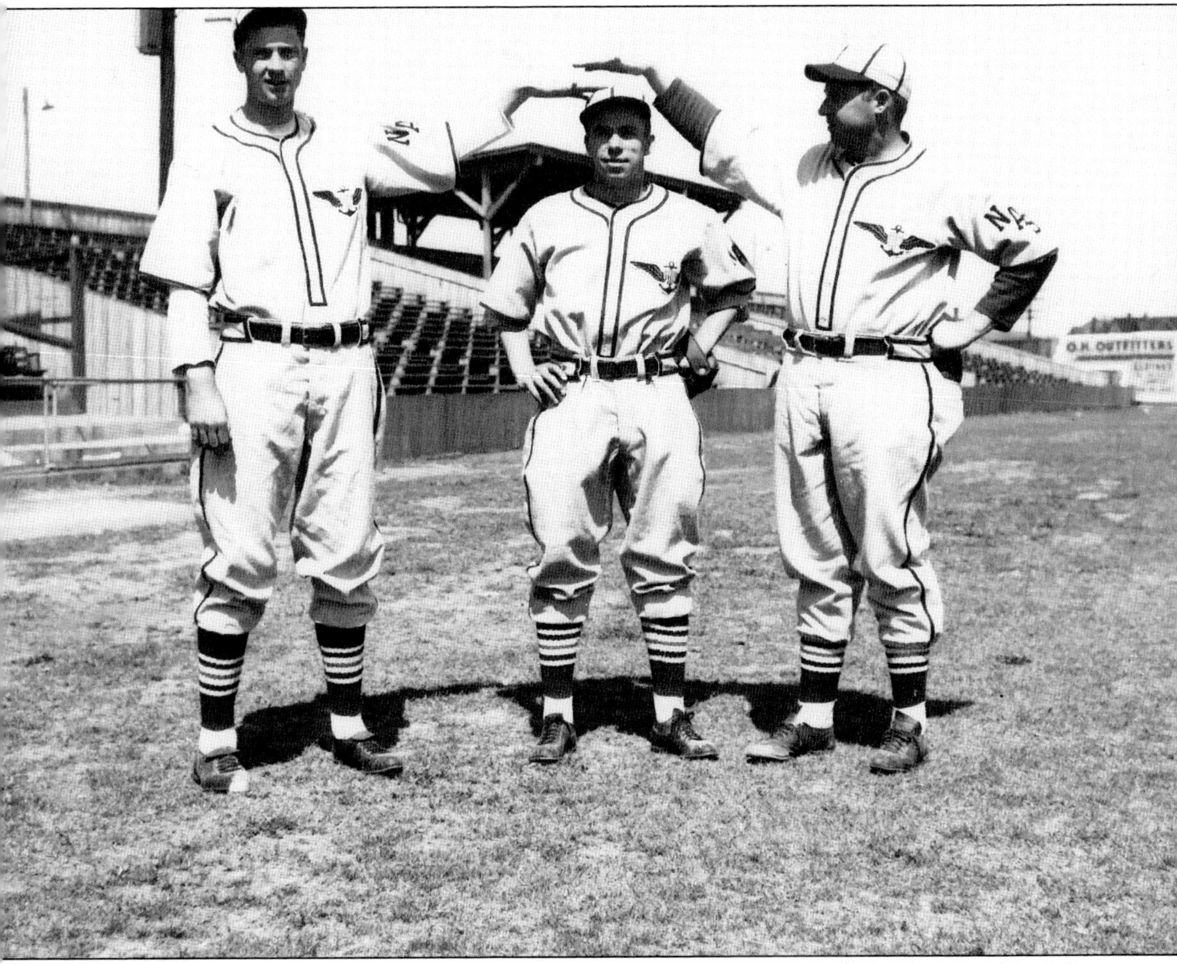

After several expansions, beginning with its inception in 1917, Naval Air Station Norfolk today occupies three-quarters of the shoreline around Willoughby Bay. During World War II, several of the country's greatest baseball players played for the air station team, known as the Fliers. Pictured here on April 13, 1943, are (from left to right) Charley Welchel, Pee Wee Reese, and Hugh Casey. Hugh Casey (1913–1951) pitched for the Brooklyn Dodgers in the 1941 World Series against the New York Yankees. Though the Dodgers lost the game, it was not because of Casey's fast pitches over the plate. His pitching was pure perfection. Casey was a tough competitor, but a heavy drinker. This would explain why Casey became fast friends with author Ernest Hemingway. During the team's spring training down in Cuba, Casey frequented Hemingway's house. It was on one of those visits that Casey and Hemingway donned boxing gloves, and totally inebriated, knocked one another silly. Hugh Casey took his own life in 1951, distraught over the break up of his marriage. Pee Wee Reese played shortstop for the Brooklyn Dodgers before entering the service. (H.D. Vollmer, photographer.)

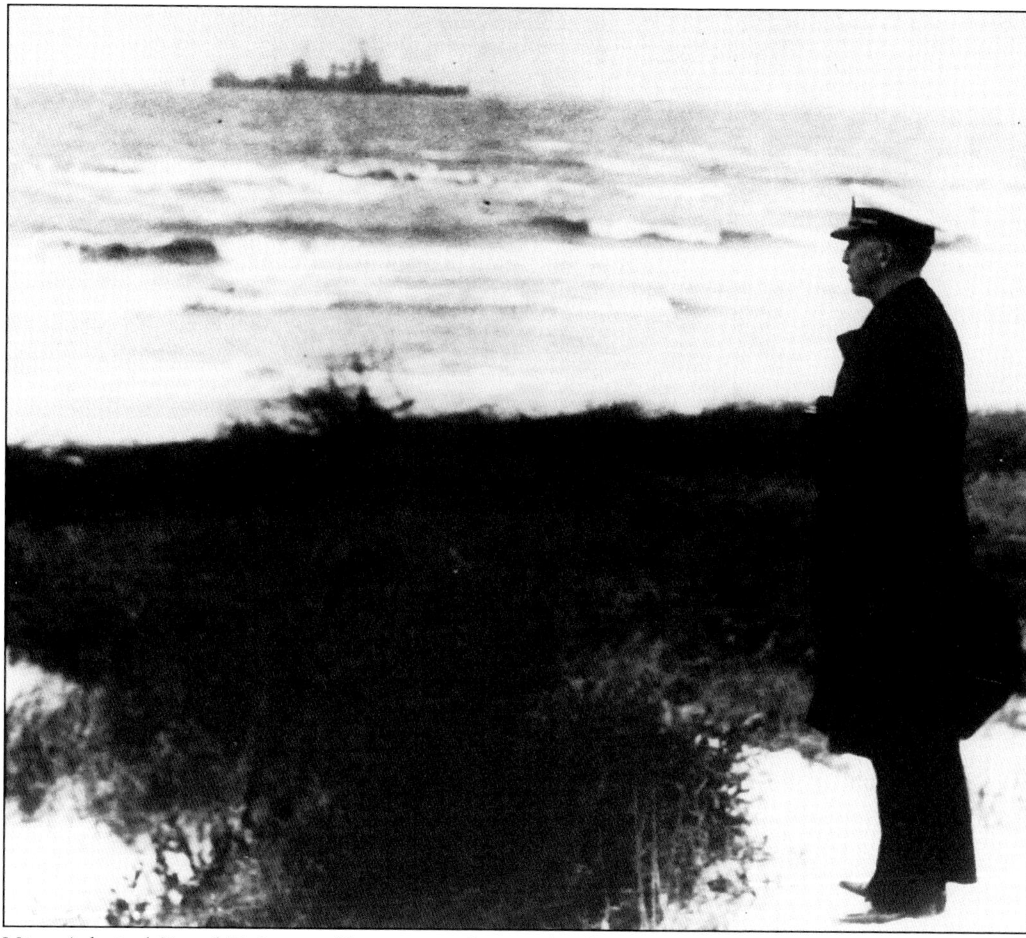

Vice Admiral Royal E. Ingersoll, commander in chief of the Atlantic Fleet in 1942, stood on Ocean View shore and watched the Operation Torch invasion force depart the Chesapeake Bay. A light cruiser is noticeable in the background. (Courtesy of the Hampton Roads Naval Museum.)

Operation Torch

The United States Atlantic Amphibious Force planned the invasion of North Africa from the Nansemond Hotel. From March 1942 through August 15, 1945, the hotel served as the headquarters of Admiral H. Kent Hewitt. Operation Torch, as the invasion was dubbed, was the first major amphibious assault of the Second World War. On October 24, 1942, ninety-nine ships departed Norfolk under Admiral Hewitt's command. During invasion planning, famous military leaders gathered at the hotel to confer on strategy. General George S. Patton (1885–1945), "Old Blood and Guts," was one of them. Patton was commander of the Western Task Force, the tantamount to having two divisions under his direction, and in that role, directed the amphibious operations near Casablanca during the Operation Torch landings in November 1942. His method of attack was splattered over the pages of newspapers around the world: "Hold them by the nose and kick them in the rear." The first of some sixty-five thousand troops to land on North African beaches charged ashore on November 8. Lieutenant General Dwight D. Eisenhower was commander in chief of the Allied Expeditionary Force, and he, too, would come to Norfolk to discuss invasion plans.

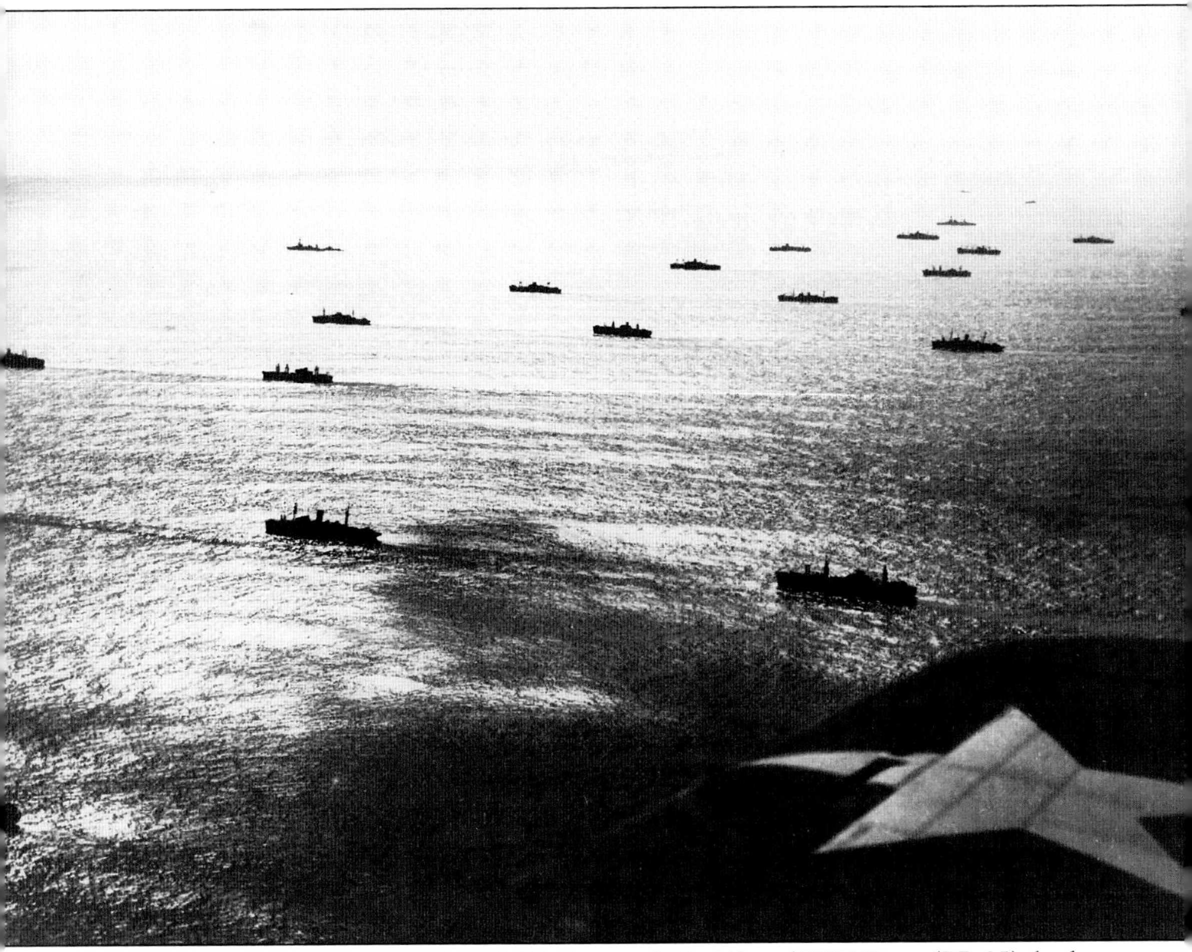

More than twenty transports joined the USS *Augusta* (CA-31) and USS *Texas* (BB-35), both visible in the distance, off the coast of French Morocco in November 1942. The photograph was taken from a Douglas SBD Dauntless bomber from one of the invasion force aircraft carriers. (Courtesy of the National Archives.)

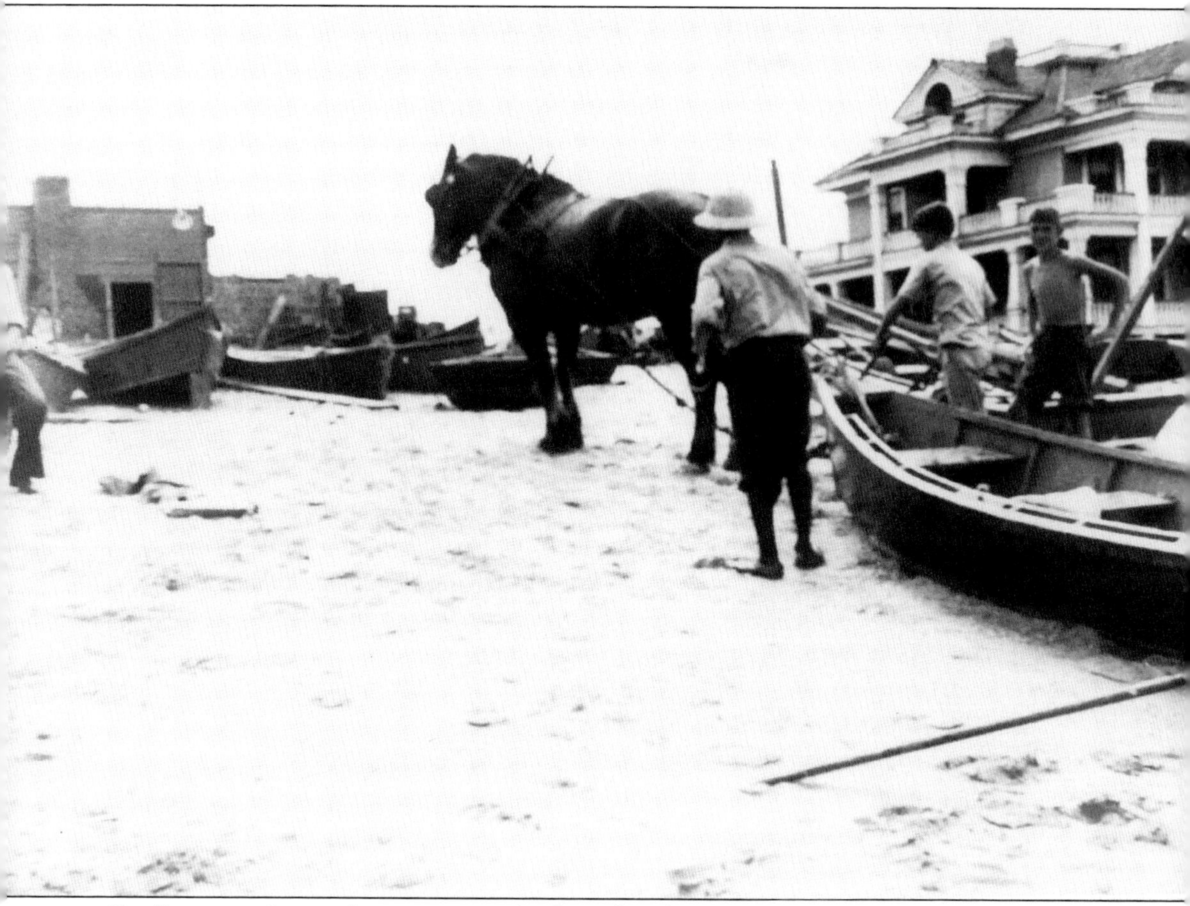

Big Ben, a sea horse of sorts, was caught doing his chores off Raiford's Boathouse, Ocean View, on July 19, 1944. Big Ben took the place of four to eight men dragging fishing boats to and from the surf. (Charles S. Borjes, photographer.)

THE STORY OF BIG BEN, THE SEA HORSE

The departure of thousands of able-bodied young men to the armed forces fighting abroad in World War II left local businesses shorthanded. When fishing season opened in 1944, R.E. Raiford, owner of Raiford's Boathouse in Ocean View, could not find reliable manpower to pull his fishing boats in and out of the surf. He solved his labor problems by employing the muscle of Big Ben, a stalwart draft horse fresh from the farm. Big Ben did not exactly take too well to the idea of streetcars and water after living a life in the quiet of the countryside. City noises spooked him and the water held absolutely no appeal. After some thoughtful consideration, Raiford got a pocketful of apples and sugar cubes, threw in a little sweet-talk for good measure, and two hours later, finally coaxed Big Ben into the surf. Raiford's labor problem could have put him out of business had it not been for a special horse. It took eight men of considerable strength to drag a 1,000-pound fishing boat off the sand into the water. Big Ben did it without breaking a sweat. The boys who frequented the boathouse gladly plied Big Ben with sugar, apples, cookies, and other sweet concoctions.

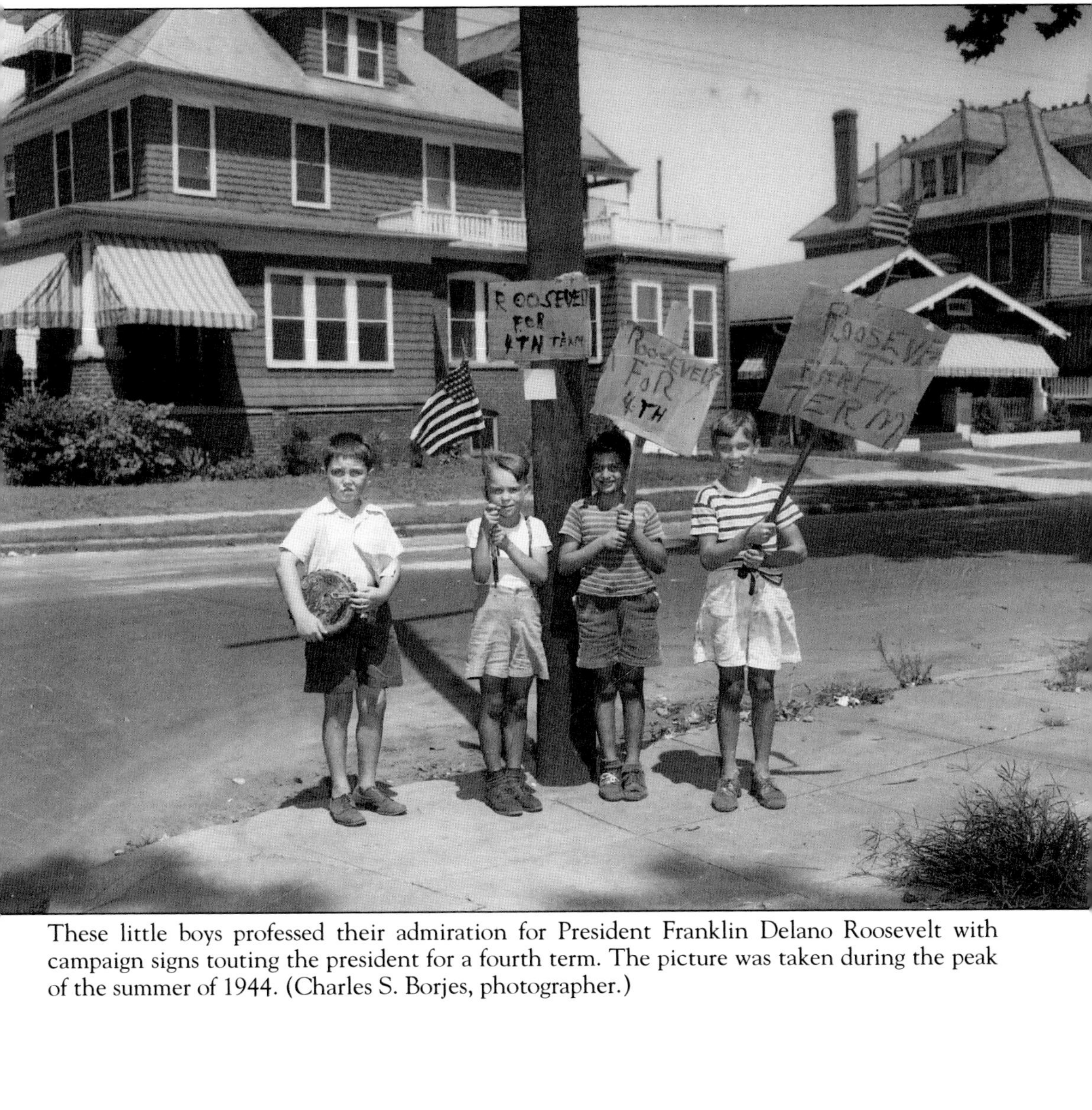

These little boys professed their admiration for President Franklin Delano Roosevelt with campaign signs touting the president for a fourth term. The picture was taken during the peak of the summer of 1944. (Charles S. Borjes, photographer.)

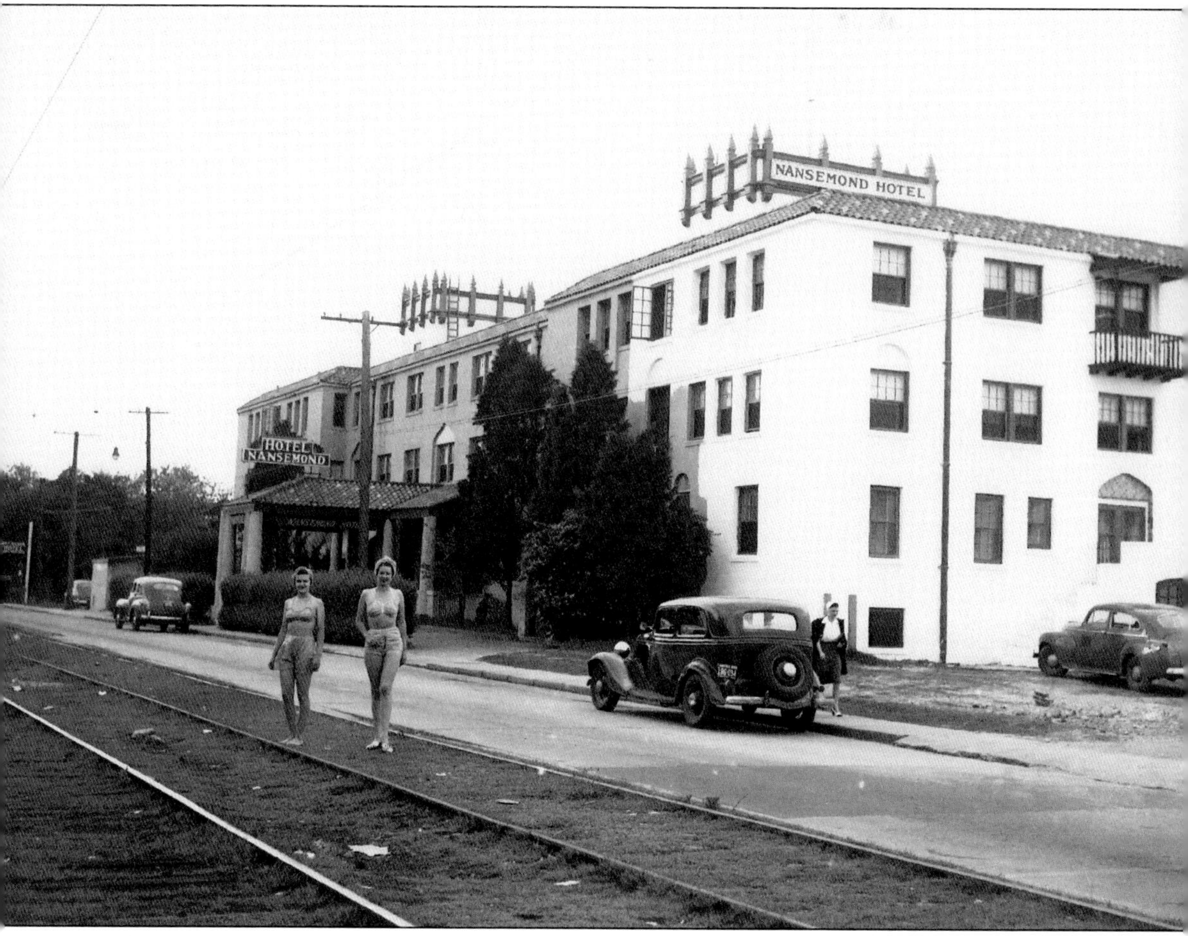

The Nansemond Hotel, occupied during World War II by Admiral H. Kent Hewitt and his extensive Navy staff, had been refurbished to its pre-war splendor and was once again full of out-of-town guests. World War II had hurt Ocean View Amusement Park and its dependent businesses. Though the parks and resort hotels did not suffer from competition with other seaside resorts, they were negatively impacted by patrons who turned away in the hopes of finding more sophisticated forms of entertainment. During the war itself, there were serious material shortages that caused many of the parks, including Ocean View, to deteriorate and, consequently, require extensive and expensive repair at the war's end. Eventually, amusement parks fell victim to the automobile since they lacked the expansive parking areas required by visitors. Real estate around Ocean View had been developed to the extent that there was little room to purchase property for parking, particularly within reasonable cost. Charles S. Borjes photographed the Nansemond Hotel on May 28, 1946.

Seven

Ocean Viewites

"My heart goes back to wander there,
  And among the dreams of the days that were,
    I find my lost youth again."
—From *My Lost Youth*, 1855
Henry Wadsworth Longfellow, American poet
(1807–1882)

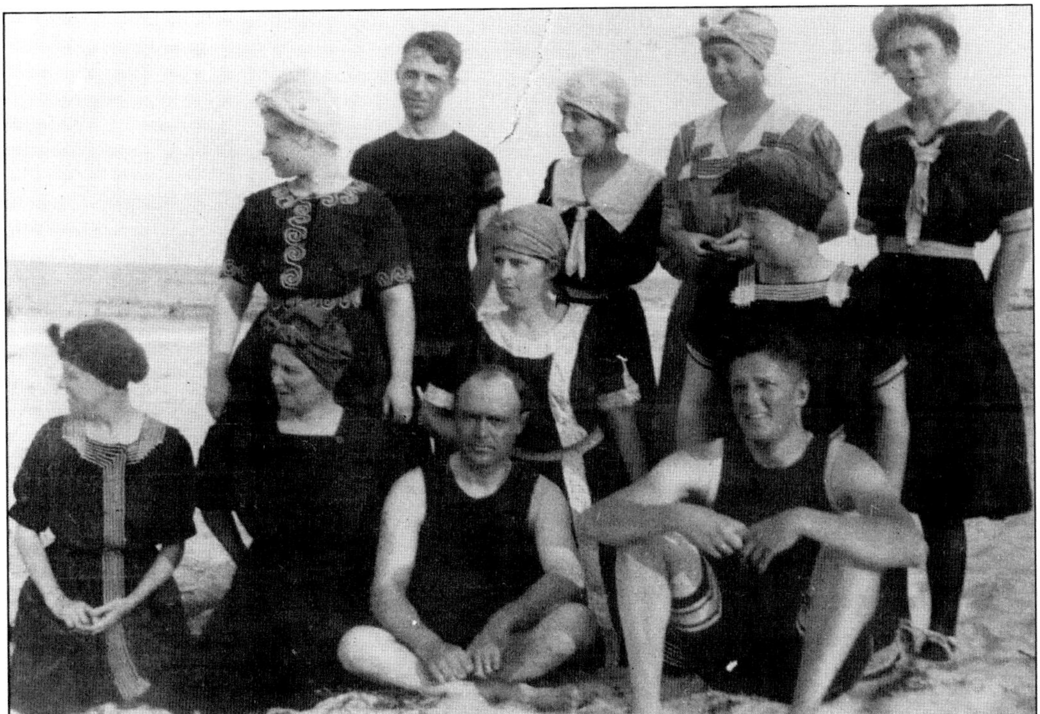

This large group of bathers had found rest and relaxation on the beautiful beaches of Ocean View, c. 1900. (Photographer unknown.)

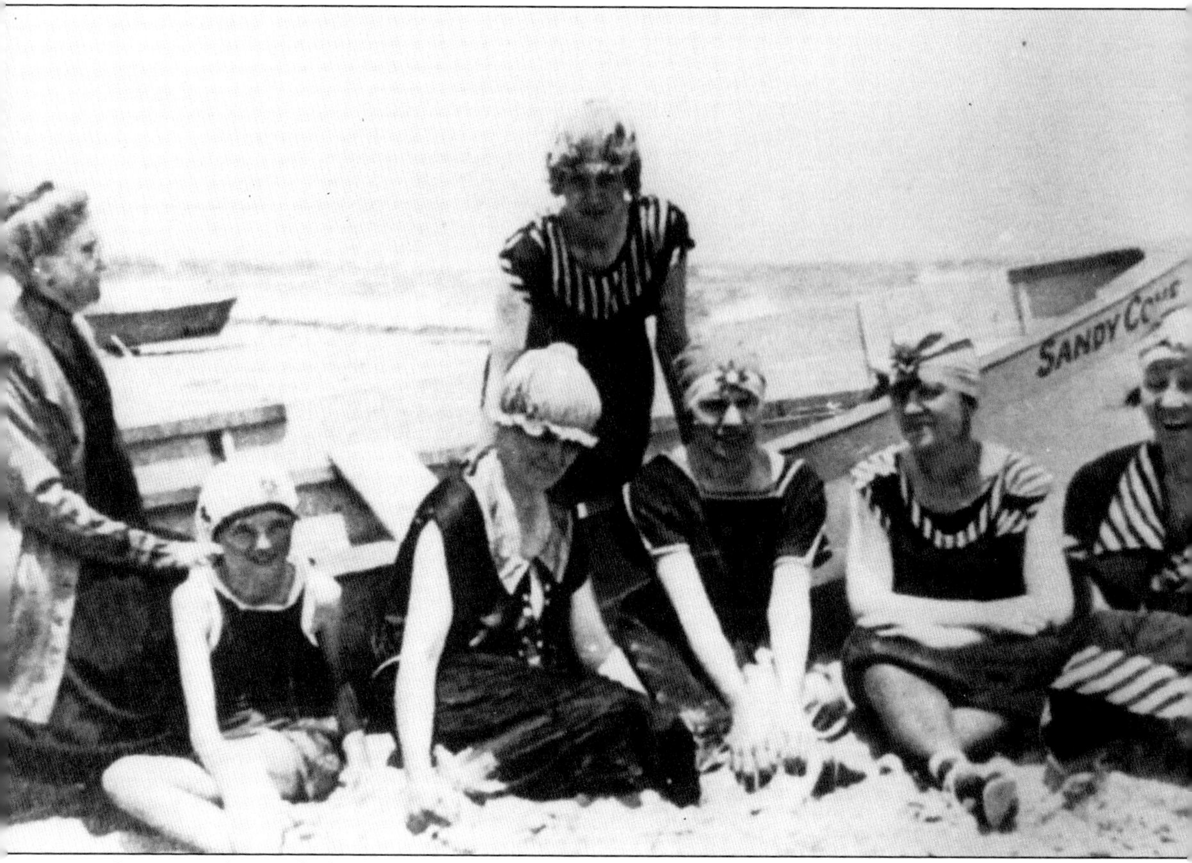

Posing in front of a little rowboat with the name *Sandy Cove* painted on the bow, these young women enjoyed frolicking in the surf at Ocean View, c. 1905. (Photographer unknown.)

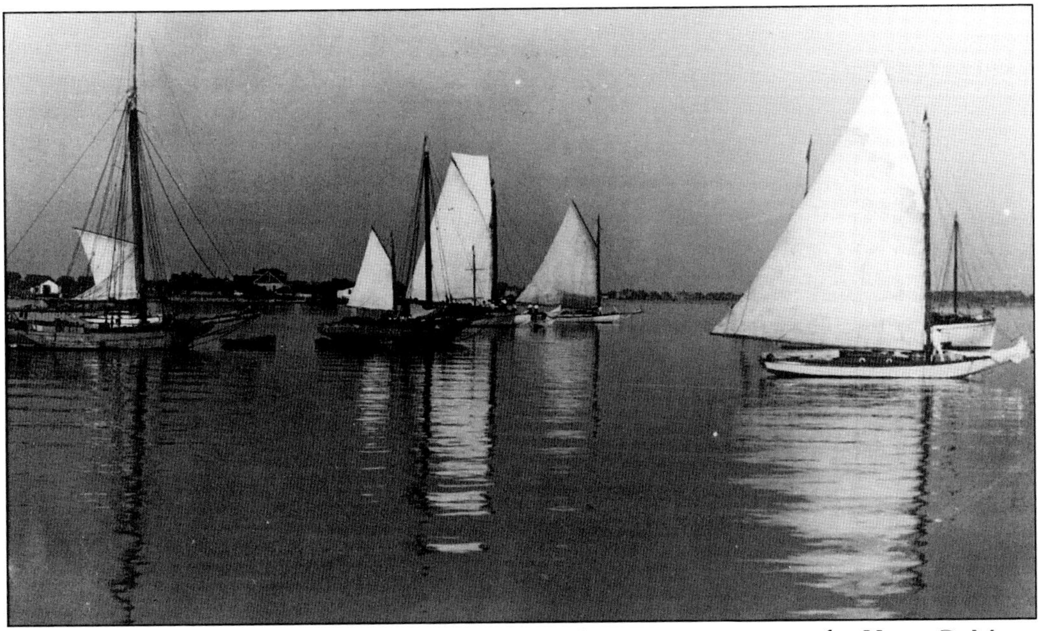

Willoughby Bay, also known as Little Bay, painted a picturesque scene for Harry C. Mann in 1910. The little bay tucked under the arm of Willoughby Spit provided protection from the currents in Hampton Roads and a safe harbor in the event of a fast-moving storm. People residing in Willoughby and Ocean View kept their boats anchored in Little Bay during the sailing season.

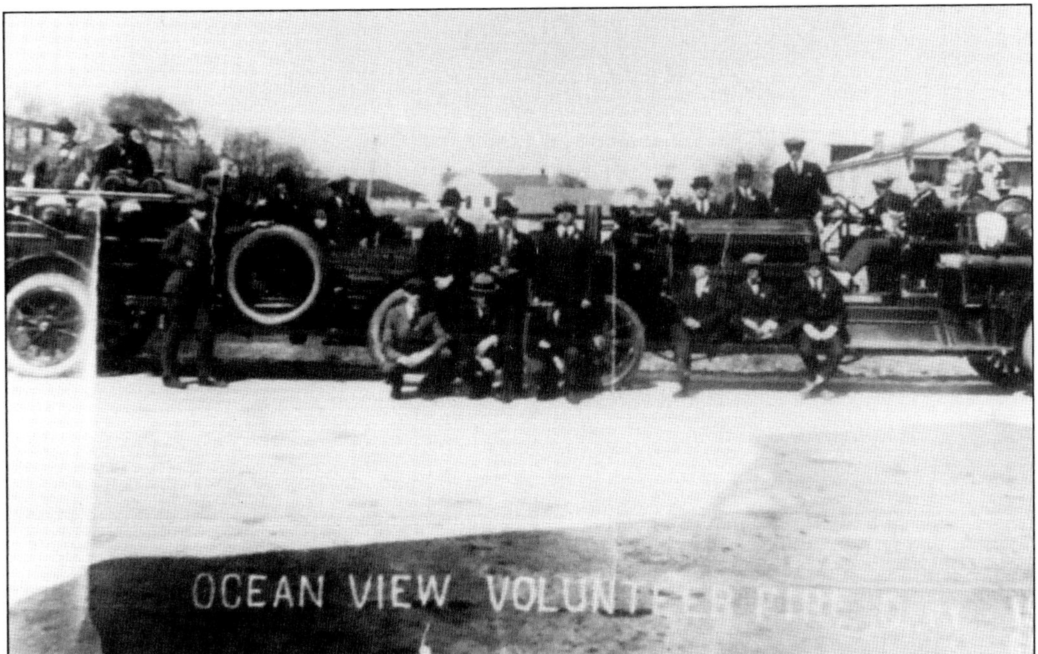

The Ocean View Volunteer Fire Department No. 1 posed for this photograph in 1922. (Photographer unknown.)

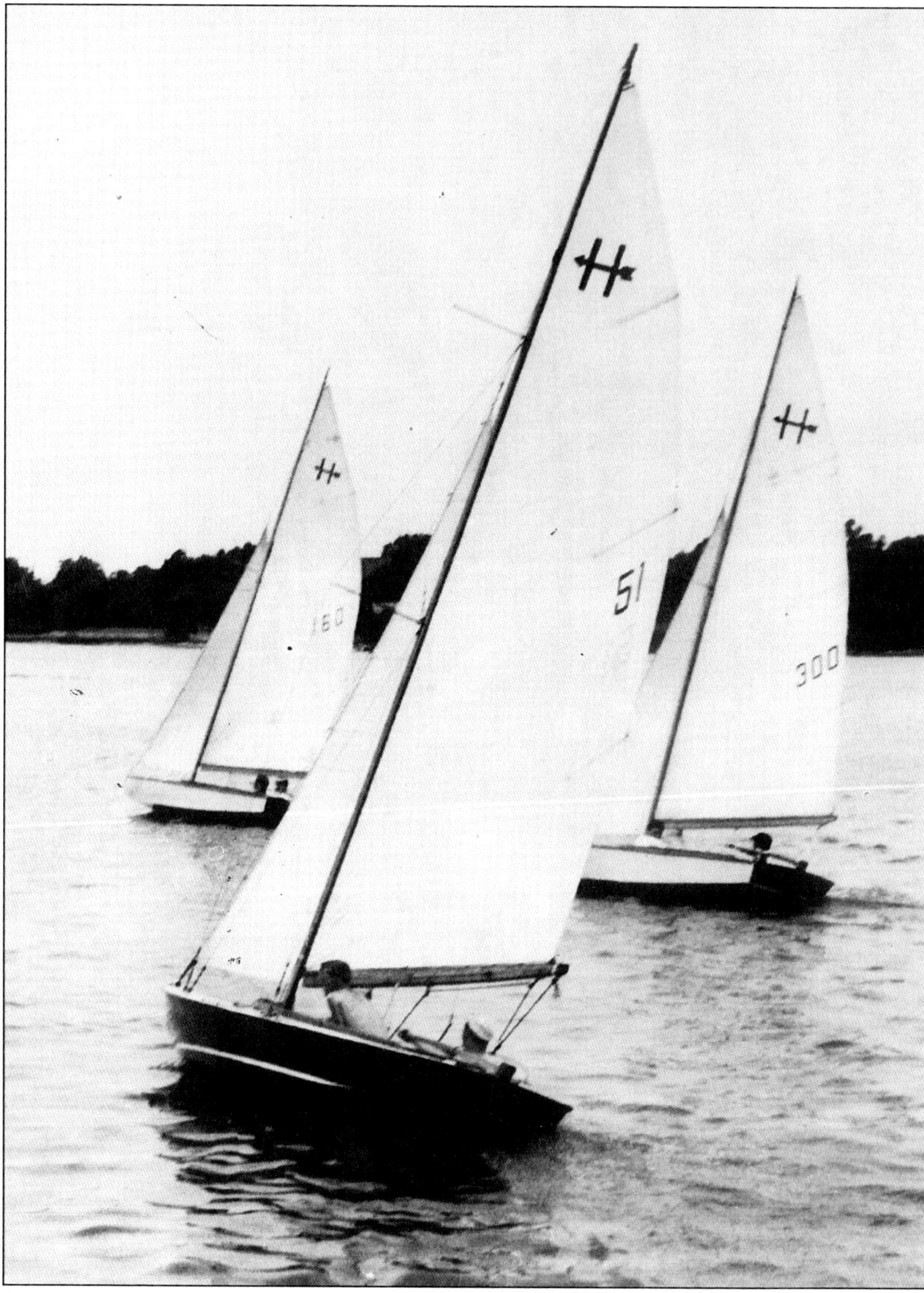

These Hampton-class sailcraft were a familiar site from the shores of Willoughby Bay. This photograph was taken about 1930 by an unknown photographer. Races were held several times a season in the waters off Willoughby, and also off the Norfolk Yacht and Country Club, situated on the Lafayette River.

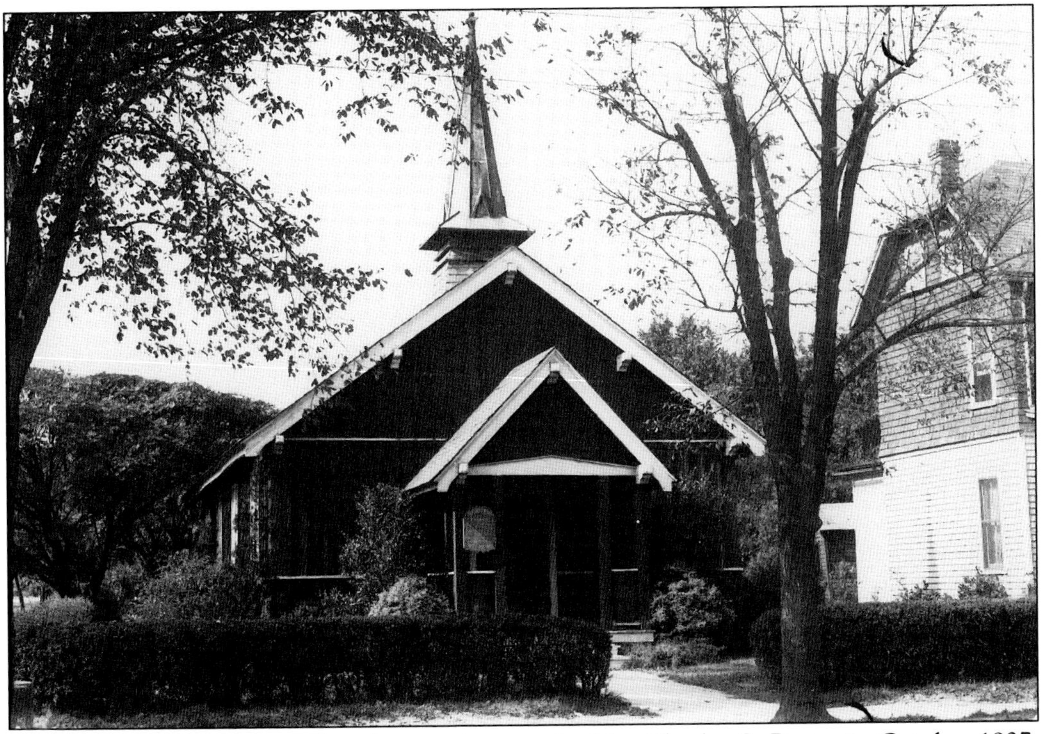

Ocean View Presbyterian Church was photographed by Charles S. Borjes in October 1937. Charles W. Brown Jr. was pastor of the church, located at 310 First View.

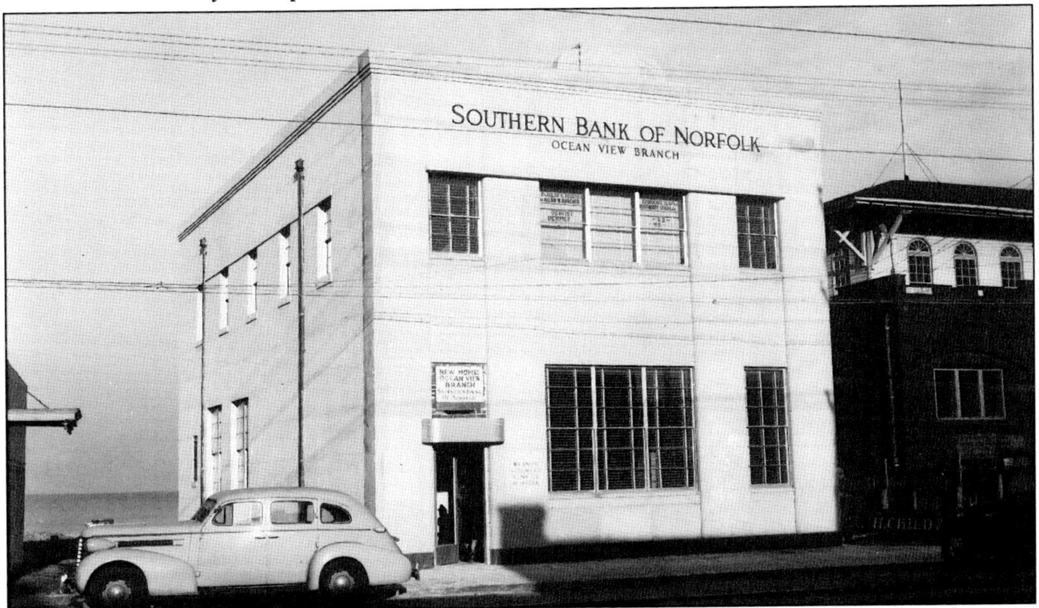

The Southern Bank of Norfolk opened its Ocean View Avenue branch in 1935, but moved to a new building by 1940 (pictured here). Chartered in 1932, the Southern Bank of Norfolk originated with the Southern Savings and Finance Company founded in 1917. The bank was headquartered in the former Virginia National Bank building at the corner of Main and Granby Streets. (Charles S. Borges, photographer.)

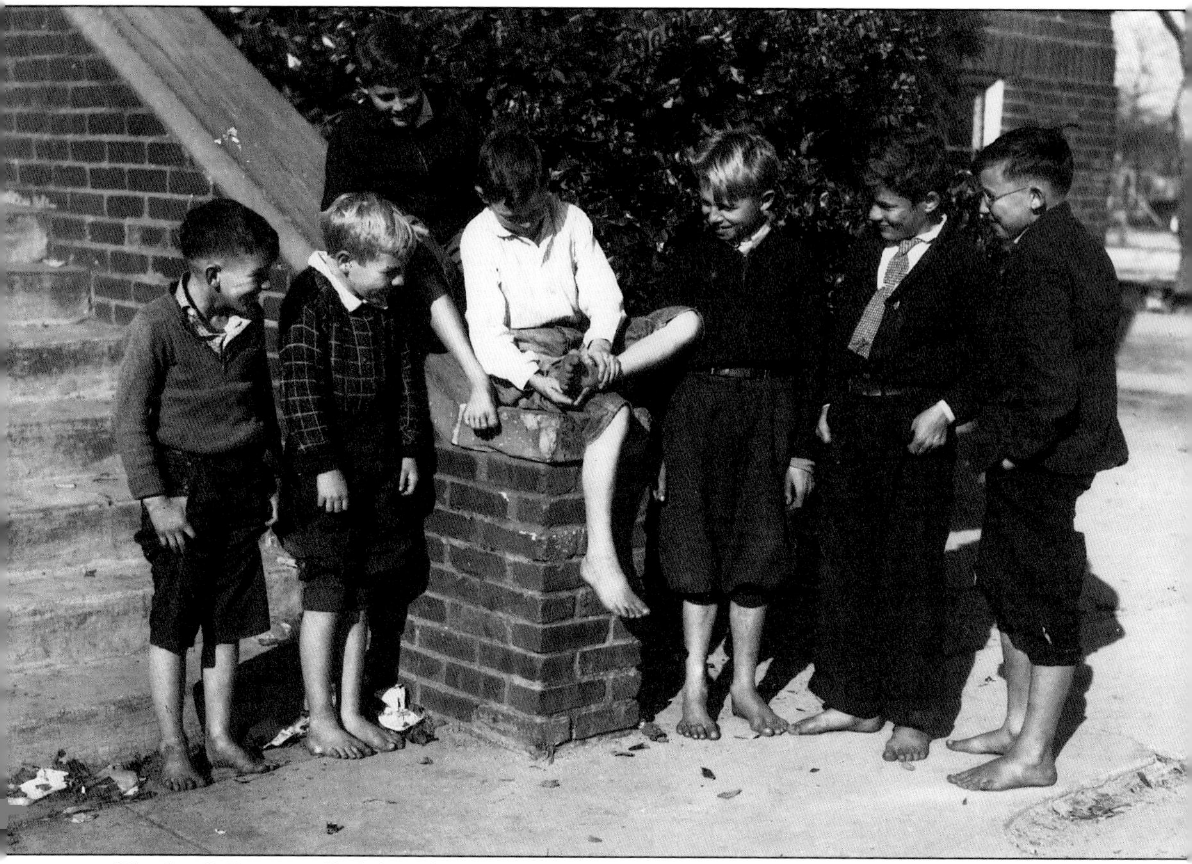

Charles S. Borjes called this photograph "The Barefoot Boys of Ocean View School." Taken on November 23, 1937, the Ocean View Elementary to which Borjes referred was the old school, soon-to-be replaced by the Art Deco–style Ocean View Elementary School less than two years later. The building in this picture was located at 701 First View in 1937 and had been in that location since 1923. The first principal of record was J.W. Campbell, who served during the 1923/24 school year. The Norfolk School Board voted to build a new school after the state fire marshal branded the existing school building a fire hazard. The new school was built on Mason Creek Road.

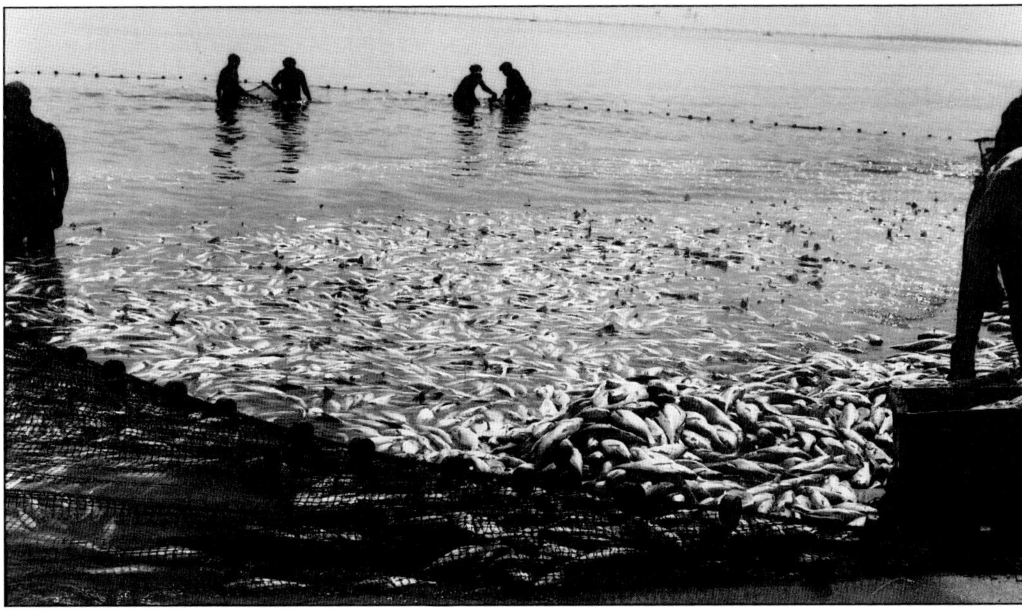

Wright's Fishery was located off Ocean View Avenue at a time when the fishing industry flourished in Norfolk. At different times of the year, fish were caught in many different ways. In the spring, summer, and fall, most of the fish were caught by haul seining, in pound nets, and in drift. Some were also taken by the trawl boats. Haul seiners launched boats from the shore that carried a net that was floated with cork and weighted with chain or heavy iron. The net was circled in the water, such as the one pictured here, and gradually pulled toward shore where the fish were emptied out of the net onto the sandy beach. They were then placed in boxes of ice and taken to the packing houses in Norfolk and Portsmouth. This picture was taken on August 8, 1938. (Charles S. Borjes, photographer.)

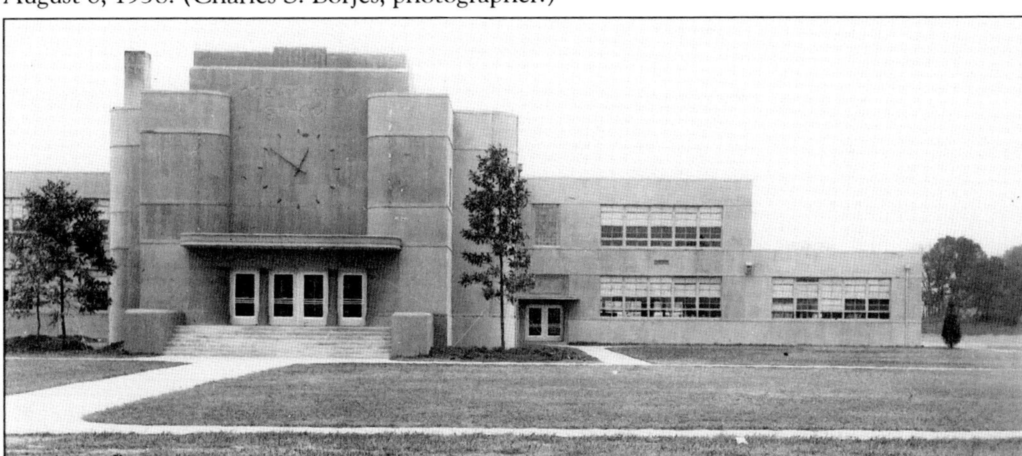

The Ocean View School moved to this unique Art Deco–style school building on Mason Creek Road in 1939. The city manager of Norfolk, Thomas P. Thompson, requested $49,500 from Harold L. Ickes, administrator of the Public Works Administration (PWA), toward construction of a new Ocean View School in 1935. President Franklin Delano Roosevelt's PWA and Civil Works Administration programs greatly aided Norfolk during the Great Depression as the city sought to improve its infrastructure. Ocean View School was photographed by Charles S. Borjes on December 28, 1939.

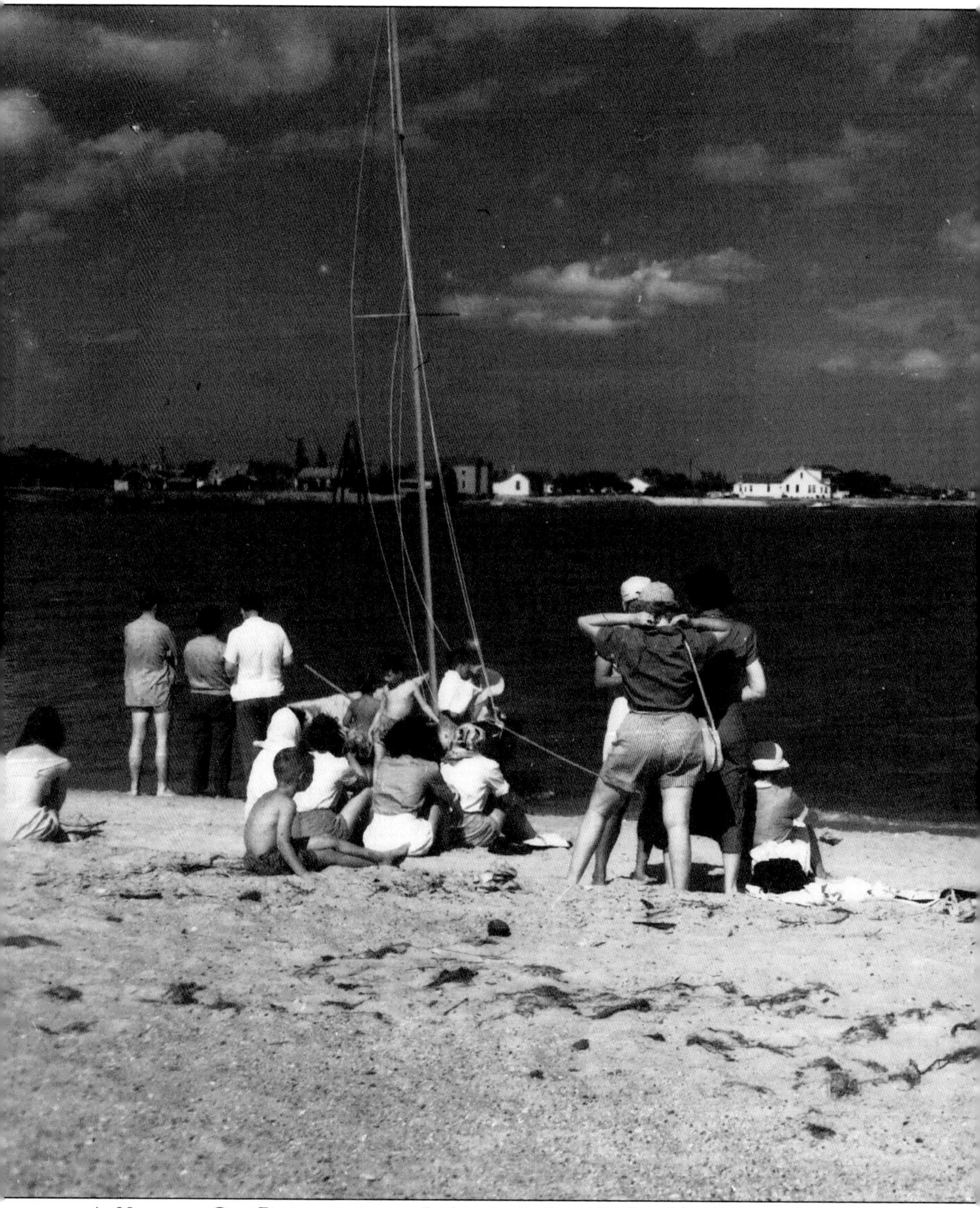

A Hampton One-Design racing craft skimmed along Willoughby Spit on June 25, 1949, during the Willoughby Yacht Club Regatta. The afternoon races had to be postponed due to gusty winds from the south. The Hampton One-Design races resumed the next morning

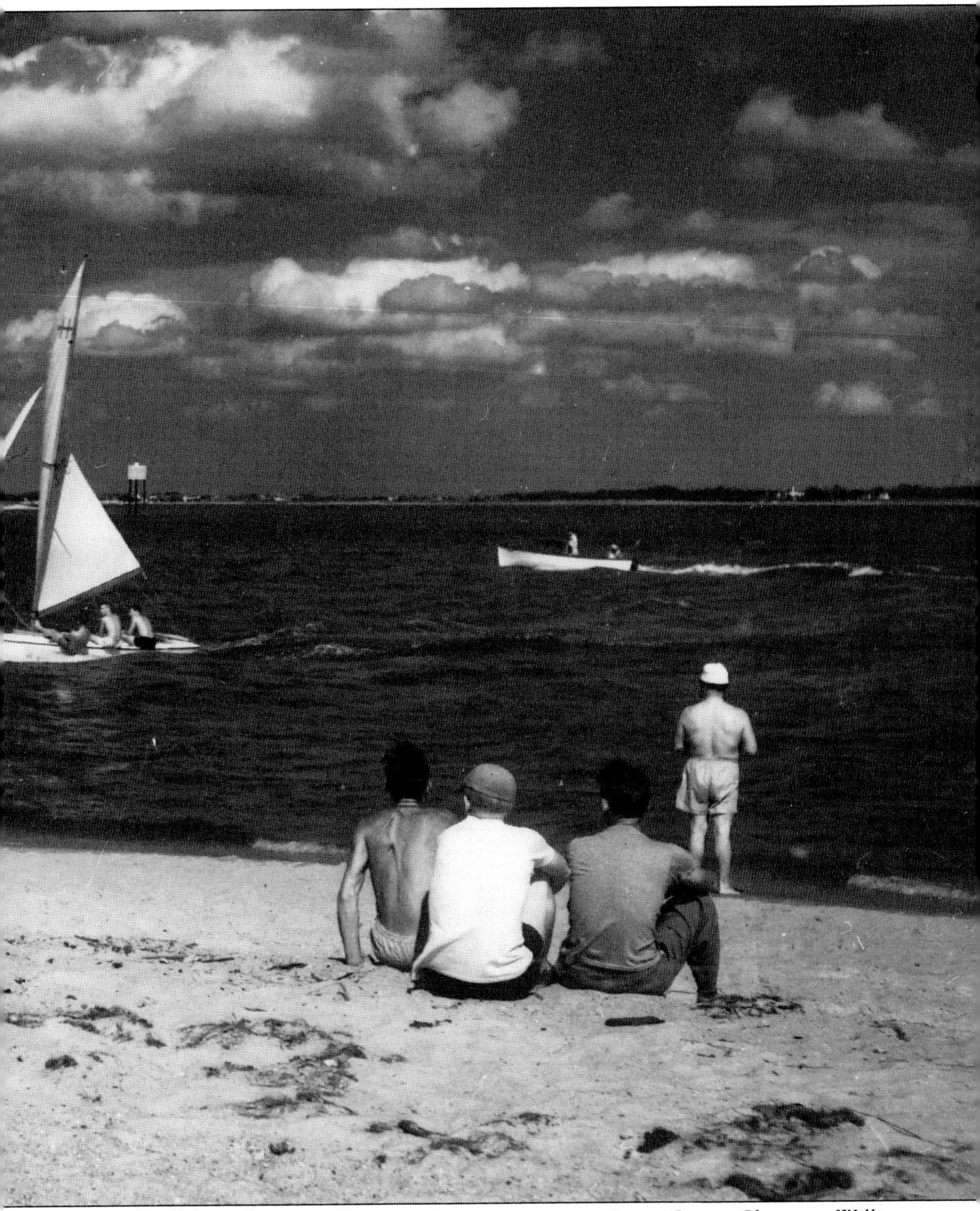

and concluded that afternoon. Winners of morning races on June 25 were Chauncey Willis, Hamptons; Tom Honeycutt, Snipes; Happy Hogshire, Moths; Charles Boykins, Penguins; and Al Purchase, Knockabouts. (Charles S. Borjes, photographer.)

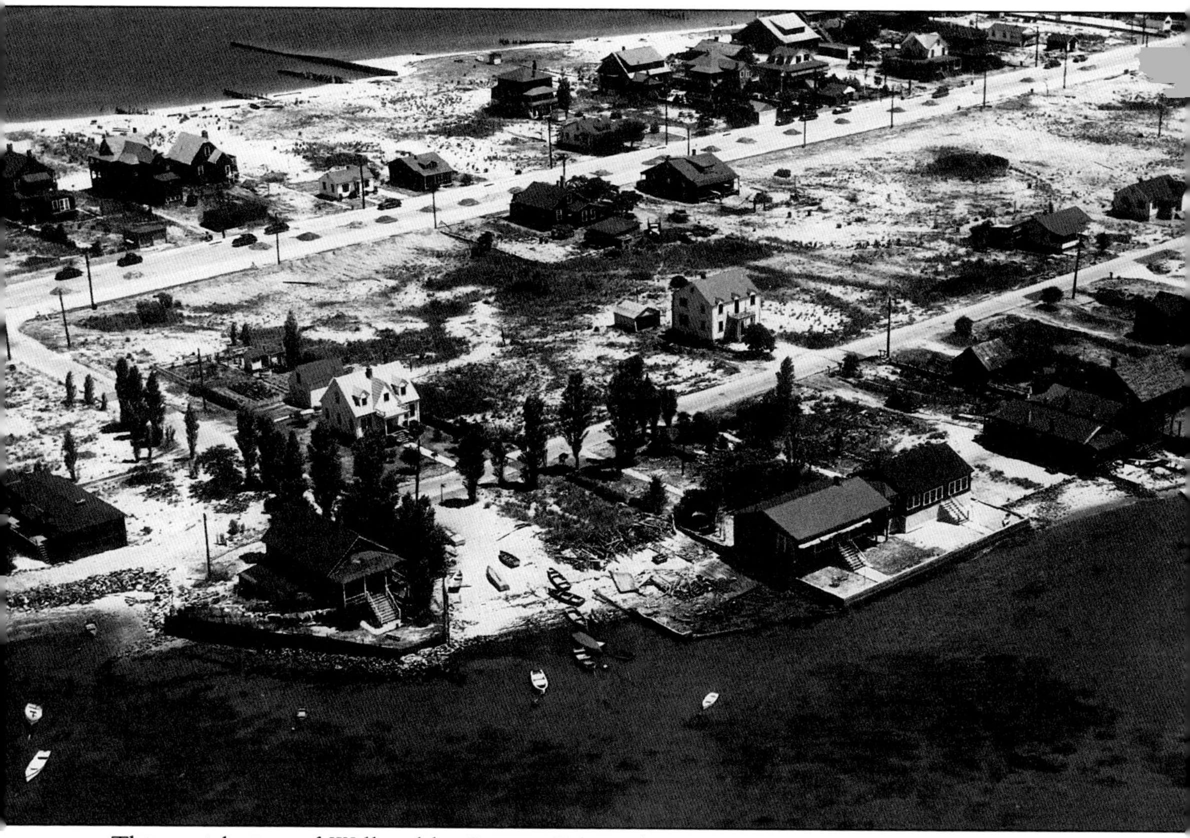

This aerial view of Willoughby Spit at Fifteenth View was taken in 1950. The ferry to the Peninsula would have been out of the picture on the lower left.

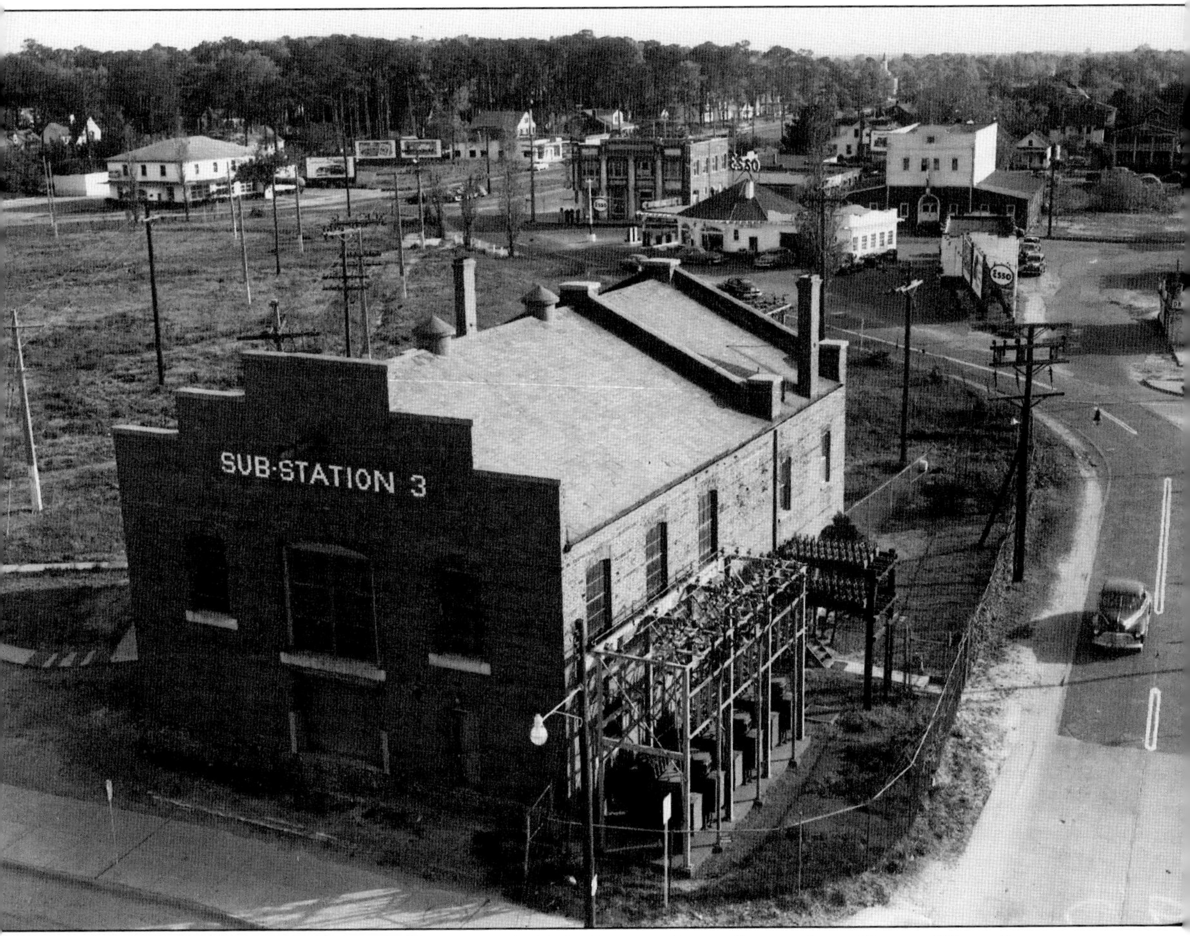

The Virginia Electric and Power Company's Sub-Station 3 was located on Ocean View Avenue across from the amusement park. The road to the right of the substation is Duffy's Lane. Duffy's Lane was a small connecter road from Granby Street, visible to the south. The intersection has changed very little over the years. Granby Street still feeds automobile traffic to Ocean View Avenue around this fork in the road via its northeast exit to the upper left of the picture and Duffy's. The picture was taken in 1950 by Jim Mays.

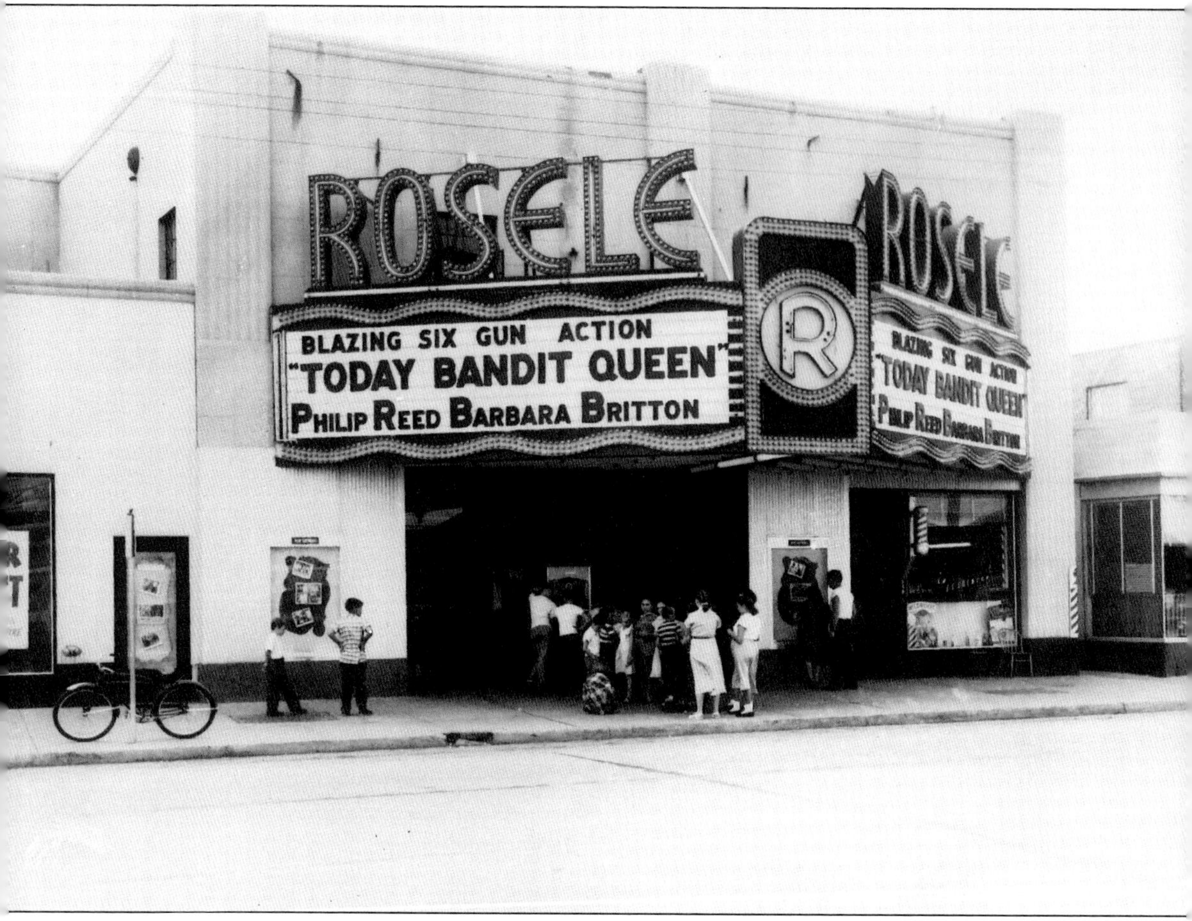

One of the favorite spots for youngsters and adults in the Ocean View community was the Rosele Theater on Ocean View Avenue. When this picture was taken on September 4, 1951, Barbara Britton and Philip Reed were burning up the screen in a B-movie titled *Today Bandit Queen*.

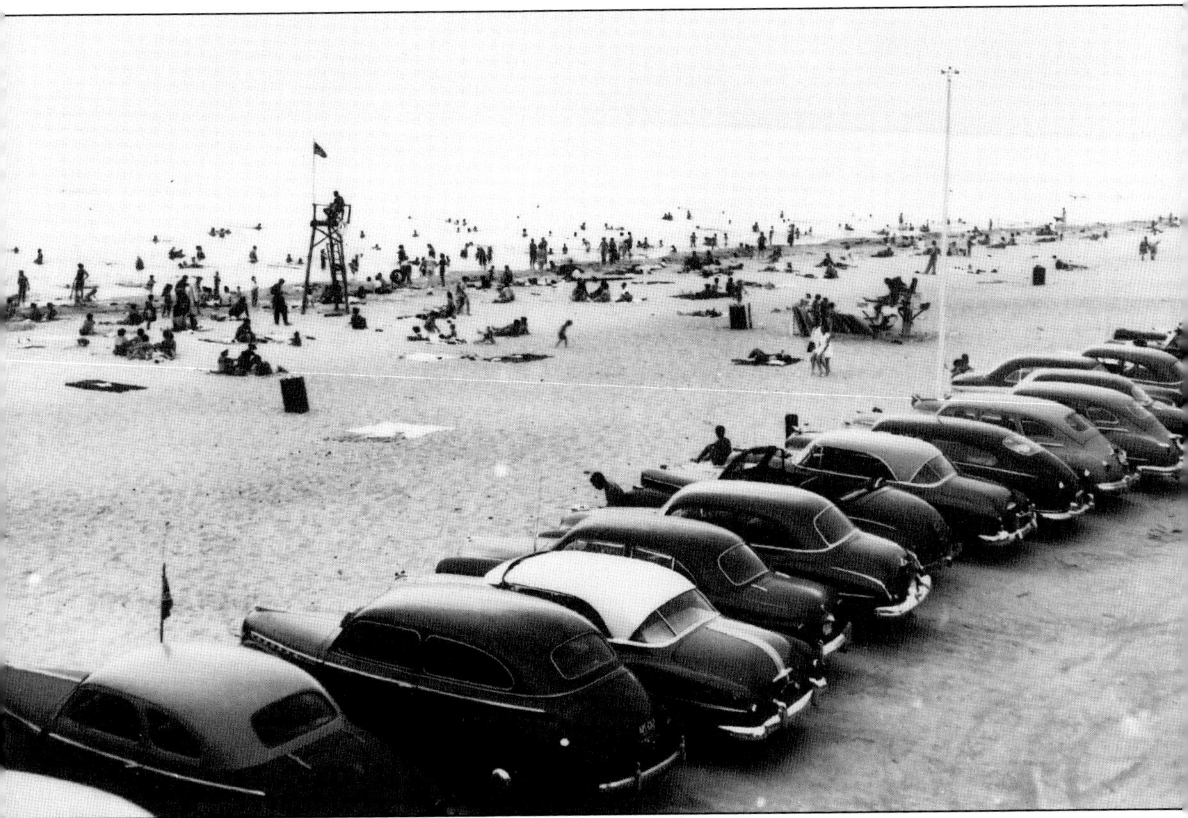

During the peak of sweltering summer heat, sleepless Norfolk residents sought relief from oppressive temperatures on the beaches and in the water. Ocean View residents recalled that the night crowds were sometimes larger than usual daytime throngs. At 9:45 p.m. on July 22, 1952, at Lewter's Beach, Ocean View, this crowd was said to be the largest ever seen on the beach at that time of night. Roy Coupland, shown at his post, was the only lifeguard on duty at night at the beach. (Charles S. Borjes, photographer.)

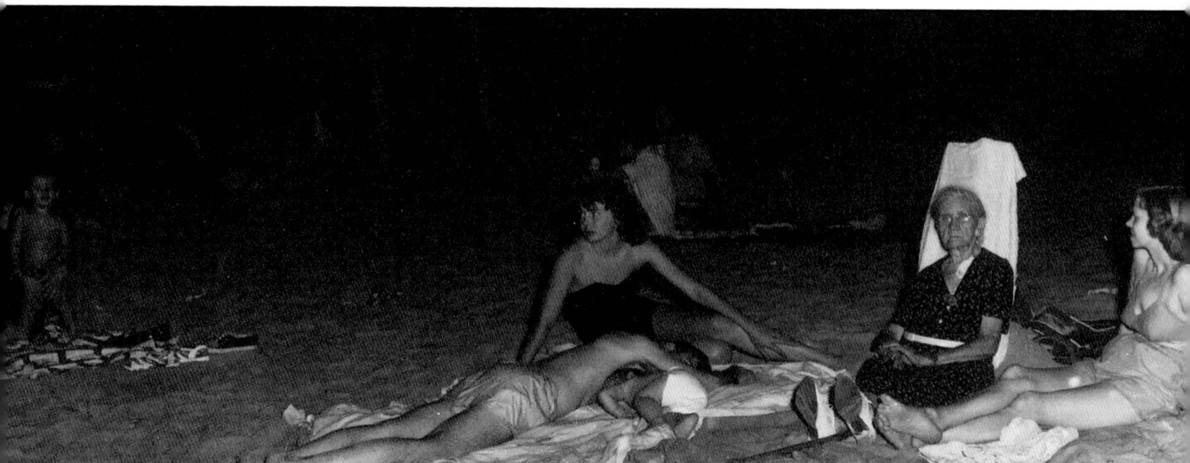

The heat wave that paralyzed Norfolk in July 1952 produced maximum readings from 90 to over 100 degrees on ten consecutive days, and skyrocketed to 103 degrees—in the shade—on July 22, the day this photograph was taken. Families flocked to Lewter's Beach in hopes of catching cooler air, but as Assistant Meteorologist Aubrey D. Hustead wryly reported, "If anyone's interested, you can tell them that it'll be freezing tonight—not at the North Pole—but just three miles from Norfolk. Straight up, that is." He added, "The airways report says the freezing level is at 15,000 feet and that's about three miles." Instead of motoring to the beach for a dip in the warm water of the bay or ocean, one weatherman jokingly suggested "jumping in your helicopter and hovering three miles up, among the ice crystals, where the flying saucers play. They're no fools." (Charles S. Borjes, photographer.)

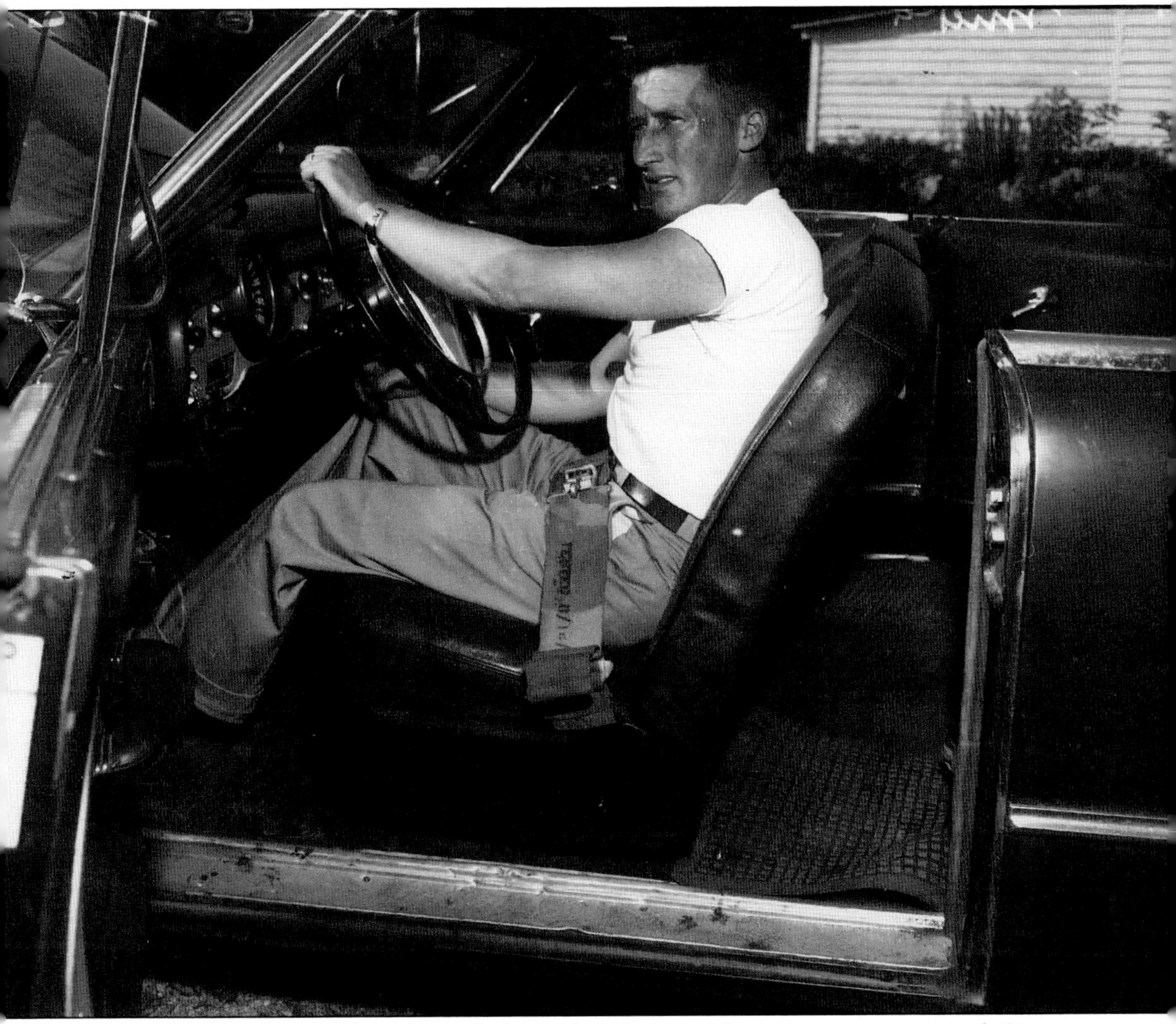

Mickey Spillane, renowned author of the Mike Hammer detective stories, visited Ocean View on June 2, 1953. The early 1950s were an interesting period in the life of the author. He had just joined the Jehovah's Witnesses and announced his retirement from writing. His retirement was short-lived. Born on March 9, 1918, in Brooklyn, New York, as Frank Morrison Spillane, Mickey began writing in high school, but it did not become his professional vocation until finishing college in 1940. Spillane served in the United States Army Air Forces during World War II, and shortly after the war, he published his first Mike Hammer story, *I, the Jury*, a bestseller. Spillane's novels were in the tradition of detective fiction as written by Raymond Chandler and Dashiell Hammett, yet laden with substantial amounts of violence, sex, and death. By 1951, Spillane's five detective novels based on the Mike Hammer character had been bestsellers and joined the annals of immediate and lasting book success stories. By the early 1960s, Spillane's "retirement" had ended and he returned to the bestseller list with *The Deep* and a Mike Hammer classic, *The Girl Hunters*. (Charles S. Borjes, photographer.)

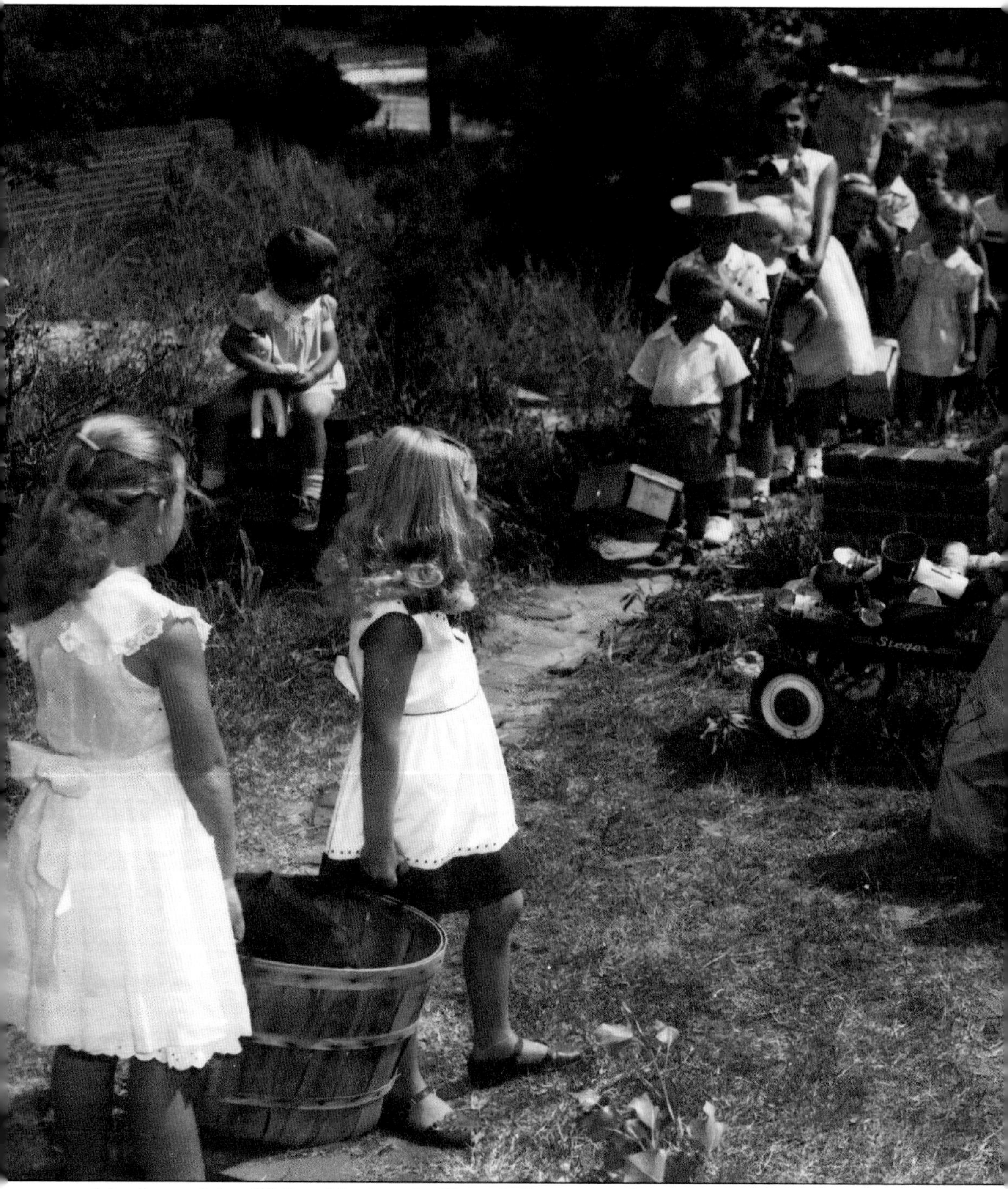

Members of the Willoughby Beach Glass Collecting and Mosquito Control squads met on August 13, 1954, to pick up broken glass, bottles, cans, and other refuse that might cause injury to bathers. Squad members ranged in age from five to twelve, and at the time this photograph was taken, the club enrolled twenty-four children. The program was under the jurisdiction of the Audubon Junior Bird Club of Willoughby Beach, whose club roster was nearly identical

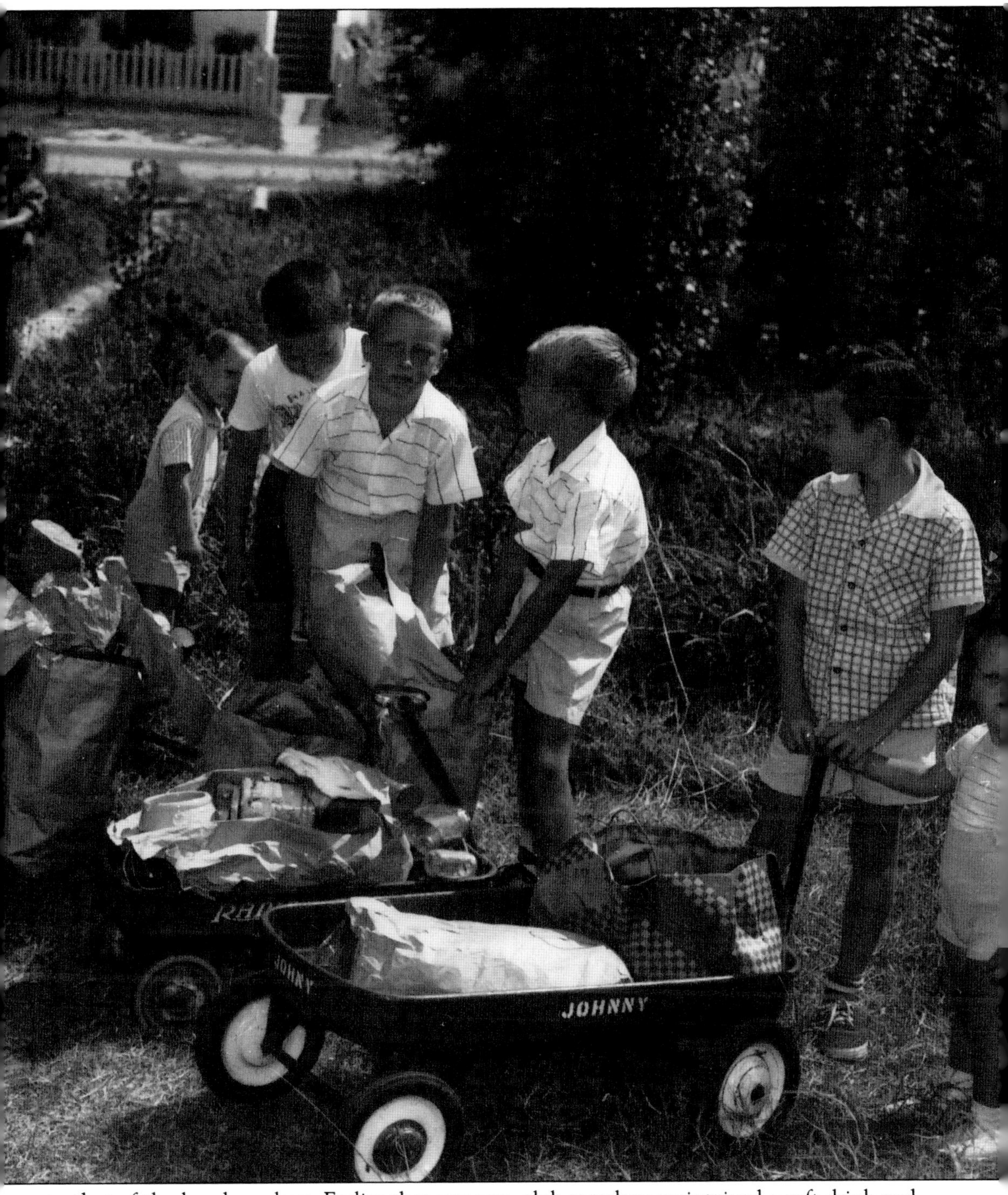

to that of the beachcombers. Earlier that summer, club members maintained a soft drink and watermelon stand on Ocean View Avenue that earned them a little profit. The children added this money to money earned from soda bottle deposits and bought two bird books, which they gave to homes for crippled children. (Jim Mays, photographer.)

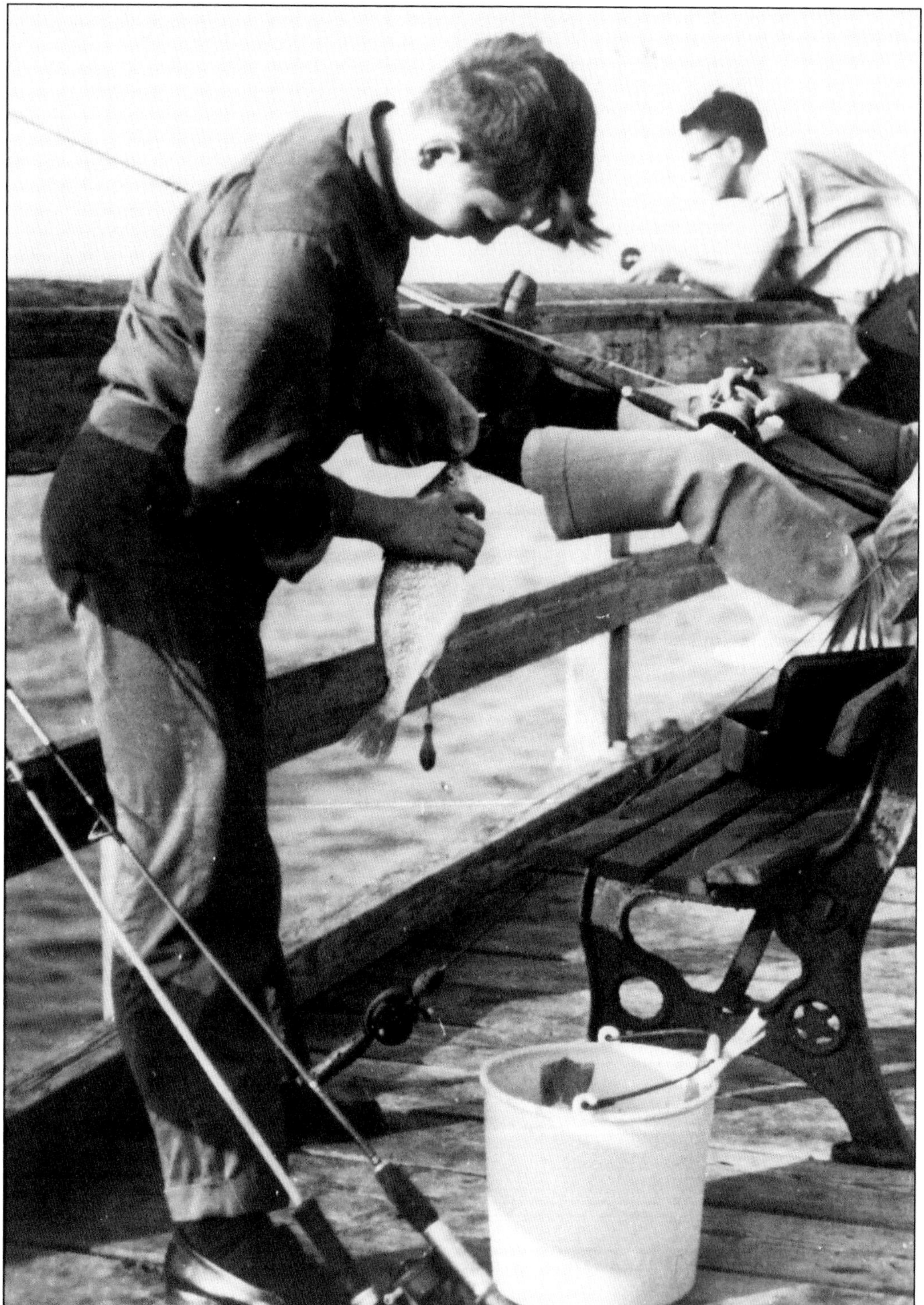

A young boy enjoyed a fishing trip at Harrison's pier on West Ocean View Avenue, *c.* 1960. Harrison's pier remains a popular place for fishing and crabbing today.

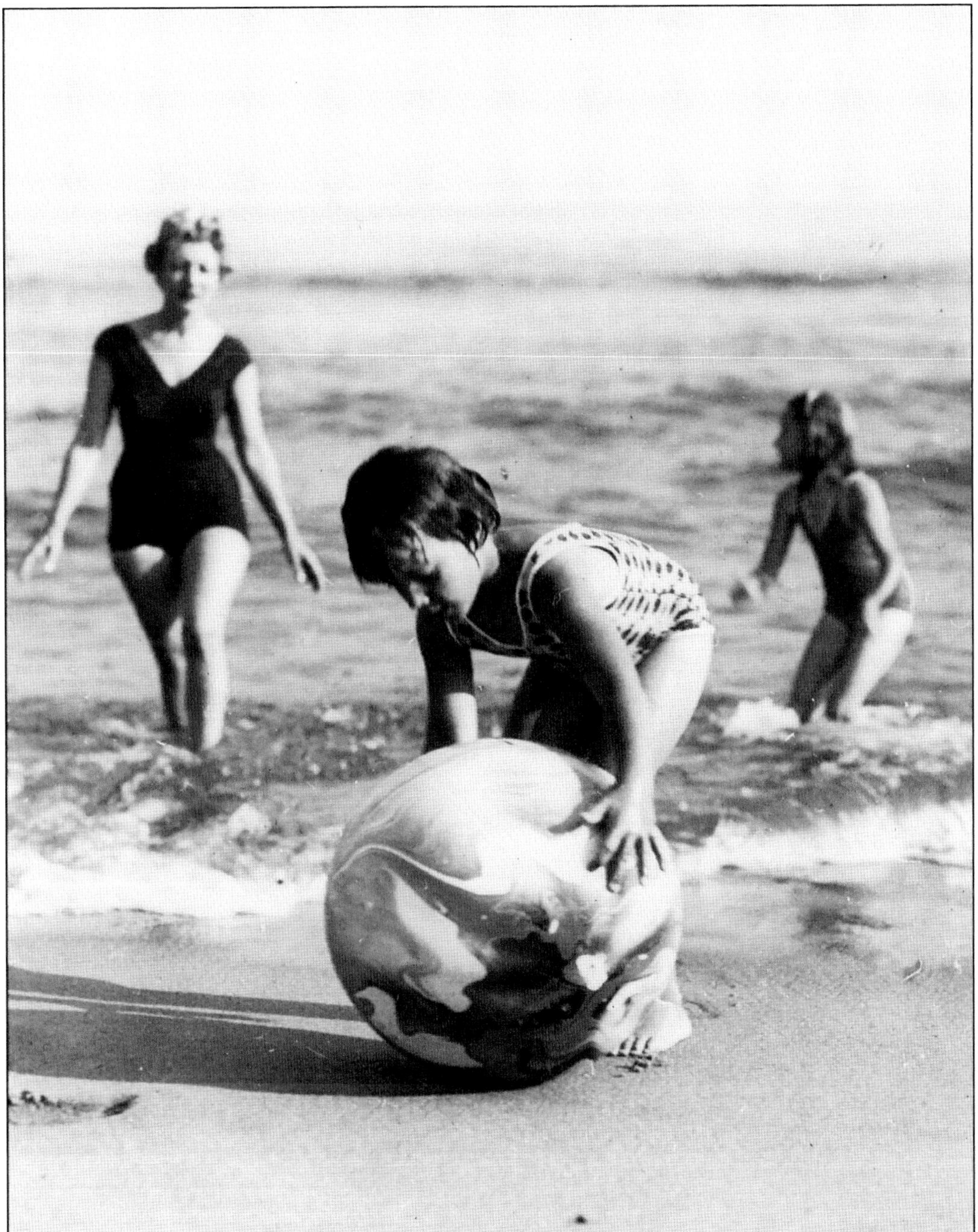

The beach at Ocean View offered a wonderful place for this little girl to play in the surf, *c.* 1960. The decade of the 1960s marked the end of an era because people gravitated toward the hotels and oceanfront attractions at Virginia Beach, and automobiles carried them to resorts such as Myrtle Beach, South Carolina, and the burgeoning tourism industry on the Outer Banks of North Carolina.

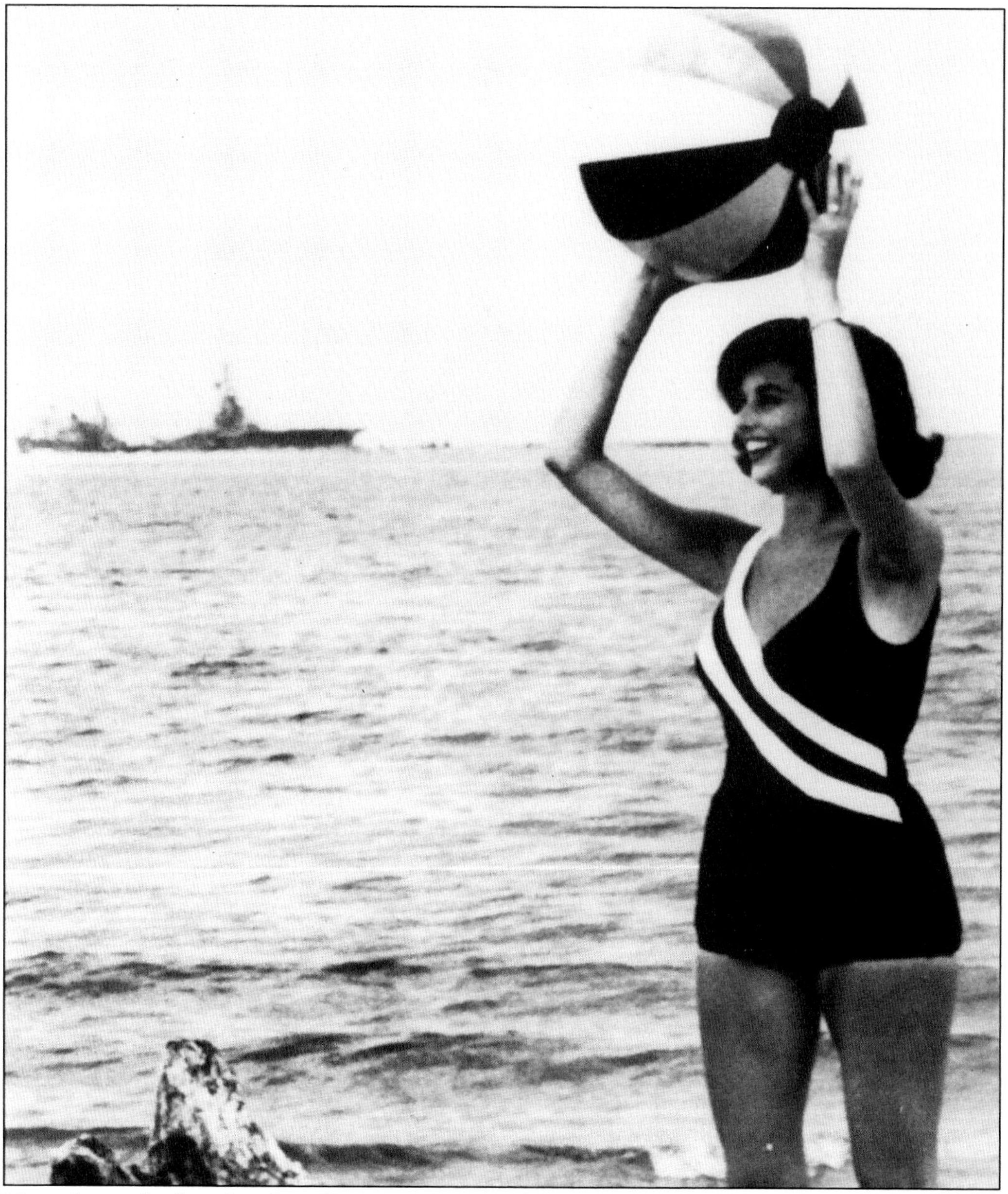

Near the end of its heyday, Ocean View's residents remained faithful to its wide beaches, quiet cottage line, and established neighborhoods. This young woman enjoyed "the View" on an exceptionally beautiful day in 1965. Memories of the Ocean View of yesteryear evoke remembrances akin to those intimated by English poet Christina Georgina Rossetti (1830–1894), who wrote these words in her poem *Remember*:

"And sometimes I remember days of old
When fellowship seemed not so far to seek,
And all the world and I seemed much less cold,
And at the rainbow's foot lay surely gold,
And hope felt strong, and life itself not weak."

(Photographer unknown.)